How-To Homeschool Your Learning Abled Kid: 75 Questions Answered

For Parents of Children with Learning Disabilities or Twice Exceptional Abilities

Sandra K. Cook, M.S. Instructional Design

Copyright © 2014 Sandra K. Cook
All rights reserved.
ISBN: 149362377X
ISBN-13: 978-1493623778

DEDICATION

This book is dedicated to my dear husband who has been our provider and my cheerleader throughout our homeschooling years. He encouraged me to continue with my Master's Degree program when I felt like dropping out—it was just so hard to work on my degree and to homeschool too. I'm glad I finished, but I wouldn't have made it through without my husband's ongoing support and encouragement. Therefore, this book would not exist if I hadn't finished my degree, hadn't focused on Universal Design for Learning, and if I hadn't learned so much from each of the families I've helped along the way.

Table of Contents

ACKNOWLEDGMENTS I
INTRODUCTION 1
OUR STORY 5

1 GETTING STARTED WITH HOMESCHOOLING 9

WHAT ARE THE BENEFITS OF HOMESCHOOLING A CHILD WITH LEARNING DISABILITIES? 9
MY CHILD SAYS SHE DOESN'T WANT TO HOMESCHOOL; SHOULD I MAKE HER? 14
CAN THE PUBLIC SCHOOL PREVENT ME FROM HOMESCHOOLING IF MY CHILD HAS DISABILITIES? 18
WHAT STEPS DO I NEED TO TAKE TO LEGALLY START HOMESCHOOLING? 21
WHAT SERVICES ARE PUBLIC SCHOOLS REQUIRED TO PROVIDE FOR HOMESCHOOLERS? 24
AM I SMART ENOUGH TO HOMESCHOOL MY CHILD? 28
WHAT IF I DON'T HAVE ENOUGH PATIENCE TO HOMESCHOOL MY CHILD? 31
WHAT ABOUT MY CHILD'S SOCIALIZATION NEEDS? 34
HOW DO I KNOW WHAT I SHOULD TEACH MY CHILD? 39
MY SPOUSE DOESN'T THINK WE SHOULD HOMESCHOOL. WHAT SHOULD I DO? 44
IS MY CHILD TOO OLD OR IS IT TOO LATE TO START HOMESCHOOLING? 49
WHAT IF I CHANGE MY MIND; CAN I PUT MY CHILD BACK INTO SCHOOL? 56

2 EVALUATION OF YOUR CHILD'S LEARNING NEEDS 61

WHY SHOULD I HAVE MY CHILD EVALUATED? 61
I DON'T WANT TO LABEL MY CHILD; HOW CAN I HELP HIM/HER WITHOUT LABELING? 67
DOESN'T OUR LOCAL SCHOOL HAVE TO PROVIDE TESTING FOR DISABILITIES? 70
HOW DO I FIND A HIGHLY QUALIFIED EVALUATOR? 74
ARE EVALUATIONS COVERED BY INSURANCE? 76
WHAT KINDS OF EVALUATIONS DO I NEED TO CONSIDER? 79
HOW DO I KNOW WHEN OR IF I SHOULD HAVE MY CHILD EVALUATED? 84
I HAVE AN EVALUATION; HOW DO I FIGURE OUT WHAT MY CHILD NEEDS? 87
I CAN'T AFFORD TO HAVE MY CHILD EVALUATED; WHAT SHOULD I DO? 93

3 ADDRESSING YOUR CHILD'S SPECIFIC LEARNING NEEDS 101

HOW DO I DETERMINE MY CHILD'S LEARNING STYLE? 101
WHAT IS MULTI-SENSORY TEACHING? 106
HOW DO I TEACH A CHILD WITH A VISUAL LEARNING STYLE? 109

How do I teach a child with an auditory learning style? 112
How do I teach a child with a kinesthetic/tactile learning style? 114
How do I use Gardner's Multiple Intelligences Theory for teaching my child? 118
How do I use the Learning Styles Inventory for teaching my child? 121
How do I know what to work on first? 123
Is my child really mentally impaired? 128
Can my child be gifted and have learning disabilities? 130

4 CHOOSING CURRICULUM 135

What curriculum would you recommend for dyslexia? 136
What curriculum would you recommend for ADHD or attention difficulties?
.... 142
What curriculum would you recommend when a child hates schoolwork? ... 145
What program should I use for handwriting? 148
What do you recommend for spelling? 149
What should I use for hands-on math? 152
How do I teach math if I don't understand it myself? 155
What foreign language is best for a child with dyslexia? 157
How do I improve my child's memory skills? 158
How do I improve my child's processing speed? 166
What is unschooling and does it work? 169
What is a unit study? 173

5 ASSISTIVE TECHNOLOGY AND TEACHING ALTERNATIVES 177

Won't using accommodations become a crutch for my child? 177
Should I have my child use a computer? If so, how much is too much? 180
Should I let my child use audiobooks? 185
Should I give up on handwriting and teach keyboarding? 187
Is there a good program to drill math facts? 188
What software do you recommend for reading instruction? 190

6 HOMESCHOOL MANAGEMENT 193

How can I get my child to stay on task and work faster? 193
How can I get my child to work more independently? 197
Can I homeschool while working? 199
How do I homeschool for little money or free? 201
How do I meet the needs of multiple kids? 204
How long do you homeschool each day? 207

How can I get my housework done when I'm homeschooling?.........................209
How do I Maintain Learning Momentum During Summer Break?....................210

7 RECORD KEEPING 213

What Do I Need to Do To Comply with State Reporting Requirements?..........213
Do You Give Report Cards or Progress Reports? 215
What is a Portfolio and What Do I Put In It?..219
How Do I Make A Transcript or Where Do I Obtain A Transcript? 221
Do you or should I give grades?..223
Does my child require an accredited high school program? 229

8 BEHAVIOR MANAGEMENT AND MAINTAINING FOCUS............................233

Should I medicate my child to manage his ADHD? 233
How do you manage ADHD without medication?...235
My child has sensory issues; how do you manage SPD? 238
My child refuses to do his schoolwork; how do I make him do it?...................240
My child hates school work; what can I do? 245
My child seems depressed; what can I do? 248

9 FAMILY MATTERS WHEN HOMESCHOOLING 255

What do I say to disapproving relatives or friends? 255
How do I handle it when my younger child is more academically advanced?...261
How do I spend adequate time with my typical child? 264
Help! I feel so stressed out! Love Breaks 267
Am I failing my Child?...270
Where can I get support or connect with other moms? 272
How well has homeschooling worked for you? 274

ABOUT THE AUTHOR 279

REFERENCES 281

INDEX 285

ACKNOWLEDGMENTS

First, I would like to acknowledge my Mom and my editor, who is one and the same person. My mom selflessly spent time editing this book for me using the skills she learned over her lifetime working as a secretary. Her corrections and input were invaluable for catching my many typing and wording mistakes.

Second, I would like to acknowledge my friend, Lorraine C., who volunteered to read my entire book to help me refine the editing, wording, and formatting so this book will be a better reading experience for you. With Lorraine's help, I feel like the book is the best it can be!

Lastly, I would like to thank and acknowledge the Learning Abled Kids' community of parents who have encouraged one another over the past decade, and who have taught me more than I ever dreamed I would know about homeschooling a Learning Abled Kid.

SANDRA K.COOK

INTRODUCTION

After a decade of running the Learning Abled Kids' Parent Support Group, I'd like to share with you answers to the most frequently asked questions I've received. The answers to many of these questions may be exactly what you need to decide whether to homeschool or how to homeschool your Learning Abled Kid. The questions have been asked by countless parents who are/were considering homeschooling or actively homeschooling their children with learning disabilities.

The variety of questions spans many topics. Therefore, if a topic is of no interest to you, feel free to just skip over that section. For example, if you have been homeschooling for a period of time, the "How to Get Started Homeschooling" series may not be of interest to you.

Skimming the questions will let you know if there is any particular answer you'd like to read, but otherwise, feel free to jump around the book and read the information which is of use to you. Where a prior section is referenced, I've tried to remember to provide you with the exact question-based title, so you can quickly find the information in the book's table of contents.

A Little Bit About Me

As a first step, let me introduce myself. My name is Sandy Cook. I have a Master's Degree in Instructional Design and I've consulted with many moms to help them develop viable homeschooling plans to meet their child's unique learning needs.

Most importantly, I'm a homeschooling mom who has spent the past decade homeschooling my two boys who have learning differences. My boys are in college and doing fabulously, so I thought this would be a good time to share all I've learned along the way with you.

I founded http://LearningAbledKids.com/ as my boys were struggling in public school and I started exploring educational options, which included homeschooling. My Learning Abled Kids' support group has more than 1600 members and is an active community of supportive, homeschooling moms with children who have learning challenges. If you'd like to gain support in your homeschooling, you can join the group at: http://groups.yahoo.com/neo/groups/LearningAbledKids/.

As you read each Q&A, keep in mind, I am trained as an Instructional Designer, not a licensed psychologist, lawyer, nor doctor. All of the information I share is opinion-based in nature and stems from my homeschooling experiences, homeschooling knowledge, consultations, and instructional design training. You should seek professional evaluations or direct medical assistance when needed in order to fully understand your child's needs.

The information within is not directly related to your child's specific needs since I have not personally met you or your child. Therefore, you alone are responsible for any and all decisions you make, and every action you take on behalf of your child, without limitation, whether your actions are based upon the information shared in this guidebook, the LearningAbledKids.com website, or other Learning Abled Kids' communications.

A Little Bit About The Information in This Book

Please note: your outcomes *__will__* vary from any results shared in this book because your child is a different child, your implementation of any specified program will be different from other implementations, and due to additional variations that exist. Therefore, there are no guarantees of any kind whatsoever, whether explicit or implied.

With the above disclosures out of the way, I know you probably have a jillion questions about the best means and methods for homeschooling your precious child. I hope this book will allow you to get the answers you need from a reliable mom who has been down this road ahead of you.

This book contains insights from my Instructional Design Training, knowledge gained through many consultations, and my first-hand experience. I'm sharing as much information with you as I can to make your homeschooling journey as easy as possible. I'll begin by answering your questions about homeschooling, followed by more in-depth information to help you design the best educational program for your child(ren). If I've done my job well, you will learn a lot from this book and it will be a helpful resource for you.

Up front I'll say the most frequently asked question is: "What curriculum should I use?" That is not an easy or straightforward question to answer because the answer varies with each individual child's needs. Throughout this book I will address how you might determine what kind of curricula are best for your child, as well as which curricula are most recommended for specific types of disabilities, learning styles, etc. By sharing all I know, hopefully you will be able to analyze and understand your own child's needs and thereby select appropriate curricula.

While my answers may or may not match your child's needs perfectly, I hope the information I share will be insightful enough to give you different ways of thinking about meeting your child's needs. Most of all, I hope my answers help you and your child find educational success in your homeschooling endeavors.

I hope you find the information valuable and that you will join the Learning Abled Kids' community online at:
http://groups.yahoo.com/neo/groups/LearningAbledKids/. Support provided by the group can become invaluable when you face new, unexpected challenges as you progress in your homeschooling. As always, I am here to help, so feel free to send me an email from the Learning Abled Kids' website or Yahoo! Group with your questions. We are also on Facebook at: https://www.facebook.com/LearningAbledKids and Twitter at: https://twitter.com/learnabledkids.

Let me ask you now, are you excited about homeschooling? Before we started, I wasn't! When I started thinking about homeschooling my boys, I really had no idea what the homeschooling community had to offer, nor if it was even the best option for me or my sons. I was relatively sure I didn't have the patience and organizational skills needed to homeschool successfully. The only thing I was certain about was the public school was not meeting my boys' unique learning needs.

First, I'll briefly share our story with you, which I hope will help put your mind at ease in regard to whether or not you can meet your child's unique needs through homeschooling. Then we'll delve into how you get started and how you can design an individualized program for your child.

OUR STORY

Our older son, who had inattentive Attention Deficit Hyperactivity Disorder (ADHD), executive functioning issues, speech-language difficulties, ocular motor deficiencies, severe dyslexia, and was going into the fifth grade reading on a kindergarten level. We had already been through due process against the school in an attempt to force the school to provide him with adequate reading services. Unfortunately, the court ordered reading services were pretty useless when implemented by our school.

In our final Individual Education Plan (IEP) meeting, my husband and I expressed concern that our otherwise intelligent son still could not read and he wanted to go to college. One school administrator snapped at us, "He will probably never read well and he is _not_ college material. You just need to lower your expectations."

It was quite evident they had very low expectations for our otherwise intelligent son. He spent some time in his reading class watching baseball on T.V., other days playing games, and some ineffective amount of time working on reading skills, which didn't lead to any meaningful progress over the five years he had been in school.

Our youngest had mild dyslexia, both inattentive and active-type ADHD, and was in the gifted program at school. He was bored to the point of creatively entertaining himself in the regular classroom with behaviors his teacher didn't find amusing. My seven year-old son's

ADHD, giftedness, and poor impulse control, coupled with his ideas of creative "fun," contributed to emerging class-clown skills. Looking back, I clearly see the problem wasn't with my son: it was the traditional school environment that did not adequately meet my young son's learning needs.

We had to "do something," but I wasn't sure homeschooling was going to be the right answer. Deciding to homeschool was extremely difficult for us. My husband and I came to the decision quite reluctantly. We felt as though homeschooling was our only viable option given our income and the distance to private schools that might actually be able to meet our boys' needs.

Our choice to homeschool was an absolute last resort—we had never considered homeschooling at all previously. However, we knew something had to change if our sons weren't going to end up illiterate or dropping out of school. Taking a chance on homeschooling was our "rescue mission" to save our sons from an otherwise bleak educational future. Depression and hatred of schooling was settling in the minds of our boys, and our boys were still in elementary school!

Quite frankly, when we started homeschooling I was shaking in my shoes. I was concerned about the responsibility homeschooling carries. I knew our boys had unique learning needs. My own personal shortcomings allowed my fears to keep me awake at night as I wrestled with my issues with impatience, organization, and even where to begin. Nevertheless, my guys were both having significant issues with public school. Neither of them fit into the traditional education box and they weren't learning much, even though they both had above average intelligence levels (as evidenced in testing).

Once we made our decision and actually began homeschooling, I felt like a TON of bricks was lifted from my shoulders because I no longer had to deal with "issues" the public school created for my boys' self-esteem, lack of learning, etc. However, I also felt like I was finding my way through an unending jungle of options with blinders on.

There were many, many choices of methods, curriculum, social opportunities, etc. There were an unfathomable number of decisions to make, most of which required hours of research in order for me to make the best decisions I possibly could. My hope is that this book will help take the blinders off of your eyes, clear the forest for a better view, and that this book will help you find success with your child without the anxiety and stress I experienced.

If you're curious about how things turned out for us, my older son graduated from our homeschool high school simultaneously with finishing his freshman year of college. He was accepted into the Honors program at his chosen college and he has been on the Dean's List every semester, having earned mostly A's and a few B's. Because of our homeschooling and his advanced studies, my older son will be able to finish college in three years. Please Note: this is my son who our public school said would "probably never read well" and was "not college material." He is definitively "college material," who is on track to graduate in three years with no major issues.

My younger son is following swiftly in his older brother's footsteps. He also took joint enrollment courses during both his Junior and Senior years of high school, graduated from high school simultaneously with completing his freshman year at college, and has earned all A's and a couple of B's in his college coursework to date. I fully expect our youngest will be as successful as his older brother. Our youngest will likewise be on track to finish his college degree in fewer years than it typically takes to earn a B.S. degree, and is receiving a scholarship that covers a large chunk of his tuition.

Our homeschool outcome is nothing short of phenomenal given the public school's prior predictions, and I thoroughly believe that homeschooling is one of the best options for educating a child with learning differences. If your child does not learn well in the traditional classroom, especially if he or she is being held back by the traditional school environment, if he struggles severely, is bullied or belittled, or has challenges that are not met by the school, you will probably be able to bring about a better educational outcome for your child by teaching him or her yourself.

Do not let your inexperience or uncertainty scare you away from homeschooling! Once you are immersed in homeschooling, and you experience this fulfilling way of meeting your child's needs, you likely will wonder why you didn't start homeschooling sooner.

For me, my beginning standard was simply to "do better than the public school." I will say, in our first year of homeschooling we easily surpassed the educational progress my sons had made in the five years they were enrolled in public school. As measured through standardized testing, my boys made more educational progress in our first year of homeschooling than they had in all of their prior years in public school combined. The rest of our homeschooling years were icing on their cakes, educationally speaking.

Based upon our experiences, and those of the many parents in the Learning Abled Kids' support group, I'm virtually certain you can meet your child's one-on-one unique learning needs. You can meet your child's needs as well as (or better than) most public schools if you are willing to consider your child's individual educational needs and be actively involved in schooling your children. Homeschooling is not always an easy journey, but it is rewarding in countless ways you may not have imagined. Homeschooling is an adventure well worth undertaking, for you, your children, and your entire family!

If you still aren't convinced, check out my previous book, "Overcome Your Fear of Homeschooling" available on Amazon at a low price. "Overcome Your Fear of Homeschooling" addresses many of the misconceptions I had prior to homeschooling, as well as concerns typical parents have prior to beginning their homeschooling adventure. It's a fairly quick and easy-reading book that may help bolster your confidence. It will give you a better understanding of what homeschooling is really like and how homeschooling can meet the needs of your child.

With that said, let's get started answering the 75 most commonly asked questions by parents beginning the journey of homeschooling their learning abled child.

1 GETTING STARTED WITH HOMESCHOOLING

What are the benefits of homeschooling a child with learning disabilities?

There are many benefits to homeschooling a child with learning differences, some of which are obvious, and others which are only seen over time. An unexpected benefit we found to homeschooling was starting with a child who is well rested and whose mind is accessible for learning when instruction begins.

You may have major battles over homework with your child, and therefore you may think homeschooling will be a continuation of those battles. Keep in mind: at the end of a long school day, your child is tired, often feeling poorly about himself, and the last thing he wants to do is more of what is difficult for him, which is schoolwork. So, you end up with protracted battles of wills to get the homework done with tears, tantrums, timeouts, and who knows what else. These battles probably make you think it would be 'impossible' for you to homeschool. I know patience was a major concern of mine before we began to homeschool, but homeschooling changed the dynamics significantly for us, and quite possibly they will change for you too.

Consider this: If your child sleeps as late as he physiologically needs to, then he will arise well-rested. Your child can have a healthy, leisurely breakfast, and you can go for a morning walk to get the blood pumping to your child's brain, then you can sit down to work on school work. I can assure you, most days will go much better than you may envision if you are currently looking at the contentious completion of homework at the end of a long school day as your vision of how homeschooling will be. Not to be mistaken, there is a needed measure of patience to meet the learning needs of a child that has learning struggles, but your battles over learning will be short-circuited with a well-planned school day and carefully chosen programs.

I was very pleasantly surprised by how well our schooling went once we got out from under the artificial schedule imposed by traditional school hours. Setting your own schedule will let you meet your child's needs much better than you may anticipate. Having access to a bright-eyed, well-rested child made a huge difference in our ability to work well together. I won't say we never had to deal with tantrums, because that wouldn't be true, but tantrums disappeared over time, once we got past the "I can't" mindset my older son acquired while he was in public school.

The greatest benefit of homeschooling is your ability to tailor instruction to meet the specific needs of your individual child. You can vary the level of instruction for each subject based upon your child's learning strengths and weaknesses and his performance in the specific subject. For example, a disability in reading doesn't mean your child has to remain below grade-level in science, social studies, or math. Individual subjects can be taught at your child's level of understanding in that subject.

For example, although my son could not yet read when we began homeschooling, he had a huge fund of scientific knowledge and was quite adept at learning information and concepts presented through educational multimedia. At home, we were able to feed my son's science learning appetite as we worked on learning to read. There was no need to hold back his acquisition of science-based knowledge solely because he struggled with reading.

Disabilities can also be circumvented by using curriculum that doesn't limit your child's learning to learning from books. For example, you can use videos, museum experiences, books-on-tape, etc. to teach science and/or history to a child with dyslexia until the child is capable of reading. You can use speech-to-text software to let a child learn how to create a composition while he is learning to master handwriting. Using alternate means of education and assistive technology allows your child to move ahead wherever your child is able, and allows you to work on remedial skills in reading, writing, or math until your child masters the foundational skills.

In addition to individually tailoring instruction, you can vary your pace of instruction on a daily basis to meet your child's individual pace of learning progress. In a traditional classroom, the class may be proceeding too fast for your child in some subject areas and too slowly in others. When your child is in traditional school and struggling, if he doesn't master critical foundational skills 'on time', he is left behind. Being left behind can become educationally devastating over time, particularly when the foundational reading, writing, and math fact skills are left behind. When homeschooling, you can repetitively teach any basic academic skill until mastery is achieved.

While homeschooling, you can also spare your child's self-esteem from the ill-effects of peer ridicule usually experienced in a classroom setting. Children are cruel, especially to anyone that is different. Given you are a kind, loving, and encouraging parent, you can help your child conquer tough concepts and skills without belittling him because the concept is difficult for him to learn.

If your child is academically advanced in some areas, you are free to advance instruction as rapidly as your child can master the subject. Each and every day you can instruct your child at his current level of understanding, in each subject, whether it is advanced or remedial instruction. Being able to work at your child's current level of understanding and being able to progress instruction at your child's learning pace will help insure a solid educational foundation.

With homeschooling, you can also provide instruction in a manner that matches your child's primary learning style(s), so he can gain optimal educational benefit from each lesson. Given that most classrooms are taught in an auditory fashion (talking and reading), if your child's learning style is visual or hands-on/kinesthetic, he will not gain as much knowledge from the lecture/reading type of teaching as he might with other teaching styles.

Multisensory teaching, using all learning styles, is the best way to maximize student understanding and learning retention, but traditional classroom teachers seldom have the time and inclination to provide the variety of activities necessary to meet all learning style needs. Some fabulous teachers have a natural knack for incorporating a lot of hands-on and visual teaching into their instruction. Unfortunately those teachers are not overly common. When you homeschool, you have the luxury of teaching almost exclusively in your child's learning style, which will enhance learning and require less repetitive teaching.

Higher academic achievement for children with learning disabilities is another important benefit of homeschooling. Although there is little in the way of published research specifically focused on the academic achievement of children with learning disabilities who are homeschooled, the research which exists has shown homeschooling has a positive affect on achievement as compared to peers with learning disabilities taught in public schools.

Your ability to work with your child one-on-one has been shown to be the most important factor in educational achievement when homeschooling a child with learning difficulties (Delquadri et al., 2004, p. 153). This is essential for you to know and remember! Read that sentence again. Make note: it is not your level of education, your income level, nor specific training that is the primary factor in successful homeschooling. The primary factor in homeschooled children having better academic advancement than traditionally schooled peers is the one-on-one teaching provided by the parent—you.

In the same study, children who have Attention Deficit Hyperactivity Disorder were studied in public school and homeschool settings. In the study, the homeschooling parents had a high school education and the teachers in the public school held Master's Degrees in Elementary or Special Education. The study results showed the "homeschool students were academically engaged about two times as often as public school students and experienced more reading and math gains" (Delquadri, Duval, & Ward, 2004, p. 140). Thus, the one-on-one teaching and your ability to tell whether your child is academically engaged at each moment of instruction are major factors that will lead to successful outcomes in your homeschooling.

With homeschooling, there is almost always an improved ability to get schoolwork done in a shorter amount of time because of efficiency in learning. When you begin homeschooling, you will be able to focus on addressing your child's specific learning needs directly through one-on-one teaching. Your child can break for food, the restroom, or get up and move when needed, so biological needs won't become the kind of distraction to learning as they are in traditional schools when a child has to wait until the next bathroom break or becomes hungry before the designated lunch time.

You can limit distractions. No time is needed for classmate's questions about material your child already understands and other distractions are eliminated, which take up time within your child's school day. Thus, homeschooling instructional time is also more efficient than most traditional schools.

Your child's positive self-esteem can also be brought forth through homeschooling. Further study data shows parents tend to focus more on what a child CAN do and parents are more positively encouraging than are teachers in traditional schools. Frequently, children with learning disabilities are also taught with lowered expectations for learning outcomes. Study data shows homeschooled students progress well beyond "traditional expectations" and can retain a positive self-image when taught with much encouragement and love by a teaching parent (Ensign, 2000, p 151). Public schools tend to focus on a child's disabilities and what he can't do. Homeschooling parents tend to focus on encouragement, focus on each small victory, and they focus on what a child can do. Maintaining a 'can do' teaching focus while teaching your child will result in your child's self-esteem remaining intact.

Another aspect of homeschooling which helps develop positive self-esteem in your child is the separation of social time from learning time. We experienced no social 'judgment' by homeschooled peers in our social outings because the kids accepted each other at face value during playtime interactions. The children had no idea which child had learning difficulties, what kind of difficulties, or how any disability might affect a child's learning.

Often in a traditional school environment, children with learning disabilities are bullied and teased by their peers. While my son was called demeaning names in public school by his classmates, among our homeschool friends there was no name calling whatsoever. When participating in homeschool events, you'll experience more civilized interactions between the children because the parents are usually right there watching and correcting any bad behaviors that may be emerging.

All-in-all, homeschooling was the best decision we ever made for our boys and it made an immeasurable difference in my older son's feelings of self-worth as well as in his educational progress. Our only regret was that we wasted so much time trying to make the public school meet our sons' needs before we embarked on the homeschooling journey. If we knew *then* what we know *now* about homeschooling, I would have jumped in feet first a whole lot faster than I did!

My child says she doesn't want to homeschool; should I make her?

What if your child doesn't want to be homeschooled? It happens! Should you force your child to homeschool? When asked this question, my answer to this question almost always begins with a question: How old is your child?

It is easier to homeschool an elementary aged child because parents are still a strong authority figure to the child. As a child gets into high school, she is often an independent thinker and has a broader circle of friends she may object to leaving behind. Leaving public school in order to homeschool, generally speaking, becomes more difficult as a child gets older. However, a child can be successfully homeschooled beginning at any age given good management of learning and social opportunities.

Truly, I think any child who is elementary aged, no matter how mature, doesn't have the ability to fully understand the ramifications of educational decisions that will affect her life. She may have reasons for wanting to stay in public school in spite of a lack of learning progress, but the longer she remains in an inadequate learning environment, the further behind her peers she will get. Eventually, being behind will take its toll on your child's self-esteem, social interactions, career potential, and in other areas which an elementary-aged child cannot fully grasp.

Thus, I think an elementary aged child should not have any direct say in a decision about whether to homeschool or not, especially if the goal is to homeschool for a year or two until the child has mastered basic reading, writing, and math skills. While your child may not have a direct say in the matter, I would highly recommend open discussions about why you are going to homeschool and about your child's fears. I recommend you address all of your child's fears with compassion and a mindset toward finding solutions to make homeschooling better for your child than she anticipates.

In dealing with mature middle school or high school aged children, I'd recommend frank discussions about the pros and cons of each schooling alternative with your child. If a child is middle school or high school age, then she is probably capable of understanding the long-term benefits of a solid education.

Depending upon what your child may want to pursue career-wise, the strength of her education may be a prime selling point on the idea of homeschooling. If your child is well behind grade level in one or more areas, or has to spend hours from sun-up to bedtime diligently working on schoolwork in order to complete her homework, discussing the benefits of shortened school days often helps build an interest in homeschooling.

As a brief side note, homeschooling leaves more time for social activities than you expect. The efficiency of one-on-one instruction will better enable you and your child to finish schoolwork within the confines of a typical school day without having any remaining "homework" to do in the evenings. While shortened school days aren't an obvious benefit until you get started homeschooling, the benefit here is that your child will have time to explore new social opportunities.

As an example, my older son used to have difficulty participating in any activity, including scouting, because he had to spend his evenings completing homework. Schoolwork took him much longer than his typical classmates, so he often came home with schoolwork he had failed to complete in class in addition to his regularly assigned homework. This meant my son's life was mostly schoolwork, all day and every night, with very little time to enjoy just being a kid. His life was school. Within a relatively short time of beginning to homeschool, my son's life became much more fulfilling from both a social and an academic standpoint. He was able to get involved in activities he never had time for while in public school, and those activities made him a much happier guy!

Parents may have greater difficulty obtaining buy-in to the idea of homeschooling with teens, and may have more difficulty gaining compliance with schoolwork in general, but the changeover to homeschooling has also been known to be a great relief to struggling teens who need more time to learn without all of the traditional school drama. If a high school aged child is behind academically, there is a good chance she will have adopted an "I'm dumb" mindset which will require an extra measure of compassion and encouragement if you are going to homeschool.

When a child worries about leaving her friends at school it is usually because the child is specifically worried about not having any friends, she's afraid of feeling isolated or not getting to see her close friends. Older children in particular have peer-based social needs that must be met. It is very beneficial to sit down with an older child and discuss difficulties she has with school, the benefits of homeschooling, and to share reassurances that her social needs will be met through a variety of outside activities and ongoing contact with her close friends. As the homeschool director, you must make sure your child has social opportunities. You can usually find activities with local homeschooling groups for your child to participate in (there is more about socialization in the "What about socialization and homeschooling?" Q&A later in this section).

If your child has been bullied or is suffering from very low self-esteem, it may be easy to convince her to give homeschooling a try. If your child is highly popular, with lots of friends and activities, there will be significant trade-offs for a solid education versus a well-established social network. Homeschooled teens can often make their lives as socially active as they want, but it does require purposeful effort on the parent's and teen's part. It isn't as easy as hopping on a bus and going to a building where there are hundreds of peers. Parents must actively seek out opportunities to socialize with other homeschoolers through local support groups, sports, and other activities. Teens must be willing to explore new activities and friendships. It takes willingness to work together to build a new social network, but often the established social network is still viable, especially with a child's closest friends.

One of the first things you should do to help your child adjust to homeschooling is to sleuth out homeschooling groups and activities in your area. Investigate social opportunities in your area even before starting to homeschool. This will allow you and your child to know what the available options are in your area, and will help your child gain confidence her social needs will be addressed right from the beginning.

With the above considerations, I think the final decision about whether or not a child will be homeschooled should always be made by the parents. It is essential for you to listen to your child's concerns with compassion and understanding, and assure her you will meet her needs in every way you possibly can, short of letting her make the final decision. If you decide to homeschool, you must be willing to do your best in meeting your child's educational needs, in supporting her emotionally, and in making sure she/he has high quality peer interactions. You must be willing to do some sleuthing to find the right educational programs and viable social opportunities.

As a marketing tip, you can obtain buy-in more easily if you enter into an agreement with your child to give homeschooling a try for one full school year or until she is caught up academically. Such an agreement often inspires a child to work harder if she truly wants to return to public school. If you make such an agreement with your teen, you can see where things stand academically and socially at the end of the agreed upon timeframe.

We initially planned to homeschool for three years at a minimum, through middle school, and planned to put our boys back into public school when they reached high school age. However, by the time our boys reached high school, neither of our sons wanted to return to public school. Homeschooling was so well ingrained in our family lifestyle that neither my husband nor I wanted to have our lives dictated by homework assignments, the school calendar, or other issues and demands that arise from public school. We had been there for five years before we began homeschooling and we had all come to love the freedom homeschooling provides our family.

With a great homeschooling experience, you may find your child has no desire to return to public school, even if she is caught up at the end of your agreed upon number of homeschooling years. Our love for the homeschooling way of life was so deep by the end of middle school that we forged ahead with homeschooling through high school. Homeschooling has been an excellent experience all the way through!

While it isn't an easy decision to make, and it is even more difficult if your child objects, I hope you can reason well with your child based upon some of the insights shared. Gaining willingness to homeschool, even if it's on a trial basis, is often the start to a great change in your whole family's way of life.

Can the public school prevent me from homeschooling if my child has disabilities?

Parents who are considering homeschooling sometimes ask if their public school can prevent them from homeschooling a child with learning disabilities. Occasionally, parents are even told they cannot homeschool a child with special needs, presumably because the parent isn't "qualified" to homeschool the child.

Looking down upon homeschooling a child with special needs is not based upon any research or data showing it is a bad idea. Most negative opinions are based upon suppositions that any teacher with a degree will be better able to teach a child than the child's parents or antiquated perceptions that homeschooling somehow stifles social development. Research actually shows homeschooling brings about better academic progress for children who need specialized, well-engaged, one-on-one instruction even if the parent only has a high school diploma. Research also shows that homeschooled students are well socialized and often more involved in their communities than publicly schooled peers (Romanowski, 2006). Thus, you shouldn't let anyone's mere opinion about homeschooling convince you that you are incapable of homeschooling your child.

As a more direct response to the question, generally speaking public school systems in the U.S. cannot prevent a qualified parent from homeschooling a child with disabilities, and a parent is "qualified" by whatever stipulations the state law specifies. For example, Georgia requires homeschooling parents to have a high school diploma. If you are in Georgia and do not have a high school diploma, you aren't legally "qualified" to homeschool your child whether your child has disabilities or not.

In all states, you will want to check your state laws to determine the requirements you must meet in order to legally homeschool your child. It is important to be aware that many states have homeschooling requirements which you must meet in order to homeschool. You will want to be sure you are both qualified in a legal sense and that you comply with the legal requirements for homeschooling in your state.

To determine your state's homeschool requirements, go to a major search engine and type in:

<your state> gov "department of education" "home school" requirements

You can copy the line above and simply change **<your state>** to the name of the state in which you live. By using this wording, your state's actual department of education rules will likely be at or near the top of your search results. Read over any rules or regulations posted about the legal requirements for homeschooling. You will want to pay attention to the specifics in regard to parental qualifications to homeschool.

Virtually every state has information about homeschooling requirements and associated laws somewhere on the State's Department of Education website. If you can't find the regulations on your state DOE website, another good resource is the Homeschool Legal Defense Association's website. They have information about state laws on their state-by-state pages at:

http://www.hslda.org/strugglinglearner/sn_states.asp, but keep in mind—your state DOE website will likely have the most current information. You may also want to check the HSLDA.org website to see what the homeschooling climate is like within your state, so you will be well prepared to deal with any issues you may encounter with your public school system.

It is completely legal in all 50 states for a qualified parent to homeschool a child with disabilities, however a handful of states have additional requirements parents must follow for homeschooling students with disabilities. Several states require additional oversight of your child's educational program as a means of determining if your child's educational needs are being sufficiently met, but most schools have the same rules for students with and without learning disabilities.

Although you may be required to submit to school oversight in your homeschooling, *do not make the mistake* of thinking the school system has a right to say you can't homeschool your child if you are complying with the laws. Neither should you let them convince you they can automatically provide a better education for your child. Federal special education laws (IDEA) do not prohibit homeschooling. Additionally, homeschooled children are generally not placed on individual education plans with public schools unless the parents desire an IEP or consent to having the school system oversee their child's education.

As an example, North Dakota requires additional oversight for any homeschooled child scoring below the 30th percentile on standardized testing, whether that child has an identified disability or not. An assumption by the state seems to be that a low scoring student would not be low scoring if the child were in public school.

Unless every single student in North Dakota's public schools scores above the 30th percentile, there is no reason to believe the school system would necessarily be able to provide a measurable improvement in your child's achievement level. The additional oversight is beneficial in making sure you've considered various options for meeting your child's needs, but there is **no assurance the school could provide better educational outcomes** for your child.

Some children are more difficult to teach, whether the child is in a traditional school or not, and low achievement scores are not indicative of whether the educational progress would be better or worse with a different educational placement. The studies previously mentioned show a child receiving direct, one-on-one, explicit instruction at home is likely to demonstrate better educational outcomes than the educational achievement of similar peers receiving instruction in a traditional, special education, group setting.

I always find it amusing that the school systems judge parents upon a homeschooled child's standardized test performance, but the schools make all kinds of excuses about the scores of low performing students within their own public school walls. Be aware, if your child falls below any monitored threshold in your state, the public school officials may try to pressure you into placing your child in their school as if that is a guarantee they can provide a better education. It is often the case they can *not* bring about better educational progress unless you have not been providing a thoughtful educational program for your child. Unless you are required by state law to place your child into public school, you should in no way feel obligated to do so.

Given that any individual state's laws may change during any legislative session, please be certain to refer to your own state's homeschooling laws when you first begin homeschooling and occasionally thereafter. Referring to the laws regularly will enable you to see if the specific homeschooling requirements have changed, or whether special requirements have been added for students with disabilities.

Don't let the legal requirements scare you, even if there are specialized requirements for homeschooling children with disabilities in your state. Legal compliance is often more of a formality than interference to homeschooling, and many states have become quite friendly toward homeschooling over the past couple of decades. As long as parents do an adequate job of homeschooling their children, and homeschooling parents are legally compliant, then the climate toward homeschooling is likely to remain amicable.

What steps do I need to take to legally start homeschooling?

The steps you must take in order to legally begin homeschooling are as varied as the number of states in the U.S. Some states have virtually no notification or reporting requirements, while others require curriculum planning, portfolio reviews, annual testing and other measures with oversight by the local school systems. Therefore, knowing your state's legal requirements is the first step in beginning to homeschool legally. To determine your state's homeschool requirements, go to a major search engine and type in:

<u>*<your state> gov "department of education" "home school" requirements*</u>

You can copy and paste the search text above and simply change <your state> to the name of the state in which you live. By using this wording, your state's actual department of education rules will likely be at or near the top of your search results.

Locate the rules for homeschooling and read through them in their entirety. Every time you see the words "must" or "required" in your regulations, pay particular attention to the specific requirement stated. Verify you are able to meet each compliance requirement. The following are common compliance questions you should seek to answer:

— Do you meet your state's requirements for personal eligibility to homeschool? (high school diploma, teaching certificate, etc.)

— Are you required to notify your state or public school system you will be homeschooling?

— Who are you supposed to notify of your intent to homeschool?

— If notification is required, how are you required to notify the school system? In writing? By meeting with someone?

— When are you required to give notification? Is there a deadline?

— What, if any, educational plans do you have to submit to the school system?

— Do you have to submit a portfolio of learning or progress reports?

— What kind(s) of documents do you need to submit on a regular basis for ongoing legal compliance?

Usually, the first required legal step is notification to let your local public school entity or state Department of Education know you are beginning to homeschool your child. In most states, you must send the public school system a "Letter of Intent to Homeschool," must fill out a notification form with your public school system, or go through specific procedures within a limited number of days before or after the establishment of your homeschool.

Outside of the initial notification of your intent to homeschool your child, the variations of requirements from state-to-state are so diverse that it is impractical to discuss specific legal requirements in a book such as this one. Some states require parents to be members of an oversight organization, others require submission of lesson plans for approval, and our state requires relatively minor compliance steps such as the keeping of annual progress reports and standardized testing once every three years.

Regardless of your state's requirements, you will want to be sure you are in legal compliance with homeschool laws for your state. Be sure you understand all of the rules for homeschooling in your state, and comply with every aspect of the law, so that you are never subjected to "educational neglect" charges for failure to properly educate your child within the laws of your state.

If you are unsure of the requirements, ask other homeschoolers in your area or call your state department of education and ask for clarification. Most states make it fairly easy to homeschool, so hopefully legal compliance will not be a burden for you.

Exercising the utmost integrity in keeping and submitting your homeschool records within the strict limits of the law will protect your right and ability to homeschool as well as the ongoing ability of all families to homeschool. When any one homeschooler fails to comply with the law, it sheds a bad light on the homeschool community and makes legislators, public school personnel, and invasive community members want to create additional laws to make it harder for anyone to homeschool. Accurate and conscientious compliance with your state's legal requirements will help keep your freedom to homeschool as a viable freedom indeed.

Although it is not a legal requirement for getting started, it will help you immensely to find a local support group for homeschoolers in your area. Homeschooling is a popular means of schooling with millions of homeschoolers nationwide, so there are support groups in every state. You can find local groups through group forum providers such as Yahoo! Groups, Google Groups, Facebook, or other social networking sites. In most of these group sites, you can search for <your state name> and "homeschool". Homeschoolers generally spell the word as a single, compound word rather than two separate words. Searching for "home school" can lead to many results that do not apply to homeschooling.

Once you make contact with other homeschoolers in your area, if you have not already figured out the required forms and legal requirements, the other homeschoolers will be able to show you examples of the required paperwork and will be able to explain the procedural requirements for homeschooling in your state. In addition, the group can help you know when, where, and how to submit required documents to public school officials. You can ask other homeschooling parents questions about your local public school's attitudes and practices when it comes to homeschooling and the group can help you find activities your child may enjoy.

Having connections with other homeschooling families in your state, and especially in your more immediate geographic region, can be an invaluable resource for information as questions come up. Connecting with a local homeschooling group at the beginning of our homeschooling experience made our transition much easier than I anticipated. Additionally, having local homeschool connections provided opportunities for park days, field trips, and other social outings that made homeschooling more fun for both me and my children!

What services are public schools required to provide for homeschoolers?

The level of services a public school system is required to provide to homeschoolers varies at the state and/or local level. At the time this book is being written, U.S. federal laws regulating services provided to homeschooled students with disabilities are limited to rules in the Individuals with Disabilities Education Act (IDEA). Under IDEA, there is no requirement that public schools provide any specific services to homeschooled children other than to evaluate and identify whether a child is a child with a disability. Thus, if you request an evaluation through your public school, they are required to evaluate your child, but the public schools are not under any obligation at the federal level to provide educational services to a homeschooled child.

While the federal law specifies public schools are required to seek to identify children with disabilities, parents are not required to identify any child to a school as a child with a disability. Because school systems are required to *attempt to identify students with disabilities*, you are likely to receive a notification from your local school system asking about disabilities your child may have or that you suspect. However, at the time of this book's writing, you are not required to disclose your child's disabilities or your suspicion of a learning disability under U.S.

Federal law. (You may want to verify that is still the case when checking your homeschooling laws, but at this time parents are not required to notify the district of existing or suspected disabilities—the district is required to seek children with disabilities under "Child Find" laws, but the parent is not required to notify the school as per IDEA.)

At the federal level, the laws regarding services to students with disabilities are open-ended. There is no direct mandate for public schools to provide or not to provide services to homeschooled students, but there are some provisions for private schools to provide services to students. Thus, if you live in a state which legally defines homeschools as "private" schools, your school system may be obligated to provide the same level of educational servicing under IDEA as is provided to private school students.

There is nothing at the federal level that prevents school systems from providing services to homeschoolers; therefore some states have implemented their own laws to provide services to students with disabilities who are being homeschooled. Here again, you will need to seek out your state's laws regarding whether schools in your state are required to provide services to homeschooled students with disabilities. The Homeschool Legal Defense Association (HSLDA) has a brief state-by-state listing which includes special needs provisioning information. The HSLDA listing may be seen at:
http://www.hslda.org/strugglinglearner/sn_states.asp.

If you decide to identify your child to your local school system in order to get special education services, the school will seek to evaluate your child to determine whether your child is, in fact, a child with a disability. You have the right to give consent to the school or to deny consent for an evaluation. If you deny consent, the school system has the right to file for due process to force you to allow them to evaluate your child, but they are unlikely to do so if you are complying with all homeschooling requirements in your state and are providing your child with an adequate education.

Only a handful of states have special requirements for identifying students with disabilities to the local school system. Some of those states provide extra support under state-level provisioning. North Dakota is one such state that is notably more invasive in their oversight of homeschooled students with disabilities or students who have low scores on standardized testing. While North Dakota is more invasive in their oversight of a homeschooled child with disabilities, they also provide additional supports and services for homeschooled students who are struggling with learning. If you are in North Dakota, you will want to be sure you understand the requirements and restrictions for homeschooling students with disabilities.

Wherever you live, you will want to seek out your state's DOE (Department of Education) website, and look for specialized "home school" requirements. Many states' public school systems provide no services whatsoever to homeschooled students, so there is little to no benefit in identifying your child as a child with a disability in those states.

If you consent to having your child evaluated by the school, and subsequently place your child on an Individualized Education Program (IEP) with the public school, you are accepting the public school's oversight of your child's education. Any services you accept will bring your child under the school system's supervision in regard to their special education provisioning and the associated legal requirements. Given you have agreed to place your child's education under the supervision of the IEP team, your public school will have the right or obligation to dictate how you educate your child based upon the agreed upon IEP.

Be aware that some school administrators have been known to tell a parent she must cease homeschooling and demand enrollment of the child into the public school. A parent always has the right to refuse the public school's services, but she may encounter difficulty with the school honoring her right to refuse services. There have been cases where school systems have filed due process against a parent to force enrollment of a child, so it is advised that you try to determine the attitudes of local school administrators before seeking services that would be "nice" to have provided by your tax dollars.

Also, public school personnel frequently do not fully understand your rights as a parent to choose how to educate your child, and schools are sometimes under the misconception that they are always more "qualified" to educate your child. They will sometimes pressure homeschooling parents to enroll a child into the public school, or may threaten legal action if you don't do what they think you should. As long as you are homeschooling within the requirements of your state's laws, you should remain confident that you have a right to refuse public school services in most circumstances regardless of the threats they may make.

Given you are not under a legal requirement to involve the public school in your homeschooling, carefully weigh whether you wish to have the involvement of the school along with IEP oversight by the school. There may be great benefits to working with your local school if your child needs speech-language therapy, occupational therapy, or other specialized programs you are otherwise unable to afford for your child. This is especially true in some of the creative school districts I've known who have provided in-home tutors for homeschooled students.

Some schools are absolutely fantastic in working with a variety of educational solutions, including homeschooling. Sadly, a high level of public school collaboration with homeschooling families is relatively rare. Just be aware: you will relinquish some control over your child's education by accepting publicly provided educational services, so it's best to know the homeschool versus public school climate prior to requesting services from your local public school system.

Before seeking services, ask around to see if your local schools provide great services with respect for homeschoolers, or whether they make homeschooling parents feel inadequate by implying the school can do a better job of educating any child. Use public services if you need or want them, but don't feel obligated to use services just because they're available.

If you cannot afford private educational services, which you know your child needs, and if your public school is willing to provide those services, you may decide it is worth working with the local school to receive services. Your decision should be based upon your personal circumstances, your ability to meet your child's needs through privately provided services, the legal requirements in your state, and the climate of homeschooling in your state (whether local school systems routinely help or hassle homeschoolers). Your goal should be to fully meet your child's educational needs while protecting your child from environments that don't provide uplifting encouragement and meaningful educational gains.

Am I smart enough to homeschool my child?

Unless a parent has homeschooled from the beginning of Kindergarten, or close to the beginning of elementary school, she often wonders if she knows enough content knowledge to homeschool her child. This is particularly true for parents who have not taken any college classes and are considering homeschooling through high school. People often ask me, "What about Algebra? Or Chemistry? Or Physics?" Then they comment, "I couldn't ever teach my child Algebra.. or chemistry.. or physics!"

"SURE YOU CAN!" I say!

Consider this, while students in homeschool settings out-pace their public school counterparts, one study observes "the low student-teacher ratio in homeschools, and not specialized training, apparently enabled parents to create effective instructional environments" (Delquadri et al., 2004, p. 153). In other words, you don't have to be a genius, or even particularly smart, to give your child the one-on-one attention he needs. This is particularly true in elementary school, as it is in middle school. I'll explain how this works in high school in a minute.

When a child is learning early skills, even if it is during the later years of schooling, they are said to be "learning to read." When a child acquires the skill of reading, he can then "read to learn." Given the main skills you have to be able to teach are reading, writing, and math computation, you need to be reasonably educated, with a high school education or having knowledge equivalent to the completion of high school, in order to teach your child the necessary skills he needs in order to be able to learn from typical educational materials.

Once your child has learned the basic skills, a large portion of his learning is gained from using the core skills of reading, writing, and math computation. You don't have to know everything your child needs to know. Your child can learn independently simply by reading a book or watching educational programming.

Most of us can handle teaching elementary school subjects without much difficulty. Middle school subjects can be more of a challenge, and high school subjects can be difficult if you don't have the needed knowledge to teach your child directly or your child isn't able to figure out the content on his own. However, as many veteran homeschooling moms will tell you, there are a wide variety of ways you can help your child learn without needing to personally know any given subject.

Two subjects I felt unqualified to teach were Chemistry and Physics. Luckily, with the size of the homeschooling market, the plethora of retired teachers, skills of other homeschooling moms, and online courses, you can often find someone to teach difficult subjects to your child or to act as a learning consultant for your child. If you are remotely located, there are great online and FREE resources through online educational initiatives. You can find a listing of several free resources at: http://learningabledkids.com/multi_sensory_training/free-multisensory-curriculum-online.htm.

There is also a wide variety of teaching videos on YouTube which help explain topics you may not personally understand or be able to teach. Your child can watch instructional videos that explain difficult topics on one of these sites, and can often gain full understanding of any concept by watching a variety of teaching videos on the topic at a variety of different sites.

Aside from using free online teaching videos, both of my sons took chemistry from highly qualified women who teach classes in their homes. My older son took chemistry from a woman who holds a Master's Degree in Chemical Engineering, and my younger son took chemistry from a former classroom teacher who has a passion for chemistry with hands-on experimentation. These outside classes had a very small class size, and each one met my sons' needs perfectly based upon their individual learning styles.

Additionally, sometimes a child and a parent have difficulty connecting on a specific subject and a child requires outside help. Such is the case with my younger son's need for assistance with Physics. We looked at in-home and face-to-face classes, but the content and scheduling didn't meet our needs. When we found an online Honors Physics class available to homeschoolers, my son decided to take the online class which allowed him to work at his own pace. The course provided my son with an instructor who explained physics better than I would have been able to, and the online class preserved the good will between my son and me.

In our case, my son would have had to wait while I studied and figured out physics concepts I didn't know off the top of my head.

Making him wait while I figured out whatever he didn't understand would have held up his ability to move forward in his lesson which would have halted his learning momentum each time he needed assistance. Since I don't really know physics, it was just better to let someone else teach my son. For any homeschooling parent, I think it is important for the parent to recognize her own short-comings and to know when it is wise to seek outside assistance.

We've known other homeschooled students who took classes online through http://christianschool.apologia.com/online-classes.asp, http://keystoneschoolonline.com/, http://derekowens.com/, and other online providers. While you may not want your child to sit at a computer to take online classes all day long, taking one or two classes in this format is an excellent way to provide courses you may be incapable of teaching or may be nervous about covering on your own.

Additionally, if you have a healthy homeschooling community near you, you may easily be able to swap instruction with another mother or two. For example, I know a mom who LOVES biology and dissection. Most moms think, "EEEEWWWW!!" so this particular mom swaps her biology and dissection instruction for art lessons for her daughter with one mom, for foreign language lessons with another mom, and a couple of other swaps for other types of instruction for her daughter. How you teach your child any given subject depends solely upon your willingness to think outside of the "I must teach my child everything" box.

So put your mind at ease! You do NOT have to be a rocket scientist to educate your child well. In fact, it's fairly easy to find online classes, computer-based resources, and teaching videos that will provide direct instruction for topics which you don't feel qualified to teach. If you are able to read, write, and do basic math, you are qualified to manage your child's education. You can provide direct teaching to your child for subjects you know and use outside resources when you are hesitant about your ability to handle a subject.

In some cases, you may find your child is sufficiently able to self-teach, so no outside resources are needed. This is usually true in a child's area of passionate interest such as my older son's desire to learn about Marine Biology. I just provided the instructional materials, then my son dove in with passion and taught himself. In summary, you CAN homeschool your child without knowing it all!

What if I don't have enough patience to homeschool my child?

One of the most frequent responses I receive when I say I homeschool my children is, "I could never homeschool my child. I don't have the patience for it!" Most parents *think* they are not patient enough to homeschool their children. Believe me; I did not think I had the patience for homeschooling either.

Before we began homeschooling, I often snapped at my sons, particularly when it came to completing homework in the evening. Their dislike for homework, resistance to it, and our relatively frequent battles over required homework made me believe homeschooling would be similar in terms of daily battles over schoolwork. Truthfully, before we began homeschooling, I was quite concerned about what I considered as my relative lack of patience and our daily homework battles.

Unexpectedly our relationship dynamics changed significantly once we began homeschooling. Most of the stress our family was under stemmed from trying to fit our unique children into the rigid and regulated schoolhouse box. Our boys encountered a mindset in school that led to higher levels of sassiness, and at the end of the school day—their fatigue caused them to whine and resist doing homework. The stress of the whole situation led to shortened tempers in all of us.

When we "de-schooled", a name homeschoolers have given to the process of getting away from the pressures of traditional public school with its schedules and demands, all of our tempers improved naturally. Whining disappeared and I had bright-eyed happy boys to work with at the beginning of our school day. Let me tell you—this makes all of the difference in the world when it comes to the matter of having patience.

Since we no longer had to arise early, race out of the house to get to school, eliminated random unexpected homework assigned by the school at inconvenient times, didn't have to spend hours doing excessive homework, etc., we all began to feel more relaxed. We got up whenever we awakened naturally, so we were fully rested each day. We leisurely got ready in the morning, and usually began schoolwork sometime before 9:30 a.m. We finished all of our school work during the day and had no homework to deal with in the afternoon as we all began to get tired.

A large dose of patience came automatically with de-schooling and homeschooling. As we distanced ourselves from the regimented and time-driven public school requirements, all of us grew in patience unexpectedly. I cannot remember the last time I snapped at either of my guys. None of us is perfect and I do get frustrated at times when things are not progressing as I had hoped, but patience has actually been an unexpected bonus of homeschooling.

Most homeschooling families I know are laid-back about their days, and they enjoy each others' company far more than they ever expected. It turns out; being with your kids 24/7 can build stronger relationships, deeper understanding, and greater patience if you don't have outside attitudes, demands, and unexpected surprises intruding into your home on a daily basis. Think back to when your children were little and you loved watching them be themselves, you loved doing activities with them, enjoyed going to the park or outside together, and you relished the time you had together. Homeschooling is an extension of that family-focused time spent together, learning, exploring, and growing in love and respect over time.

Therefore, you shouldn't let any lack of patience you may feel at this very moment keep you from homeschooling. If you are like most homeschooling families, patience will come with the removal of outside pressures applied by traditional school schedules and expectations that don't fit your family's individual needs.

Aside from the natural reduction in stress we experienced when we left the public school system, I gave myself constant reminders of why we were homeschooling to help maintain my new focus on maintaining patience. Here is why:

After five years in public school, my older son was depressed. He cried in the evenings, wouldn't look anyone in the eye, and he hardly spoke a word to anyone outside of our family. He was convinced he was incapable of learning. He was kicked on the playground, had his head bashed into the concrete to "knock some sense into him", was called moron by his peers, and told by his teacher not to bother to do assignments because he couldn't do them anyway. To say his self-esteem was low would be a gross understatement.

One thing I knew I had to do in our homeschooling was to help restore his self esteem. I knew I could never belittle him, yell at him for his struggles, nor treat him with any disrespect if I was going to help him recover from the trauma of his public school experience. One of my primary homeschooling goals was to recover my son's sense of self-worth. Does that mean I never got frustrated with him or never on the verge of loosing my temper? Definitively not.

There were several times I had to put myself in a timeout as the frustration welled up inside me. I would say, "Mom will be back in a minute." I would head to our upstairs bathroom, in the far recesses of the house, and cry. I'd grit my teeth and clench my fists, and call up to God, "Why me? Why do I have to deal with this?"

It was at those peak moments of frustration and crying out that I would remember I came to homeschooling to save my little boy from feelings of worthlessness and from the lack of compassion he experienced because of his learning struggles. I would remember the bright, bubbly, happy little guy he was the first day of kindergarten. I knew that joyful boy was still inside my now frustrated, depressed, "I can't do it," son whom I was in the process of rescuing. So, I would splash my face with cold water, blot it with a towel, put on a smile, and head back downstairs cheerfully saying, "Now, where were we? Let's try again and maybe this time it will seem easier!"

Truthfully, I grew in my personal level of patience and compassion as much as my boys did educationally. I now have more patience than I ever dreamed, and so much of it that other people marvel at it! I now know what the heart of sacrificial love is and I know the immense satisfaction found in putting your child's needs before your own.

As adults, we can understand the ramifications of growing up to be illiterate, of being unable to follow a career path that is a passionate interest of ours, and most of all—we are the adults, so we have to lead our children by example. It's not always easy, and patience is not always our first response, but I am fully confident that if I could grow and change through homeschooling, you can too. You will grow with the natural reduction in stress you will find from not having to deal with a typical, traditional school, and you can grow further in exercising patience if you put good self-coping strategies into place. A place to cry in the recesses of my house was an invaluable resource for me.

As my sons regularly say now, as I have said to them regularly to encourage them to retain patience and perseverance over their sometimes difficult schoolwork, "Patience is a virtue!" It was my way of encouraging myself as I encouraged my boys. So, I say to you, "Patience is a virtue," and you can have it too.

What about my child's socialization needs?

Socialization of children who are homeschooled is a matter deeply misunderstood by many people including relatives, friends, school personnel, and even parents who are just beginning to homeschool. Unless you are actively involved in the homeschool community already, awareness of the great opportunities homeschoolers have to socialize is usually non-existent. That said, you must actively seek opportunities for your child to interact with others and to make new friends.

Luckily, in today's society, there are a lot of opportunities for homeschoolers to participate in activities, sports, learning co-ops, etc. with other homeschoolers. However, depending upon where you live, finding these kinds of social opportunities may be easy or challenging. Almost all large metropolitan areas have large homeschooling communities and opportunities of all sorts can be found. Small communities may have fewer opportunities, but you may be able to create opportunities. Thankfully, today's Internet-connected society makes it easier for you to connect with other homeschoolers even if you are remotely located.

No matter where you live, you have to find social opportunities for the sake of your child. The quickest way to find local homeschool groups is to visit any major Internet search engine and search for "homeschool" and your city, county, or larger geographic area. For example, you could search for "homeschool northeast Georgia" or "homeschool Jefferson County, AL".

When you find a homeschooling group(s), write or call the contact to receive information about their activities or information they may have about other groups' activities nearby. Ask the contact person about opportunities of interest to you and/or your child, find out if or when the group meets, then get involved. You can ask, "Do you know of any local art classes for homeschoolers?" "What sports opportunities are available for homeschoolers?" or "Is there a local learning co-op?" If you are looking for specific opportunities, just ask and one might be available.

If your child is interested in an activity, and you can't find a program already in place, consider helping coordinate the activity for other homeschoolers. For example, my younger son wanted to take golf lessons, but we couldn't find a golf program for homeschooled students. I called our local golf course and asked them about starting a program in the afternoon for homeschooled children. They jumped on the opportunity and my son took golf lessons there for three years.

Many businesses which offer activities for families or children are interested in catering to homeschooled children while the majority of their clientele are in school. It is a win-win situation for businesses. They have to be open anyway, so offering classes for homeschooled children enables them to serve the community during a time when they would otherwise have very few customers. It just makes sense for businesses who offer services for children to offer opportunities to homeschooled children during the normal school day.

Many of businesses are willing to offer classes at discounted rates for homeschoolers too, especially when they are made aware that almost all homeschooling families are single-income families. Serving homeschoolers provides income the businesses would not have otherwise even if it is at a discounted rate.

So, if there is an activity your child would like, call businesses to see if they'll start a program, then tell other homeschoolers about the opportunity. You will undoubtedly have others who are interested in participation as well. Most homeschooling activities are started because a parent took the initiative to start something on behalf of her child.

Through homeschooling, our guys have participated in many opportunities offered by individuals and businesses. My sons' activities have included sprint kayaking, rowing, golf, tennis, creative writing, fencing, basketball with a former Globetrotter, Engineering, Chemistry, bowling league, swim league, Airsoft shooting, orienteering, drama, weekly park days, a middle school field trip group, and more. Our guys have toured the Federal Reserve Bank, the Tennessee Aquarium, Georgia State Botanical Gardens, gone to JapanFest, Michael C. Carlos Museum, The Heritage Center, Elachee Nature Center, the Zoo, the High Museum of Art, attended the Atlanta Symphony in an exclusive performance, and have participated many other field trips exclusively for homeschoolers.

Being actively involved with our local homeschooling community has provided us with numerous opportunities for expansion of our social circles and educational experiences.

Socialization with homeschoolers is vastly different than it is in public school as well. Given your child has disabilities, there is a possibility your child has been belittled or bullied in school. Socialization of the bullying-type is more **harmful** than helpful and can reduce a child's self-esteem for a lifetime.

While many people perceive a child will not be 'properly' socialized if he is homeschooled, the truth is many children with disabilities are not treated kindly by peers in a traditional school environment. Bullying is a common experience for children with disabilities, leads to depression and distrust, and is definitely not 'proper' socialization. Additionally, some kids with disabilities mimic behaviors of peers in school; including bad behaviors. Socialization through homeschooling can help turn around a child's low self-esteem and help to eliminate bad behaviors learned through improper socialization in public school.

When your child is homeschooled, his education will be handled one-on-one, at home by a loving parent—you. When your child then goes to social enrichment or sports activities with other homeschooled kids, those kids will have **no idea** your child has learning differences. *Because homeschooled children learn apart from each other, typical homeschooled children don't shun a child who has learning disabilities, because they have no idea whether learning is easy or difficult for other children.* Homeschooled children tend accept each child at face value, unlike in public school where every child in the class knows if your child is 'slow' to learn, comparatively speaking. Your child is far less likely to be teased in a homeschooling group.

Additionally, if a child with a Learning Disability (LD) experiences any form of teasing or taunting at a homeschool activity, many parents are usually close-by to correct the offending behavior immediately. The respectful interactions with constant adult supervision teach your child he is worthy of being treated well, and it teaches the other homeschooled children that teasing is an unacceptable behavior. The same level of oversight and control is just not possible when there are a couple of classes at lunch or on a playground, 50-60 children, with only one or two supervising adults.

On a broader spectrum of socialization, children in public schools are grouped in artificially constrained groups of same-aged peers. Throughout the rest of a person's life, he will interact with persons of all ages and all abilities. Homeschooled children often interact with children of a wider range of ages on field trips, park days, and in other activities.

At outings, it is not unusual to have kids of all ages from the very young up through seniors in high school. Since homeschooling is generally family-based, all of the children in a family come to most activities. The older children help the younger children, and the younger children share their exuberance with the older children. The social opportunities most often lead to joyful interactions for just about everyone involved. Consequently, homeschooled students are usually found to have appropriate interactions and communicate well with children across a wide variety of ages.

Homeschoolers also interact frequently with a large number of adult figures through outside activities, frequent field trips into the community, and when talking to any number of adults who ask them why they aren't in school on any given day. It is not uncommon to have doctors, field trip leaders, or other professionals comment about how articulate and well-behaved the homeschooled children have been during a visit, and I believe this is due to the form of broad socialization that comes naturally with homeschooling.

Interactions of homeschooled children with a wide variety of people helps equip the children with social skills that enable them to interact well with society at large. Studies have found homeschooled children to be very adept at social interactions with a wide variety of people in a broad spectrum of social situations (Romanowski, 2006).

Let me contrast for you "public school versus homeschooling" socialization as they are experienced in practice. Here, for your consideration, is each of these types of "socialization" as they affected my son:

When we sent our older son off to kindergarten, he was a talkative, bright, happy, and outgoing little boy. He was bubbly, excited about learning, and his most frequent exclamation was, "Mommy! I know something! Know what? …" He was like an information sponge and very excited to learn new facts.

By the time we began to homeschool, my son had been bullied, called names, kicked, pushed around, and teased so severely that he would not look anyone in the eye. He would hardly speak to anyone, and his self-esteem was lower than the belly of an ant. You would be hard-pressed to find a more socially withdrawn child. Throughout the school year prior to homeschooling, our son cried about going to school with some degree of frequency. He was so abused at school that it robbed him of any readiness to learn, so his educational progress was non-existent.

That's what "socialization" in public school did to my son. Outcomes of this devastating kind are hardly what people are thinking of when they worry about "socialization" of children who are homeschooled.

When we began homeschooling and went to park days, my son would not talk to the other kids, but they would include him in their play. He played alongside them, but did not talk to his peers for nearly two years. Since he had always been included and accepted 'as is', he slowly began to feel comfortable around the other homeschooled children. Over time, my son came out of his social shell, and began making singular comments here or there to his friends.

By the end of our third year of homeschooling, my son would chat with the other kids to some degree. Today, people would never know he had a problem with shyness or that he was so withdrawn, but our homeschooling friends have remarked about the transformation they have seen in my son.

These days my son laughs, chats, and talks with other people openly. I credit homeschooling for the return of my son's social abilities and for the restoration of his self-confidence. I shudder to think of where our son would be today if we had left him in our local public school environment which was destroying him day by day.

If your child's self-esteem and joy are being crushed by an oppressive traditional school environment, I implore you to consider homeschooling as a way of rescuing your child from a situation that is killing the very spirit of your child. If your child is bullied with any regularity at school, you may find homeschooling to be one of the best possible moves you can make to save your child, socially speaking.

A different kind of social concern emerges if you live in a remote location. If you are remotely located away from other homeschoolers, another avenue of thought for you is the possibility of Skype-Pals. Many homeschoolers we know have pen pals, and a new trend is to have friendships with other homeschoolers who are remotely located. We have a couple of friends who have Skype Pals in foreign countries, and they help each other work on their foreign language skills.

For students who live far from a larger city, they already have an area of common interest—remote living. By asking within online homeschool groups, you may be able to find online friends for your child. Of course, you should always practice good Internet safety protocols, monitor online interactions, and screen to be SURE you know who your child is communicating with online. While it can be difficult to get started building online friendships, they can be a great way for kids to connect.

All of this is to say, don't let concerns about socialization hamper your decision to homeschool. You will have to search out opportunities, but if you are anywhere near a metropolitan area, you should be able to find groups and activities for your child to participate in with relative ease.

We have simply found homeschooling socialization to be a much easier area to fulfill than we suspected before we joined the homeschool community, and it has been far better than the type of socialization we experienced through our public school. I hope you are excited about the social opportunities you find and that you find some that are as fabulous as those we experienced.

How do I know what I should teach my child?

At the lowest level of academics, the critical skills to teach are reading, writing, and math computation skills. If a child can master these basic skills, then he will be prepared to engage in learning at a higher level. When a child has learning struggles in one of the critical skills, it is a good idea to focus on direct teaching of the critical foundational skills with intensity for a period of time.

When concentrating on your child's critical skills, don't dilute your child's learning by focusing on broad coverage of academic subjects. Covering "everything" is often counterproductive to making effective progress in the critical skills. For example, reading inferences, poetic phrasing and beats, etc., can wait until a child proficiently reads grade-level books. Teaching of grammar, parts of speech, writing genres, etc., can be delayed until a child is able to write decent sentences and paragraphs. Math is naturally hierarchical, so you wouldn't teach a child percentages or sophisticated math concepts until he understands adding, subtracting, multiplying, and dividing.

I'm not suggesting you withhold any instruction that your child is capable of understanding because there are accommodations that can be made for reading, writing, and math to allow your child to learn higher level concepts. Rather, I am suggesting if you are trying to teach your child to read, spending an hour and a half to two hours on reading itself is sufficient for "literature" instruction for the day. Lessons to teach higher level concepts can be added as the amount of reading instruction your child requires lessens over time.

With that said, there are requirements in many states to cover specific topic areas. For example, in our state we are required to teach reading, language arts, math, social studies and science. For a child with learning disabilities, social studies or science are often their "fun favorites," so including them in your school day will make the day less tedious, not to mention they will allow you to meet the legal requirements. However, you do not have to "teach" science or social studies as separate subjects if you use a bit of outside the box thinking.

If you have a non-reader beyond third grade, I'd highly recommend focusing a large portion of your formal instructional time on teaching your child to read. You can use what is known as "non-fiction narrative" books for reading practice, which will enable you to cover history and science without directly studying those subjects separately. Just consider it "efficiency in learning."

Non-fiction narrative books are based upon true stories, events, or scientific concepts, but may not be 100% fact oriented. For example, a book that tells a story from the view of Pocahontas helps your child learn about the lives of Native Americans without teaching history directly is considered a "non-fiction narrative." The "Magic School Bus" series focuses on scientific concepts, and this series was a hit with my boys. They also loved the "Magic Treehouse" series, which covered historical, scientific, and geographical information. By using non-fiction narrative books, you can overlap instruction by teaching other subjects while practicing reading.

If your child has difficulty with reading, you will find it beneficial to check out Hi-Lo books. These books provide non-fiction titles of high interest with low reading levels. There is a list of Hi-Lo publishers at: http://learningabledkids.com/home_school_info/specialty_curriculum.htm.

To select Hi-Lo books for your child, look for books with your child's Interest Level (IL), which will be his chronological grade level based upon his age, and his current Reading Level (RL). For example, a child who is chronologically old enough to be in the sixth grade, but reads on a third grade level, would need books with an IL6, RL3 specification.

To determine which topics you may want to teach your child, you will find most states have "standards of learning" published for public schools to use to meet the local education standards. For homeschooling purposes, you can access the standards on any state's website (it doesn't have to be your own state unless you are required by law to follow your state's standards). Any list of state educational standards will suffice in helping you know what topics you should teach your child.

Some states' standards are easier to understand than others', depending upon the amount of educational jargon used in writing the standards. Thus, if you are not required to teach from your particular state's standards, look at other states' standards until you find a listing of standards you feel will be easy for you to work from.

I'd like to say too—no person or school covers every single tidbit of content listed in any standard. Additionally, standards vary from state-to-state and sometimes even within school districts. There is a national movement toward uniform standards of learning, called "Common Core," to be implemented across all 50 states, but no specific, pre-defined set of informational facts are essential for every child to know other than the possibility of core skills in reading, writing, and math. In fact, I feel "Common Core" will stifle innovation and creative thinking, so I personally don't feel like common core is a wise path to take educationally. Therefore, selecting a standard (any standard) to go by, working from that standard, and varying it based upon your child's interests, will be sufficient for providing your child with a well-rounded education.

Do not feel like you have to teach your child every single thing about every subject under the sun. Homeschooling parents sometimes have a tendency to worry about what their child doesn't know. Try not to worry at all as long as you are regularly teaching your child, she is learning, and you're covering a reasonable breadth of subject content. Your focus should be on what your child is learning and her forward progress.

If you prefer to use an actual book about what to teach your child, you may want to use the "What Your _th Grader Should Know," where the blank is 1st, 2nd, 3rd,...th, book series. These books are good resources for planning and checking off topics as you teach them. Following the suggestions for each grade-level will give your child a well-rounded education. The book series includes books for each grade level from Kindergarten through Sixth grade and you can search for the various grade level titles on Amazon (What Every ?th Grader Should Know).

Once a child reaches 7th grade, he is usually entering into more advanced analytical learning. If your child is reading and ready, you can start him on beginning high school courses like Physical Science, Biology, and Pre-Algebra. If your child is still not ready for high school, you can proceed with a general 7th grade curriculum. Advance only in subject areas where your child is academically ready, and use standard 7th grade curricula where your child may still need to improve his core skills and abilities.

High School students generally study topic-based courses such as Biology, American History, British Literature, Geometry, etc. For High school requirements, I highly encourage you to follow the general High School Graduation requirements for High School diplomas in your state. It is also advisable to be aware of differences between diploma requirements for college-bound students versus those who plan to enter into a skilled trade. Assume your child may want to go to college, and prepare at the higher level, unless your child clearly expresses total disinterest in attending college.

As an alternative to planning your child's high school course sequence, you can buy a packaged curriculum and not worry about specific standards of learning or specific high school requirements. There are many providers of entire grade-levels of curriculum like Sonlight, A Beka, Alpha Omega Publications, etc.

If you are a secular person, you may want to check pre-packaged, comprehensive, grade-level curricula to determine if it will be offensive to your personal beliefs. There are many options for Christian Homeschoolers because homeschooling was initially most popular among those who homeschooled for religious reasons. Today there are many programs provided for high schoolers of any background, whether religious or secular, via online charter schools (K12, Connections, etc.), and through high school programs sponsored by universities, and other initiatives. You can find an extensive list of online programs at: http://learningabledkids.com/college_and_high_school/virtual_high_schools.htm.

If you don't find a comprehensive high school program to your liking, you can purchase textbooks from any of the many textbook publishers who publish for the public school markets. Often, you can find used textbooks offered very cheaply on Half.com or eBay. The public school systems switch to new textbooks every couple of years and dump the old books with used book resellers.

Many of these books also have audio-book versions available for purchase, which can be very helpful if your child cannot read well yet. Do NOT let his inability to read hold back his high school education. You can find audiobook versions through the publishers themselves or via audiobook providers like http://www.learningally.org/ or Audible.com.

Although you can't possibly teach your child everything there is to know, don't fret! There will be gaps in your child's education, just like there is for every single child in public school. Take just a moment and think back to your classes from high school. What percentage of the specific information you learned in high school do you remember and use in your everyday life today? If you're like most people, you only remember a small portion of what you learned. Much of what kids learn they forget anyway, so don't fret about the details as long as you are covering topics rather thoroughly and your child is learning well overall.

Understanding concepts, why things happened, and how things happened is much more important than being able to recite trivial facts like all 50 state capitals, the date any given war started, who fired the first shot, etc. If your child understands that World War I came before World War II, the reasons the wars happened, and general chronological timeframes, he will understand the wars as well as most of the general public. Given your child can recognize the names of states versus countries, and knows the general region of the U.S. for any given state, again—he will understand states as well as most of the general public.

How detailed you want to be in your educational requirements should depend, to a large degree, upon your child's inclination toward learning trivia and his desired profession. If a child wants to become a scientist or loves science, knowing detailed facts of a scientific nature will be much more important than knowing how to diagram a sentence. If a child doesn't understand and can't diagram a sentence, dare I say it—let it go. It's unlikely he'll ever have to diagram a sentence as an adult for any reason. While it is a topic listed in many standards for learning, the ability to diagram a sentence is not an essential bit of core knowledge for the vast majority of adults.

Cover what you can, try to be fairly thorough, but don't sweat memorization of details or worry about trying to cover everything. I'm SURE there will be some people who will gasp at the previous paragraph, but really—all college students and adults I know have been fine despite random gaps in their knowledge base.

My spouse doesn't think we should homeschool. What should I do?

If you're struggling with the question of whether to homeschool or not, or are feeling uncertain about your choice to homeschool, I hope the info provided here will be both encouraging and uplifting to both you and your spouse.

Before homeschooling, my husband wasn't at all convinced it was a good idea either. My husband had his doubts about my organizational skills and ability to stick with projects through to completion. Truthfully, I had my doubts too. However, we both clearly knew public school was not working for either of our boys. He wasn't fully "sold" when we began, but knowing the facts helped open the door to his willingness to give homeschooling a try.

Given your or your spouse's uncertainty, I would suggest researching to find great articles, videos, and books about homeschoolers' achievements, homeschool successes, and information

about how homeschooling works. One of the best starting points is to determine the (un)likelihood that your public school will ever meet your child's specialized learning needs well. If your child has learning struggles, you will want to look at the U.S. Department of Education's statistical proficiency data:
http://www.learningabledkids.com/DownloadablePDFs/AchievementLevelsForStudentsWithDisabilities2010.pdf .

This data shows academic proficiency for elementary, middle, and high school students in each state across subject areas. Keep in mind, there have been numerous cheating scandals lately where school systems have modified their students tests to make it appear the students are achieving at higher levels. Thus, when looking at the above report, remember that the data, if correct, is likely the best-case scenario.

In states like Georgia, which has been rocked by a major school cheating scandal, the aggregate data must come under suspicion particularly if personal experience leads you to think performance isn't nearly as high as the school system's *self-reported* data. In other words, despite what this table indicates, if you've had bad experiences with your public school, you are likely to continue to have bad experiences.

There are studies which show that homeschooling works well for most families. I specify "for most families" because sometimes the child or parents have problems which make homeschooling extremely difficult to handle. I have known families who were committed to homeschooling, where the child's needs were so extensive and draining that the toll of teaching the child at home was an insurmountable difficulty for the family. Subsequently, the child was placed into a public school program, which allowed the family to function more smoothly and to have more love and patience with each other at the end of the day.

On the other side of the coin, I've known a few families with a child who was constantly struggling, had social issues, discipline problems, etc. in public school. Having to deal with the constant school demands, rigid procedures, and the child's issues became disruptive to the entire family. The situation placed stress on everyone in the household. Bringing the child home to a loving, stable environment was the key to quieting their lives down.

You have to do what works for your family overall, so what I say here is not a blind recommendation toward homeschooling at all costs for every family, but rather for consideration of your personal circumstances in regard to whether homeschooling will be a viable solution for your family. How well homeschooling works for your individual family will depend upon all of your children and the personalities within your household.

When considering whether to homeschool or not, homeschooling works best when you have buy-in from both parents. Without mutual agreement, there is tension that develops which is counterproductive to a good homeschooling environment.

When one parent is spending days teaching children, evenings grading papers, reviewing or scheduling lessons, and chauffeuring children to social activities, it is a full-time job. Household dynamics change both in management of the home, and in family interactions, thus everyone in the home is affected by homeschooling and spousal support is a life-saver. Full buy-in from both parents helps with homeschooling success in the long-term.

With some situations, like our family's, one spouse may be skeptical in the beginning, but is willing to give homeschooling a try. If one spouse objects, but is willing to give homeschooling a try, then give homeschooling a whirl. In our case, and in several other cases I know, one year of homeschooling was all that was needed to show that homeschooling provided a better quality of family life and better educational advancement than public school. Hopefully, if you give homeschooling a try, you will have a good outcome and will continue homeschooling with more confidence.

When seeking to 'convince' your spouse, you should not nag, beg, or plead. It works best to talk openly about concerns and address them with research about homeschooling and by forming an educational plan.

If your spouse isn't sure you're qualified to teach your children, share research data with your spouse. For example, the research shared in the next paragraph shows one-on-one teaching from a loving parent goes a long way toward helping a child make learning progress, even without any specialized teacher training whatsoever. The parents in the study were parents with high school diplomas.

One of my favorite studies observes "the low student-teacher ratio in homeschools, and not specialized training, apparently enabled parents to create effective instructional environments" (Delquadri et al., 2004, p.

153). "The results showed that the parents, although not trained to use methods such as direct instruction or mastery learning, engaged their students at higher levels of academic responding than the public school instructors achieved with their students" (Delquadri et al., 2004, p. 153).

The Delquadri study shows that students with learning disabilities make more progress in a one-on-one homeschooling environment than they do in the classroom. That alone is a good reason for homeschooling. You can find a lot of good research information about homeschooling at the National Home Education Research Institute (http://nheri.org/).

If your spouse is concerned about your organization and planning, start planning! Having a plan laid out for what content you are going to teach, when you are going to teach, and how you are going to meet your child's individual needs will show your spouse you have the ability to organize and plan. Whether or not your spouse objects on the grounds of planning and organization, you will need a plan to get started, so it won't hurt to lay one out as evidence that you are going to approach homeschooling thoughtfully.

If your spouse is concerned about socialization of your child, research and find homeschool co-ops, play groups, park days, etc. in your area. Look for activities your child can do with other children outside of your academic day. Refer back to the prior Q&A in this "Getting Started" series for additional information about how socialization for homeschooling can be of a more positive and beneficial nature than socialization for a child with learning difficulties at a typical public school.

Share information you find about local homeschool socialization opportunities with your spouse. Again, this is information you'd need to find if you are going to meet your child's socialization needs while homeschooling, so it will not be lost effort.

When my husband and I were discussing homeschooling, I printed articles and study data about homeschooling for my spouse to read. He would read the information in the evenings or on the weekend, and we would discuss the pros and cons of the matter. As I shared information with my husband during the school year, while our sons were still in public school and having difficulty, he became more willing for us to give homeschooling a try.

We had our fateful, change of course IEP meeting at the end of the school year when our school administrator told us we just needed to lower our expectations. She insisted our son would "probably never read well" and—as she said with emphasis—"He is **_not_** college material." At that point my husband had become convinced enough about homeschooling to say, "I'm DONE HERE." –And he meant DONE with public school!

Our goal when we started homeschooling was simply to "do better" than the public school. Our older son had been in public school for five years, received specialized reading instruction, and yet was going into the fifth grade unable to read competently on a first grade level.

Lucky for us, it wasn't at all difficult to perform better than our public school. We surpassed every expectation the public school had ever expressed. In our first year of homeschooling, my son went from a 0.9 grade reading level to a 6.2 grade equivalent, which surpassed any expectation we had dared dream for ourselves. From there, homeschooling enabled both of my sons to make excellent progress on an ongoing basis.

Although the teachers and administrators at our school were "highly trained," as they liked to remind us, they had our son's educational provisioning completely W-R-O-N-G in saying he wouldn't read well and wasn't college material. Our son entered the honors program at a large university, has been on the Dean's List each semester, and is quite capable of reading well at the college level. If you have a gut-instinct that your child is capable of learning at a higher level than your child's school says—it is important to listen to your instincts.

If your child has specialized learning needs, you can also show readiness to teach him by obtaining any specialized training that would be beneficial for meeting your child's individual needs. Although, as the previous study showed, specialized training isn't required to have decent progress when compared to the provision of one-on-one instruction, the extra training does add strength to the instruction you provide.

As an example, since my son had severe dyslexia, I completed a 56-hour course in the Orton-Gillingham Methodology used to teach children with dyslexia to read. With this training, I was well-qualified to teach our son how to read, and the training was invaluable for understanding how to meet my son's learning needs best. I do believe having specialized training enabled me to accelerate my son's learning progress, especially given the one-on-one teaching I was able to provide.

Truthfully, your spouse's doubts can be a blessing because they will help you become better prepared for homeschooling. My spouse's doubts helped me focus on training, planning, and preparation for the realities of homeschooling my sons. When we began, I had a plan for our entire first year, had obtained specialized training, and we were able to make good progress by following our plans. Initially, we agreed to homeschool until our older son could read, and we thought we would send him back to public school when he reached reading proficiency. Once we got into the homeschooling lifestyle, and saw the wonderful benefits for our family, we never had any desire to return to the public school nation.

By the end of our first year of homeschooling, we had a HUGE reduction in our stress levels as a family and a great improvement in our boys' learning. By the end of our first year of homeschooling, I had complete buy-in from my spouse for further homeschooling. From there, the rest has been history, as they say. While spousal doubts can be frustrating when you want to homeschool now and your spouse doesn't, tackling any doubts head-on can better prepare your entire family for the realities of homeschooling.

Is my child too old or is it too late to start homeschooling?

Is it ever too late to rescue your child from an inadequate education? Never! Sometimes a child is in middle school or high school before parents realize there is a significant problem and the question of timing can be of concern. Beginning to homeschool during high school requires careful consideration and effective planning to insure your child has the needed credits for his future college or career plans. Whatever your child's tentative plans may be, you can rethink your child's education at any point in time.

If your child is past the 10th grade, and if your child is significantly below grade-level when you begin homeschooling, circumstances can make it more difficult for your child to receive a typical college-prep diploma "on time." However, if you are willing to postpone graduation a year or two, your child can conceivably catch up.

Let's look at considerations for beginning to homeschool at various grade levels.

If your child is behind, the sooner you get started with homeschooling, the more likely you are to be able to provide enough remedial instruction to make a meaningful difference in your child's educational outcome. If you begin homeschooling when your child is in third through fifth grade, he is probably not as far behind as he will be if you wait until middle or high school. It is generally easy to catch your child up to his grade-level peers during his remaining years of schooling if you have a good number of school years remaining.

If you don't start homeschooling until mid to late high school, you will only have a couple of years to overcome an 8-10 year deficit in learning. Needless to say, that makes the job much more challenging, but there are various ways to approach the problem. Just beware the later you begin, the more intense your instruction will need to be if you are going to help your child reach grade level in all subject areas.

If your child is entering or in sixth grade, you are at a juncture that will provide good timing for instructing your child to meet his critical learning needs prior to high school. Given that it generally takes three years of intense, one-on-one instruction to take a non-reading child to a level of reading proficiency, starting in sixth grade gives you a sufficient window of time for one-on-one instruction. Although I have not been able to find specific data on remediation progress for written expression or math computation deficits, I would imagine that daily, intense, one-on-one instruction for a period of three years would also be sufficient to overcome basic deficits in any of the foundational skills. Thus, timing if your child is in sixth grade is relatively ideal as far as getting a late start on remediation goes.

Typical grade-level instruction provides one year of academic progress for one year of instruction. If your child is behind, and you want to catch him up, your child will need to progress 1.5 to 2 or more years academically for each single (calendar) year of instruction. In order to provide the needed intensity of teaching, you will need a targeted program that will meet your child's specific learning needs. You will need to provide intense, direct instruction (whether by you personally, a tutor, a computer learning program, or whatever means you can find), on a daily basis, for more than an hour per day, to enable your child to make sufficient progress.

If you do the math, three years of instruction at 1.5 years worth of progress allows your child to make 4.5 years of progress during three years of intense instruction. If you are able to work with sufficient intensity, and your child is academically engaged enough to allow 2.0 years worth of progress for each of three years, you can bring about 6 years worth of academic progress in a three year period. In three years, my son went from 0.9 (a kindergarten level) to a 13+ grade equivalent, which was an average of four years of progress for each of the initial three years we spent working on intense reading remediation. I count that nothing short of a miracle, and thank the Lord for our progress.

For remedial reading instruction, research shows that one-on-one teaching must be given for two hours or more per day, every day, for a period of three years to take a child with classic, phonemically-based dyslexia from a non-reader to a reading proficiency at a sixth grade level. We followed the recommended intensity guidelines in providing my son's program. If you intend to bring your child up to grade level, you will have to provide intense remedial instruction, whether you provide the instruction yourself or hire someone else to teach your child.

Thus, if your child is in sixth grade and only two or three years behind, you should easily be able to double up on instruction for the foundational reading, writing, and/or math computation skills. If your child is behind in all areas, and the foundational skills are the only direct instruction you provide (as mentioned in the prior Q&A about what to teach), the middle school years should be sufficient for catching your child up. If you can lift your child's foundational skills to grade level, it will permit him or her to have a more typical high school experience, whether by homeschooling or traditional school.

If your child is in eighth grade, as you can probably guess, catching him or her up to the same level as peers will either require more intensity of instruction or an extension of your child's high school education by a year or two. If, by chance, your child is just about to enter high school or has already begun high school, your homeschool planning will need to vary from what may be considered as typical high school academics. Homeschooling can be ideal for catching a child up when remediation begins late in middle school because you can delay entry into high school if your child is not yet academically ready.

In elementary and middle school, academic learning is usually general in nature across each subject area. For example, students study math or English. In Math, students study mathematical computation skills and foundational concepts. In English, study consists of learning to read, proper grammar usage, spelling and writing skills-both compositional and handwriting.

However, when a child reaches high school, he studies specific topics in depth. In Math, the students study Algebra I & II, Geometry, Trigonometry and Calculus. English studies consist of American Literature, World Literature, etc. In high school, subjects are no longer skill-based. They are content based, and a child is expected to have mastered the basic skills needed to complete high school level coursework.

Thus, if your child is entering or is in high school, you need to be aware of the necessary requirements for high school graduation, especially if your child desires to go to college. If your child wants to go into a specialized trade after high school, he will need the basic academic skills in order to be successful in training, but you may not need to worry as much about the specific coursework required for college admission.

An important note: If your child goes for a college preparation diploma, he can go to college or seek any other training he desires with that diploma. If you decide to bypass the college prep coursework required by colleges, your child may not be able to attend a desired college. That isn't written in stone, but a higher level of preparatory course work will give your child a broader range of post high school options when it comes to further education and future employment.

Whatever approach you take in regard to high school completion, given a disability in reading, writing, and/or math, you can take one of two approaches here too. The first is to provide sufficiently intense instruction to overcome the learning disability, and the second is to use assistive technology or accommodations rather than focusing on actually overcoming the disability.

As an example, a child with dyslexia can usually learn to read given sufficient direct instruction in reading using Orton-Gillingham teaching methods, or the child can use text-to-speech software, audiobooks, recorded books, etc. to hear the content read to him or her. While the ability to read outright always serves a student well because he can then function in any environment where reading is required, using text-to-speech technology can provide an opportunity for the student to understand written content.

Unfortunately, text-to-speech is not a viable option in every scenario. Thus, I advise working as diligently as possible to help your child acquire the foundational skills themselves, whether in reading, writing, or mathematics. Using text-to-speech software and audiobooks can help your child advance in content knowledge even though he can't yet read. Therefore, I actually recommend a combination remediation and use of assistive technology.

Aside from the actual remediation versus using assistive technology balance, there are two different trains of thought in helping your child complete high school or earn a diploma. First, if your child does not care at all about college, and just wants to finish high school for employment purposes, you can approach high school remediation from one of two angles.

First non-college angle: Forget the traditional path. In this case, you could seek to work with your child diligently until he becomes sufficiently proficient in reading, writing, and math, and then have your student study for the GED. Local community colleges often offer GED prep classes too. Your child won't be able to pass the GED exam without proficiency in the core academic areas, so working on the core academic skills will be your #1 goal. Obtaining a GED is a perfectly viable way to provide necessary completion of a high school level education to permit a student to get a job, get into a community college, or pursue other career goals.

WARNING: There is a tendency among some parents to be laid back about working diligently on foundational skills because a person can get his GED "anytime," but this is often a disservice to your child if you want him to be able to get a good job and compete well with his peers. If your child ends up in his mid-late 20s before obtaining a GED, employers will tend toward questioning why he didn't finish sooner. If a child obtains a GED "on time" or near to his chronological graduation date, then employers are more likely to dismiss a GED as an alternate education path. Just be aware that anytime a person has a GED, a potential employer may ask why the student got a GED instead of a high school diploma.

Second non-college angle: Delayed or altered traditional path. In this case, you would take a year or two to diligently work on overcoming learning deficits and build the foundational skills necessary for success in traditional high school. While you don't have to work on the foundational skills to the exclusion of all other coursework, you will want to provide a robust chunk of time to provide one-on-one remedial instruction for your child. Meanwhile, you can also let him complete a course or two in his primary areas of interest by using accommodations.

For example, if your child can't read, focus on his one-on-one reading instruction, but let him advance in math, science, or social studies as fast as he would like by using audiobooks, text-to-speech curricula on the computer, or you could read his textbooks aloud to him. You can use a program such as Keystone National High School, Alpha Omega (www.aop.com), or other at-your-own-pace high school program to make progress in high school while working on remedial skills.

You can also opt to work on any high school level course independently by acquiring the teaching materials and helping your child by using the audio book versions, reading aloud to him, taking his dictation, or guiding him through the use of assistive technology. The goal is for your student to complete high school, even if it takes him an extra year or two.

The key is to focus intently on overcoming the areas of learning difficulty without getting into a mindset of *having* to finish high school within a specific timeframe or "on time". When it comes to the grand scheme of life, it really won't matter if your child finishes high school this year, next year, or even the year after. What matters more is that he is able to read, write, and do math with sufficient ability to enable him to do whatever he would like to do as an adult.

High achievement in reading, writing, and math is not entirely necessary given the ability to use audiobooks, dictation software, and a calculator, but understanding what is 'read', knowing how to communicate in writing, and knowing how to calculate to pay bills are all essential skills for independent functioning. These same skills are needed to be considered for viable employment opportunities.

If your child is in high school and wants to go to college, I would recommend a more in depth approach similar to the second option above. Again, timing for completing high school doesn't matter all that much.

What matters is completion of the required course work over time.

If your child wants to attend college, then working as intensely as possible to remediate learning difficulties, along with following a planned sequence of coursework, will enable your child to have a college prep diploma within a year or two of his typical chronological high school time frame. If a student is passionate enough about going to college, working through the summers in year-round schooling can enable him to complete high school relatively close to "on time."

Remember, working on specific remedial skills does not prevent completion of typical high school courses, because you can use assistive technology or one-on-one assistance to work around your child's disabilities. Your goal is to help your student become proficient in the deficit skill areas while simultaneously advancing in high school coursework.

Given that kids with learning disabilities are able to learn, and many are average or above average in academic ability, it is possible for your child to graduate with a college prep high school diploma. The key is in providing the necessary assistance to work around your child's disability (_not_ in doing the work for your child) by reading aloud, taking dictation, or teaching your child how to use assistive technology. By working on the necessary foundational skills and teaching a child how to use assistive technology to work independently, you can actually help your child prepare to be independent and successful in college.

Given a diagnosis of a learning disability, a child generally receives accommodations in college such as having a note-taker, being able to record lectures, having a text-to-speech version of textbooks, answering test questions on a computer, etc. Given the academic aptitude to understand college-level content, a child who is able to qualify for and use assistive technology can be successful in college even if he is not a stellar reader, proficient at writing by hand, or can't remember his math facts.

So, even if your child is in high school and struggling, don't feel like it is too late! In fact, if your child is in high school and struggling—particularly if he wants to go to college—it may be ideal to pull your child out of school and start working diligently to get him on track for high school graduation now.

If your child is in high school and behind by a couple of years or more, I can assure you that it is highly unlikely the remaining few years of school will suddenly bring about a dramatic change in your school's provisioning. If your child is significantly behind going into high school, chances are good he will end up failing and/or repeating some high school subjects. If his struggles get to be an embarrassment to him—he may drop out rather than stick it out to the end and statistically dropping out is a strong possibility.

Therefore, if you are at all inclined to homeschool, high school is NOT too late to start! You will just have to remain highly focused on providing intense instruction in remedial areas to help your child achieve his educational and career goals. Your child can graduate or get a GED given the proper support and instruction, and your key is to focus on what needs to be done over time without worrying about being on time for high school graduation. Time doesn't matter nearly as much as academic proficiency.

What if I change my mind; can I put my child back into school?

One thing I always tell parents is whatever decision you make about homeschooling, your decision is not set in concrete. You can change your mind at any time. If homeschooling turns into a disaster for you and your child, you can re-enroll your child in a traditional school. There are, however, issues you must be aware of regarding accreditation, particularly if you are homeschooling a high school student. Let's talk about elementary and middle school first since they are the easiest to discuss.

If you are homeschooling a child in elementary or middle school, you will generally have no difficulty re-enrolling your child in school at any point. At the elementary level, re-enrolling is usually as easy as showing up at the school's office, filling out paperwork, and the school will enroll your child at his or her chronological grade-level. I've only heard of an occasional elementary school that requires placement testing to accept a previously homeschooled child for enrollment in the public school. Testing is usually a placement screening tool used to determine if a child needs any remedial help, and does not generally affect grade-level placement.

When a child is in middle school, it is not unusual for the school to require a child to have some level of competency-based testing prior to grade-level placement. Given that many classes are segmented into remedial, typical, or advanced levels, the school will want to determine the best placement for your child. Seldom is there any sort of issue in middle school with placement regardless of whether prior homeschooling occurred using an accredited program or not. Again, your child is likely to be placed in his chronological grade level, possibly at the remedial level if you haven't had sufficient time to raise his remedial skills into the average scoring range.

Making the decision to re-enroll a child in public school during the elementary or middle school years is generally pretty easy and straight forward. You may want to access and read your state's rules for enrolling a "transfer" student into a school to see how placement will be handled. Usage of an accredited program is not usually required and changing your mind about homeschooling is easier in the early grades.

If you are homeschooling a high school student, you will want to give more careful consideration about how you will approach your homeschooling. If you are homeschooling a high school student, you will have much less flexibility in reversing your decision, because most public high schools will not recognize your homeschool instruction "as is" unless it is through a program accredited by one of the large, regional accrediting agencies. Even with accreditation, there are many public high schools which will not accept the coursework your child has completed at face-value.

To be clear, accreditation is *not required* for homeschooling in most states. However, few public schools accept the coursework outright as documented by a parent. Thus, if you think there is any chance whatsoever you will want to enroll your child in public school, you will want to check the rules in your state through your state's Department of Education website to determine how or if the schools accept coursework from homeschooled students.

If you decide halfway through high school that your homeschooling isn't working for you or your child, and you aren't using an accredited program, your child may have to begin high school again in order to gain credit for coursework through the school. This can be a difficult and devastating blow to any student. Therefore, if you are at all unsure about whether you will homeschool through to the completion of high school, it is a good idea to consider using a program which is likely to be accepted for transfer credit into your local high school.

Some schools will accept high school coursework completed through an accredited program as documented. Some schools won't accept the work. Some school systems require a child to pass proficiency exams before giving credit for home study / homeschool coursework even if it was completed through an accredited program. Whichever way your school system handles the matter, being aware of the education rules in your state will let you make a sound decision about whether or not you wish to use an accredited high school program.

Be aware that all accreditation is not created equal and there are many accrediting organizations. Many types of accreditation are not recognized by high schools or colleges. Public schools and universities generally recognize accreditation through one of the large, regional accrediting organizations:

- Middle States Association of Colleges and Schools (MSA)
- New England Association of Schools and Colleges (NEASC)
- North Central Association of Colleges and Schools (NCA)
- Northwest Commission on Colleges and Universities (NWCCU)
- Southern Association of Colleges and Schools (SACS)
- Western Association of Schools and Colleges (WASC)

By going through an accredited program, prior work is reviewed and credit is given, but not all accredited schools are accredited by one of the seven agencies above. Be sure you're aware of the type of accreditation any given school has, and you should also know that accreditation can be revoked at any time. It is often best to check with the specific accrediting agency to be sure the program you are selecting is indeed accredited.

Aside from national or statewide high school programs, there are sometimes local options for accrediting oversight as well. Local programs will oversee a students' coursework for accrediting purposes. Most of these programs allow a student to begin schooling through them prior to the students' senior year of high school. All of the schools require a student to study under their supervision for at least one full academic year prior to certifying the student's previous coursework.

You can search for such programs by looking at the listings of accredited schools in your state, by asking questions of local homeschoolers, or searching online for "umbrella" homeschool programs. Once a child reaches his senior year in high school, I don't know of any accredited school program that will certify a students' prior course work without requiring some duplication of effort. There may be a school out there for that purpose, but I do not know of one at this time.

Important questions you should ask yourself when starting to homeschool a high school student in regard to whether you want to use an accredited program are:

1. How likely is it that you will change your mind and stop homeschooling?
2. Do you plan to homeschool for the entirety of high school?
3. How likely is it that something will happen in your life which will require a change in your homeschooling plans?
4. If something interrupts your ability to supervise your child's schooling, is he or she motivated enough and mature enough to complete studies independently?
5. Do you need your child's diploma to be readily accepted at all universities or for scholarship purposes?

These are questions you should consider in determining whether you want to use an accredited program or not. Keep in mind, an accredited program is not required by all colleges and universities, or for homeschooling itself. Whether or not you need or want to use an accredited program depends upon your individual child, your child's needs, and your life circumstances.

We opted for an accredited program through high school because of the Georgia HOPE scholarship funding. It is provided from day #1 in college when a student has an accredited diploma. However, it's not paid until the completion of 30 credit hours of college coursework, if the student does not have an accredited diploma. For us, it was important to have funding for college from the first day of attendance, not after the first year of paying for college ourselves. We have a large number of homeschooling friends who did not use any accredited program and their children were readily accepted to colleges of their choosing.

There is a lot to consider when deciding to homeschool, but most of the weighty decisions don't enter the picture until high school. Hopefully you have time to consider the possibilities for different programs, and to determine your likelihood of homeschooling until your child graduates from high school. Your decisions at the beginning of high school can determine your limitations if you decide to make changes half way through high school, so I hope the information I have provided here will help you think about the various possibilities and considerations that lie ahead.

With this Q&A, I am concluding the basic questions of how to get started with homeschooling. There is still a lot coming up in this book to help you figure out how to meet your child's specific learning needs.

Next Up: We will begin the "Testing and Evaluation Series." I receive many questions about testing and evaluation. Should I have my child tested? Does our school have to provide testing? What if I don't want to label my child?

Answering these questions helps you answer the question "What curricula should I use?" which is probably the most asked question of all. If your child is evaluated and you receive meaningful evaluation results that explain your child's needs, you can provide the specific types of instruction your child requires. I hope the next series of questions and answers is enlightening and helpful when you make decisions regarding evaluations of your child's learning needs.

2 EVALUATION OF YOUR CHILD'S LEARNING NEEDS

Why should I have my child evaluated?

The top reason you should have your child evaluated is for the sake of educational efficiency and the elimination of frustration, wasted time, and misplaced effort due to guesswork in trying to meet your child's needs. Having a comprehensive evaluation:
- helps you understand your child's specific needs;
- acts as a guide for selecting programs;
- helps you provide the right kind of support and appropriate learning experiences;
- and allows you to gain professional assistance more easily, if it is needed.

You may think you know what type of disability your child has, but many times the specific symptoms do not reveal the root cause of a child's actual problem(s). Also, there are often multiple issues present, and if you only address one area, you may find yourself frustrated by a lack of progress because you don't fully understand all of the learning issues you are dealing with. Working on every area of need helps your child make more meaningful progress over time.

As an example, suppose your child is having difficulty with reading. Many conditions cause difficulty with learning to read—Auditory processing issues, lack of phonemic awareness, working memory and processing issues (requiring brain training programs), scotopic sensitivity (which requires colored glasses or overlays), ocular motor problems (requiring vision therapy), attention deficits, absence seizures, etc. While there are many conditions that cause difficulty with learning to read, many people immediately assume their child has "dyslexia" if the child is smart but struggling with learning how to read.

If you assume your child has dyslexia and purchase a program designed to teach a child with true dyslexia to read, but your child has some other cognitive or physical problem, you will be applying the wrong solution to your child's learning problem. Thus, it is imperative you obtain an accurate assessment of your child's learning abilities and disabilities in order to provide the correct solution to your child's learning difficulty.

The only way to accurately identify the root cause(s) of your child's learning problems is to have a thorough evaluation by a qualified doctor—a neuropsychologist (most preferably someone who specializes in the evaluation of learning disabilities) or a psychologist with an educational focus. Please be aware—there are both excellent and lousy evaluators, and both useless and excellent evaluation reports. The lousy evaluators are a waste of time and money, but the good ones can be worth their weight in gold, so be sure to select your evaluator carefully! There is an upcoming Q&A about how to find a highly qualified evaluator, so you will want to read that section before seeking out an evaluator.

A high quality evaluation will assess all areas of cognitive and academic functioning including processing, perception, memory, executive functioning, attention deficits, phonemic awareness, comprehension issues, as well as levels of achievement and ability in core academic skill areas of reading, writing, and math. A comprehensive evaluation of this kind more accurately diagnoses learning or cognitive difficulties and will help determine what type(s) of learning intervention your child requires.

Many times when parents decide not to get an evaluation, they go through several programs, wasting time and money, before finding a program that works for their child. By the time the parents find the right program, **if** they ever find the right program, the child has usually had several disappointing, frustrating, unsuccessful and sometimes demeaning learning experiences. The child ends up feeling "dumb" because he can't get it even with "special" instruction.

However, it isn't the child's learning that's the problem—it's the instruction that does not meet the specific needs of the child. In my opinion, it is your job as a parent to seek out the proper solution for your child and to provide that solution. You don't want to wear yourself and your child out by taking stabs in the dark with programs that may not meet the needs of your child at all.

I cannot stress strongly enough how important it is to obtain a comprehensive evaluation for the sake of your child in choosing the right program. I've known several parents who've wasted two, three, five or more years trying glasses, color overlays, neurological brain training, tutoring, yelling at the child for not trying "hard enough," when the child actually lacked phonemic awareness and could have been taught to read in the first couple of years, if the parent was using the right kind of program.

With the most frequently asked question being, "What program(s) should I use?" (usually without any preliminary evaluation) most parents who ask this question end up more confused than ever as every other parent shares what worked for his or her own child. What works for your child will depend totally upon specific learning issues affecting your child. What worked for my child most likely won't work for your child, and what worked for any other child most likely won't work for your child either. The primary risk in not having an evaluation is that you will waste time working with a program that worked for someone else, but is not a good match for addressing your child's specific needs. Most times guesswork causes a parent to lose time and money, and results in frustration and failure.

Without an evaluation, you will be engaging in guesswork in trying to meet your child's specific needs. Sometimes parents get lucky and they guess right, or their child's problems are singular in nature, so finding the right solution is relatively straightforward. However, I have seen the majority of parents waste time and money trying various solutions before obtaining an evaluation.

Learning is already difficult for children with learning disabilities, so added frustration from using the wrong type of program will really hamper your efforts and your child's willingness to work with you in the long run. Over time, if your child is constantly failing or not making progress, he will become less and less willing to try. How many times would you attempt to climb a tree if every time you started, the tree branch you grabbed hold of broke off? Eventually, you'd give up.

For kids with learning disabilities, it is a similar feeling of ongoing frustration and defeat. They will continue to give their lessons another try for some period of time, but after repeated failure your child will not try any more.

So, in short, having an evaluation allows you to properly select which programs to use, to know what foundational academic skills you need to work on, and helps you understand how to teach your child most effectively. Secondarily, having testing and evaluations early and throughout a child's academic years helps establish a paper trail. Why is this important?

If a child decides to go to college, he will have to take college admission exams and will benefit from learning accommodations in his college classes. Having an established paper trail helps the universities and test companies determine the types of accommodations the student needs.

Given a child who has never been evaluated for learning disabilities, and parents who worked to overcome the child's disabilities, the child may very well work in what is classified as a 'normal' range of performance. If a child's resulting educational achievement is such that he can get into college, but the child reached that point through specialized instruction and accommodations, then the child's level of achievement can cause problems if the child requires accommodations at the college level.

Let's consider two examples of students with dyslexia. In the early grades, both students struggle gravely with learning to read. From kindergarten through seventh grade these students work hard to become proficient readers, and they become competent readers and writers in ninth grade. Throughout their high school years, the students perform well enough that they decide they want to go to college.

As with many colleges, there is a foreign language requirement for a B.S. degree at these students' chosen colleges. Since these two students took many years to acquire reading and writing skills in their native language, it will—because of their dyslexia—take both students as long to acquire the required level of skill in a foreign language at college. Most colleges are willing to grant a "Foreign Language Waiver" if a student has a documented learning disability. If the student does not have a documented disability, he will be required to complete the foreign language requirement.

Given our two students, one had documentation for his disability from second grade onward with a comprehensive evaluation every three years, and annual achievement testing. He presented his evaluation information to his college's Student Disability Center and was granted a note taker, audio books, a foreign language waiver, a reader and computer for all exams to make sure he doesn't misread the college level words, and to be sure he can type his answers with spell-checker. (This is a true scenario!)

The second student didn't have comprehensive evaluations throughout schooling, and in fact didn't have any because his parents didn't want him "labeled". He overcame his disabilities through diligent homeschooling just like the first student, so his disability is now "invisible". When he went to the Student Disability Center and applied for accommodations, he had no evaluation data to present. The university provided an evaluative assessment and determined this student can both read and write, and therefore he does not "need" a foreign language waiver. The student is found to be competent at an 'average' level of performance, so he is granted no accommodations whatsoever.

As the second student progresses through college, he struggles to keep up with the volumes of college-level reading, and finds he cannot pass his required foreign language class. Despite his three attempts to pass the foreign language class, three semesters is not enough time for him to reach a satisfactory level of proficiency in the first course of a required two course series in a foreign language. The student cannot complete his degree because of the foreign language requirement and he walks away from the university with no degree to show for his time. (Also a true scenario that has hurt more than one student).

The first student above is my older son. Our trail of documentation actually began very early and was essential for establishing his need for accommodations in college, including a foreign language requirement waiver. He was required to take anthropology courses instead of studying a foreign language. Because we had full documentation of our son's learning history, and it was evident to the college psychologist who read my son's history of evaluative reports that my son had worked really hard to overcome significant learning disabilities, my son was granted extensive accommodations, many of which we did not even request, but the college felt were essential for assuring my son could be successful in college.

My son was granted accommodations we didn't even ask for because the university felt it was important for him to have strong assistance in order to level the playing field for him to compete academically at the college level. The college's goal was to put my son at an 'equitable' level of difficulty by providing accessibility to learning for the same content as everyone else.

We didn't ask for a reader or audiobooks, because my son can read. The Director of Disability Services said it was important for my son to have audiobook versions of his textbooks to help my son with the pronunciation and understanding of new college-level words specific to his field of study. The terminology in a college level course can be similar to learning a whole new language. The reader for exams was provided to make sure my son has an opportunity to hear sophisticated, multi-syllable words for clear understanding and to avoid misreading words during the exam.

The foreign language waiver was quickly granted because foreign language is not essential for my son's chosen degree and would be an extremely difficult subject for my son to pass. Our trail of documentation made it evident to the university that our son is smart and capable of college level work, but it was also clear he had overcome significant disabilities to reach a college level of proficiency in English.

Sadly for students like the second one, the inability to earn the desired degree is like a sledgehammer to the self-esteem. While the student can get a job in retail, at a restaurant, or get a trade job, it feels like his dream career is now the impossible dream. Having the career he wants is an unattainable goal without a college degree.

A student with notable disabilities often can't be successful in college without accommodations. Although the parents thought they were doing their son a favor by not labeling him, the decision not to have comprehensive evaluations when he was young had long-term ramifications that were not understood in the early educational years.

Thus, you must be far more forward thinking in regard to your child's future needs when your child has disabilities that may require special supports and/or accommodations.

Please remember the purpose of having an evaluation is to figure out how to meet a child's needs properly, and not merely to "label" the child. The label is only harmful if you chose to use it as an excuse or misuse the diagnosis otherwise. The way I see it, diagnosing a learning disability is no different than diagnosing a cold versus allergies versus pneumonia. You don't know what treatment (or remediation program) to use until you know what the actual problem is. An evaluation and diagnosis can be of great benefit in properly meeting your child's needs.

Having an evaluation can be critical in the span of your child's educational career to insure that his learning needs are understood and met when he becomes an adult. If you evaluate your child and meet his specific needs, he is far more likely to obtain both educational and career success.

I don't want to label my child; how can I help him/her without labeling?

Not wanting to "label" a child is the number one reason parents give for not having their child evaluated. Consider this: is there a long-term educational benefit in avoiding a label? Or, is a child better served by having his learning needs accurately identified and addressed?

Let's talk about concerns parents often have about having an evaluation and labeling their child. Parents are often concerned about the lifelong ramifications of their child being labeled as a person with a disability. There is an underlying question as to whether there is any real benefit in having an evaluation that results in a diagnosis label.

Perhaps I was able to convince you there is real benefit in having your child evaluated in the prior Q&A, so you can properly address his educational needs. I do hope so, as it is the most efficient route to take. The college-based scenario shared in the previous question is also a critical consideration for evaluation and diagnosis.

Often in the early years, parents simply don't know what a child will want to do for a career. Therefore, it is best to prepare for whatever choice your child may want to make—and that includes laying the groundwork for college beginning in elementary or middle school. If you haven't read the previous question and answer, please go back and read it, so you will more fully understand the ramifications of choosing not to have your child evaluated for learning disabilities.

Perhaps after reading the prior Q&A you are still concerned about the "label." Let's look at the label issue from a broader perspective in regard to benefits to your child versus costs when your child interacts with society.

First, it is really difficult to properly address a child's learning difficulties without an evaluation or a "label". As I touched on in the prior Q&A, a proper diagnosis is critical for providing the correct treatment.

If a person has pneumonia, bronchitis, allergies, or whatever, then we say the person is "sick". Being "sick" doesn't enable you to obtain the right kind of medical care. It's like saying the child has a "reading disability." That broad designation doesn't provide enough specific information for you to adequately provide the proper treatment/remediation your child needs.

Continuing with the example of being "sick," your child's illness must have a diagnosis and a "label" to determine what kind of medical care is needed. A person with a runny nose, coughing, chest congestion, etc. will be treated very differently, depending upon whether the illness is pneumonia, or bronchitis, a cold, or allergies. Without precisely identifying and naming the illness, the doctors would have to approach treatment through guesswork.

While guessing, your child's medical treatment would go something like this: "Your child has a runny nose, and cough, and chest congestion. He might have an infection, or maybe a fungal infection, or something else. Since it looks like it might be a cold, we'll just give it some time and see if he gets over it." What if it is pneumonia, a fungal infection, or allergies? If we're sitting around waiting to see what happens (as is often the case when parents want to wait to see if a child will 'outgrow' his learning struggles), the child will be getting sicker the longer we don't address his actual problem. If the child has allergies instead of a cold, he could feel better tomorrow with a good antihistamine. If the child has something else, treatment is going to be more difficult the longer you wait to get a proper diagnosis.

Does that scenario make sense as an example? In the case of learning disabilities, it is very similar. Given any number of causes for a child to struggle with reading, if we just say the child has reading problems, we don't have enough detail to select the proper solution.

If a parent assumes her child has "dyslexia" but, the child actually has short-term working memory and recall problems, then the parent may seek reading programs, none of which will actively work on strengthening memory and recall skills. A parent may spend hours—days—months working on phonemic awareness, pronunciation, and sounds, when the child really needs programs to improve memory and recall skills.

The parent and child will both become frustrated by putting in so much effort without seeing meaningful progress in the child's ability to read well. Having a proper diagnosis and "label" will allow the parent to obtain a memory improvement and rapid recall program, which will allow her to focus on fixing the root cause of her child's reading difficulty.

For your child, as an individual with learning needs which must be uniquely met, it is difficult to argue that an evaluation would be of no benefit. In fact, every parent I've known who didn't want a label has agreed it would be helpful to know precisely what her child's learning problems are, which would enable the parent can get the right kind of learning support. Even in knowing an evaluation will provide valuable insight that can be used to help their child, some parents still hesitate to obtain an evaluation.

Parents are still stymied by the thought of labeling their child when it comes to interactions with society. Consider this, *it isn't the labels themselves that are harmful, but rather how the labels are used which can be detrimental.* The evaluation, diagnosis, or use of a label is not harmful in and of itself.

A label only becomes harmful when the label is used as an excuse, as a demeaning way of addressing a child, or any number of ways a label may be abused. Misuse of a label really is an entirely different matter than getting a proper diagnosis in order to effectively help a child learn.

When you are homeschooling, *no one* *needs to know your child has a labeled disability other than professionals that you choose to work with your child.* Sometimes parents figure they're providing the educational assistance themselves (no professional help), so they don't *need* a label. However, having an identified disability helps you know, specifically, how to help your child learn. It all goes back to the example of your child being sick.

Additionally, as discussed in the previous Q&A, if a child has no documented history of a disability, it can deeply affect his ability to complete college, if he decides he'd like to get a degree. Having a documented history of your child's learning struggles can help your child receive accommodations or waivers at the collegiate level.

Always keep in mind that having an evaluation leads to instructional efficiency. Saving yourself from guesswork helps you and your child experience success more easily and helps you search for appropriate solutions with more accuracy. Having a specific diagnosis will help you understand your child's needs, and it will enable you to seek viable teaching assistance. I believe there is great benefit to having an accurate diagnosis for the sake of your child, particularly if you are homeschooling.

Doesn't our local school have to provide testing for disabilities?

To give the briefest answer to the title question, yes, they do! However, the real question is, "Do you want the school to test your child for learning disabilities?" It's a loaded question. I covered a lot of information about school testing in the "What services are public schools required to provide for homeschoolers?" Q&A in the previous section. I'll try to repeat myself as little as possible here, so please refer back to the prior section for a fuller explanation.

In this Q&A, we will go deeper into discussion about the legal requirements as well as the pros and cons of having a public school evaluate your child. Additionally, some parents have no financial means for seeking an independent evaluation, so going through the school may be their only choice. For those parents, I want you to be fully aware of the possible problems and benefits you may encounter.

If any child is suspected of having a disability, under the Federal IDEA "Child Find" laws, the public schools are charged with identifying children with disabilities. The school system is required to evaluate a child for learning disabilities, if an evaluation is requested in writing on the basis of a suspected learning disability.

However, homeschooling parents aren't required to have a child evaluated by the school system. In other words, the evaluation is an optional, one-way street. If you want the school to evaluate your child, you can give them a written request for an evaluation and they are required to evaluate. If you do not wish to have the school evaluate your child, you are not required to let them evaluate your child.

As far as U.S. laws go, "Under 34 CFR §300.301(c)(1), an initial evaluation must be conducted within 60 days of receiving parental consent for the evaluation or, if the State establishes a timeframe within which the evaluation must be conducted, within that timeframe. The IDEA 60-day timeline applies only to the initial evaluation. Public agencies are not required to make the eligibility determination, obtain parental consent for the initial provision of special education and related services, conduct the initial meeting of the IEP Team to develop the child's IEP, or initially provide special education and related services to a child with a disability during the IDEA 60-day initial evaluation timeline" (http://idea.ed.gov/explore/view/p/,root,dynamic,QaCorner,3,).

That said, keep in mind those public school resources, available time to serve many children, and the scope of evaluation is often limited. You can have your child tested by the school, but it is highly unlikely that the evaluation will be deeply comprehensive.

Although schools are supposed to evaluate for all areas of suspected disability, they often only evaluate in limited areas and leave many possible areas of disability unexplored. Areas such as processing issues, attention functioning, executive functioning and memory deficits are often not fully explored, if assessed at all. You are more likely to get testing results that tell you your child has "a reading disability," which you probably already know or suspect.

The results will often not have the depth you need in order to effectively select programs and teach your child. I've never seen one of our local school's reports that are more than five pages, and they are usually three pages. By contrast, I've seen private evaluations range from ten to forty pages in length, and the longer evaluation reports read like an instruction manual for teaching the specific child. There is a huge difference in the depth and breadth of evaluations when you compare public school testing versus private testing by a highly qualified neuropsychologist.

If your child has underlying deficits with memory, executive functioning, attention, or processing which remain unidentified, then those issues will probably go unaddressed. You will end up being frustrated by only knowing a piece of your child's full learning profile. Unaddressed issues always make learning more difficult for a child.

As an additional area of concern, some public school systems give families grief about homeschooling a child who is identified as having a disability. The schools often think their "highly qualified" teachers can do a better job than any "untrained" parent. The school administrators will sometimes deride parents and make them feel incapable and unqualified to homeschool their child—more out of ignorance than out of any actual data that proves the public schools are better able to teach your child than you.

You can convince yourself you can do a better job, and possibly convince the school administrators, by checking your public school's proficiency data. The proficiency data often leads parents to the realization that you can do at least as well as the public school (You can see the most current data at the U.S. Dept of Education Website or see a table of 2010 data at: http://learningabledkids.com/downloadablepdfs/achievementlevelsforstudentswithdisabilities2010.pdf).

Remember from our earlier Q&A, research data shows better academic progress for children taught one-on-one by a caring parent who is focused on what a child can do, rather than being taught by a teacher focused on what a child can't do. Additionally, unless your school system can demonstrate high levels of academic achievement for every child they are already working with, they don't really have any right to judge the level of success you may or may not achieve in teaching your child.

If you request an evaluation by the public school system, just be sure you are prepared for and willing to deal with additional bureaucracy from the school in relation to their concerns about your ability to homeschool your child. Not to fear-monger either, but just to make you aware—there are some bullying-types of school districts out there who believe they know better than any parent how to educate a child. I have known a handful of families who have ended up in legal wrangling with public school systems. The school administrators thought they had every right to force the parents to enroll their child in public school, because the child has special educational needs.

While in most cases, the parents prevail, there have been a couple of cases I've known where the judge had a definitive bias against homeschooling and ruled in favor of the school district, thereby forcing the parent to enroll the child in school. While it is not necessarily typical for schools to go to the extent of filing a court action, it is very common for schools to try to intimidate, belittle, or otherwise try to convince the parents they are not capable of homeschooling a child with disabilities. I provide this information simply as a precautionary "buyer beware". Just be aware you could be opening an ugly can of worms, depending upon how your public school system works with homeschoolers or students with disabilities.

That said, sometimes people live in great school districts where the schools do a fabulous job. They work compassionately with the child and family, and they really want to do all they can to help a homeschooling parent out. I've heard from parents who have had wonderful experiences receiving at-home services from their local public school, including specialized programs taught in their homes, enrichment opportunities, etc.

Your best bet is to ask around in your community to find parents of children with learning disabilities who have or had their children in public school. Ask the parents bluntly if they think the schools do an adequate job of meeting the needs of children with learning disabilities. Don't ask parents of typical children, because they don't know how well schools handle IEPs, IEP meetings, evaluations, etc.

There is often ignorance about special education provisioning by those in the community who have not actually been involved in trying to have the needs of a child met through special education. The only people who really know whether schools meet the needs of children with learning disabilities are the parents of children with similar disabilities.

You can usually determine whether the local school system will be of great assistance by how other parents of similar children feel about the schools in your area. They will sing praises, say the school was alright, or they will whip out their soapbox and tell you like it is! If you have several parents whip out their soapboxes and complain vigorously, it'd probably be best not to seek services from the school. You are unlikely to gain meaningful educational benefit for your homeschooled child if the school does not do an adequate job of helping those who are already enrolled in the school.

If you decide to ask for an evaluation through your local school system, you can simply write your local school a letter saying, "I believe my child has a learning disability, and I would like to have him/her evaluated under the IDEA Child Find provisioning. Please consider this letter as consent to evaluate and let me know when and where I should bring my child for his/her evaluation."

You don't have to tell the school which disability you suspect. In fact, they are more likely to perform a more comprehensive evaluation if the door is left open to any disability. If you say, "I think my child has dyslexia," the school may severely limit the scope of their evaluation. If you name any specific condition, they are much more likely to evaluate only to rule in or rule out the specific condition you named. If they rule it out, then you still have no specific answers as to what your child's disabilities are. By leaving your request open-ended, simply letting them know your child is struggling with learning and you don't know why, they will be forced to start with a broader analysis and narrow in on specific causes for your child's difficulties.

Given you want to have an evaluation, and decide not to go to your local public school, you'll want to seek a highly-qualified evaluator who will perform a comprehensive assessment of your child's learning strengths and weaknesses, including processing, memory, attention, and other areas of neurological functioning that affect learning. The next Q&A will help you know how to find a highly qualified evaluator.

How do I find a highly qualified evaluator?

If you are spending your hard-earned dollars and time getting a comprehensive neuro-psychological evaluation for your child, you want an evaluator (psychologist or neuro-psychologist) who is proficient and highly qualified to assess the learning needs of your child. You do not want to pick a random evaluator based upon search criteria, due to sales pitches on their website, or a directory listing. Blindly picking someone can, and probably will, result in poor results for your money.

I hate to admit it, but we have selected bad evaluators before, and a lot of other people within the Learning Abled Kids' group have had that experience too. Choosing a poor evaluator is costly in many ways and will make it more difficult for you to afford a better evaluation should you need a better one. Therefore, it is usually best to go for the best possible evaluator you can find without worrying about finding a cheap or convenient provider.

So, how do you find a great evaluator? The best place to find a fabulous evaluator is among those who know what good and bad evaluations look like. One of my favorite resources for referrals is the Council of Parent Attorneys and Advocates (COPAA) - http://www.copaa.org/find-a-resource/find-an-attorney/.
Special Education attorneys and advocates deal with public school problems and they routinely seek independent evaluations to help their clients determine the root causes of a child's learning problems.

Since Special Education attorneys have to acquire solid and comprehensive evaluations to force schools to properly address a child's needs, they know who provides the best evaluations in the local area. The attorneys know which evaluators will do a comprehensive job of evaluating and who will produce a detailed report which will clearly explain a child's needs.

If you go to the COPAA website, look for an attorney or advocate in your state or a nearby adjoining state, then call their office and ask if they have a list of recommended neuro-psychologists. Ask specifically who they'd recommend for a comprehensive evaluation for learning disabilities.

Alternately, you can check with your state's National Parent Technical Assistance Center (NPTAC,
http://www.parentcenternetwork.org/). The parent centers are advocacy organizations in each state. NPTAC helps parents navigate "the system" in order to obtain supports and services for children who have disabilities.

Your Parent Center can make recommendations for evaluators in your area, but they are not necessarily focused on the quality of the listed providers' evaluations and reports. Your state's National Parent Technical Assistance Center is more of a 'referral source' where anyone willing to provide services may be listed and their name will be given out for referrals. The NPTAC is a good place to receive information on licensed practitioners in your area who provide the type of evaluation you are seeking, but you will need to check references from the provider to determine the quality of his evaluations.

A great place to ask questions about evaluators is within the Learning Abled Kids' support group. Did you know we have a support group with over 1600 members? You can join the group at http://groups.yahoo.com/neo/groups/LearningAbledKids/. Once in the group, you can search the archives for past posts about evaluators or inquire about a specific doctor you have found through another avenue to see if anyone has used that doctor. You can also ask within the group if anyone has a great evaluator they can recommend in your geographic area or state.

As an additional option, you can search for groups that share information about disabilities in Yahoo, Google, CafeMom, or similar group sites. To find groups dealing with special education in your state, search for your state name along with the disability condition you suspect your child may have. Although recommendations are more varied among parents, who may or may not have found a great evaluator yet, you will generally be able to eliminate poor evaluators or find an evaluator that people like "well enough". Sometimes you'll get lucky and find an evaluator that is highly recommended by several people. If you find such an evaluator, he or she is likely worth their weight in gold.

When you are asking other parents for referrals, be sure to ask detailed questions about the number and types of tests the evaluator used, whether the evaluation takes place over multiple days, and inquire about the extensiveness of the results reporting. Being able to understand your child's evaluation results is just as important as having the evaluation done in the first place!

Are evaluations covered by Insurance?

Given that evaluations are usually quite expensive, parents often ask me if evaluations for learning disabilities will be covered by their insurance. Whether an insurance company will cover the cost of an evaluation often depends on the resulting diagnosis code(s) as well as your insurance policy itself. That makes my answer about insurance coverage somewhat muddled, and the precise answer usually has to be obtained through your insurance company.

While most insurance companies do not cover the cost of "educational" testing, when the outcome is a diagnosis of a medical nature requiring medication or therapy, the insurance is more likely to cover the cost of the evaluation. Unfortunately, if the resulting diagnosis determines whether the insurance company will pay for the evaluation, you won't know until after the evaluation is complete whether your insurance will cover the cost. You would have to go into the evaluation expecting to pay for it, and then you'll be pleasantly surprised of you don't have to pay for it out of pocket.

Examples of medical diagnoses sometimes covered by insurance include Bipolar Disorder, Attention Deficit Disorders, or low muscle tone (hypotonia), etc., which are often classified under "Other Health Impaired" or "Emotional Disorders" by school systems. These conditions are treated by medicines to balance brain chemistry or through physical or occupational therapy and are not classified as "learning disabilities". They are, in fact, medical conditions treated by medical professionals. Although the conditions often interfere with learning, and special supports and services may be needed to improve a child's ability to retain information, the treatment itself is medical or therapeutic in nature.

Non-medical diagnoses include dyslexia, dysgraphia, dyscalculia, executive dysfunction, Asperger's Syndrome, etc. These disabilities cannot be treated with medications. Learning Disabilities are neurological differences which require specialized instruction or alternate teaching methods. These disabilities are classified under Specific Learning Disability (SLD) or Autism Spectrum disorders by school systems and cannot be cured through medication or physical therapy.

For example, our insurance company covered our younger son's psycho-educational evaluation because his primary diagnosis was ADHD. Our insurance paid 80% of the evaluation cost because medication was recommended for our son. ADHD is considered a 'medical' problem treatable by medication, so the insurance covered the cost of the evaluation even though our son also has mild dyslexia and dysgraphia. The latter two are learning disabilities, but somewhat secondary in nature to his ADHD.

Our older son was diagnosed with ADHD which was noted to be "secondary" to his LD issues. In other words, my older son's inability to attend was due to his inability to understand the printed materials. His ADHD was not due to a chemical imbalance in his brain. Since the ADHD was not "primary", medication was not recommended. We were told our older son's ADHD would disappear when his LD issues were overcome (indeed, his ADHD disappeared after he was able to read).

Although both boys had ADHD, because medication was recommended for our youngest, our insurance paid for his evaluation. Since our older son did not have a recommendation for medication, and his recommendations were based upon educational programming, the insurance would not pay for our older son's evaluation(s).

Insurance companies will usually pay for Speech-Language evaluations, Physical Therapy evaluations, and Occupational Therapy Evaluations. However, whether or not they pay for the recommended treatment(s) depends upon the diagnosis. Sometimes vision insurance will cover developmental eye exams, but vision therapy itself is almost never covered by insurance. Our insurance covered the cost of the developmental eye exam, but not the cost of my son's vision therapy.

If your insurance company's payment is dependent upon the diagnosis and upon your policy's specific provisions, it can be a 'gamble' financially going into an evaluation. You don't know what your child's final diagnosis will be, nor whether the insurance company will actually pay for the evaluation until it is all said and done.

Given the uncertainty of insurance coverage, I think it is best to be prepared to pay for the full evaluation with your own money. Then, if the diagnosis aligns with insurance coverage, you can be pleasantly surprised and relieved when the insurance does end up paying for all or part of the evaluation.

Hopefully this information will be of use to you in determining what your insurance coverage may be. I'm sorry the answer to this question isn't more straight-forward. I wish insurance always covered the cost of evaluations to identify learning disabilities, but sadly more often than not, the insurance does not cover evaluations related to educational matters. If the insurance companies did cover the cost, I believe more kids would have their learning needs assessed and identified early.

What kinds of evaluations do I need to consider?

There are many kinds of evaluations, which are related to meeting a child's educational needs, including:
- Neuropsychological evaluations,
- Developmental eye exams,
- Occupational Therapy (OT) evaluations,
- Physical Therapy (PT) evaluations,
- Speech-Language Pathology (SLP) evaluations,
- Central Auditory Processing Disorder (CAPD or APD) evaluations,
- Functional Behavior Assessments (FBA), etc.

These are all types of evaluations that may help identify a child's areas of need.

The number and types of evaluations can seem like one huge alphabet soup, and parents often wonder whether they need one, some, or all of the different types of evaluations. Hopefully I can help clarify the various types of evaluations so that you can target your time and money toward the evaluations which will be most beneficial for you and your child.

I will start by sharing some of the primary evaluations and the types of data that is gathered through that type evaluation.

— **Occupational Therapy (OT)** - An OT evaluation can be beneficial if your child is having difficulty with the physical act of handwriting, holding a pencil, fatigue from sitting to do school work, or other issues related to posture, eye-hand coordination, object grip, various motor skills (fine motor, oral motor, visual motor), and self-care skills. An OT evaluation can also assess sensory integration in addition to other areas. This type of evaluation seeks to identify functional limitations your child may have which impede his ability to perform well in his day-to-day learning environment. Educationally-based evaluations will pay particular attention to areas where a child's academic performance is impacted, such as handwriting. Occupational Therapy can help your child learn to hold a pencil properly, learn how to maintain good posture, coordinate eye-hand movement, better integrate visual information, etc. In the broadest sense, Occupational Therapy focuses on fine motor skills more than gross motor skills, but OT is not limited only to fine motor therapy.

— **Physical Therapy (PT)** - Physical Therapy, in the broadest sense, focuses on gross motor abilities in a person. These abilities enable him/her to navigate the environment, walk, run, jump, stand up, sit down, etc. The PT evaluation focuses on large body movements of the arms, legs, trunk strength, etc. The PT evaluation also considers motor planning issues such as being able to swing, run and kick a ball, catch a ball, or walk on a balance board. Physical Therapy is often considered when a child is having difficulty with the above-mentioned skills, particularly when the deficits impact a child's ability to complete basic tasks such as getting dressed, walking, sitting upright, or prevent participation in physical games, sports, playground activities, etc.

— **Speech-Language Evaluation (SLP)** - Most often a child is taken for a SLP evaluation if he or she is having articulation difficulties. These are evidenced when a child is unable to speak certain sounds clearly or properly, stutters, or otherwise has difficulty communicating verbally. A common example would be when a child says the sound of /w/ instead of the sound of /r/.

It is usually obvious when your child has a need for speech-language therapy; however, sometimes it isn't quite as evident whether a child's difficulties are developmental or neurological. Conditions such as Apraxia, where a child doesn't say the sounds he intends to say and words are spoken strangely, requires a comprehensive evaluation and extensive therapy.

For a child with reading disabilities, he may lack phonemic awareness and not realize there are differences between spoken sounds. For example, your child may confuse the sound of /v/ with the sound of /f/ or the sound of /d/ with the sound of /t/. In such cases, the sounds are formed similarly when speaking, with very slight differences in the placement of the lips or tongue. Phonemic awareness issues often require specific, explicit, and direct instruction regarding the precise differences between the printed letters and their representative sounds when spoken.

In any case, when your child reaches school age, if he is having articulation, apraxia, or phonemic awareness issues, having a speech-language evaluation followed by therapy will help your child overcome related learning and communication difficulties as the child advances academically.

— **Psycho-educational Evaluation** - If your child has a singular learning disability or condition, a psycho-educational evaluation might be sufficient for determining the nature of a child's learning struggles. Psycho-educational evaluations are performed by school psychologists, and although there are some who delve more deeply into learning processes, most of the assessments offered through school-based professionals are designed to rule in or rule out specific disabilities such as dyslexia, dysgraphia, dyscalculia, etc.

Many times the summary reports will specify your child has a "reading disability," "written communication disability," or a "mathematical computation disability" without detailed specifics about underlying neurological processes such as processing speed, attention functioning, executive functioning, memory/recall processes, etc.

When your child has a mild, and seemingly straight-forward learning struggle that only affects one area (such as reading), a psycho-educational evaluation can be sufficient for ruling in or ruling out a specific learning disability. However, if a child's problems are complex, and it seems there's something *more* going on with a more pervasive affect across most areas of learning, I think it is usually better to seek an evaluation from a licensed neuropsychologist (next bullet).

— **Neuropsychological Evaluation** - If your child has perplexing ways of responding, forgetting, inability to remember what he is told, has difficulty in multiple areas of learning (isn't learning to read and can't remember math facts), or you suspect there is something other than a singular area of learning disability, I recommend a comprehensive neuropsychological evaluation by a highly qualified evaluator. Neuropsychologists assess the neurological processes necessary for planning, sequencing, memory and recall functioning, processing speed, different forms of comprehension and expression, attention, as well as assessing for specific disabilities like dyslexia, dyscalculia, and dysgraphia.

A neuropsychologist is going to assess the full spectrum of brain processes used in learning. This level of evaluation will give you a deep, robust exploration of your child's functioning in relation to learning, relationships, self-care, etc. While a neuropsychological evaluation is more costly than a simple evaluation provided by a typical school psychologist, if your child has complex issues, full understanding of his disabilities will be essential for making meaningful educational decisions. Having a precise and accurate diagnosis will enable you to provide programs that will enable meaningful academic progress.

— **Functional Behavior Assessment (FBA)** - When your child exhibits ongoing problems with inappropriate or uncontrolled behaviors, a FBA can help determine the purposes behind (or function of) the behaviors your child displays. FBAs are particularly useful with children who have limited verbal communication or are otherwise unable to verbally let providers know their individual needs, wants, and meanings behind behaviors.

FBAs can lead to better understanding of your child, can enable providers to better manage your child's behaviors without unnecessary restrictions, and without building frustration due to the lack of communication. FBAs can help providers develop plans for meeting your child's needs before his behaviors reach a point of frustration and disruption.

Through the FBA, providers can develop a Positive Behavior Intervention Plan, which enables the providers to respond to or modify a child's behavior through positive reinforcements. If your child's behaviors are difficult to manage, a FBA can be helpful for understanding how you can better help your child.

— **Developmental Eye exam** - When your child cannot smoothly move his eyes back and forth, right to left, or cannot sweep his eyes fully to the outside or inward toward the nose for reading, then he may have difficulty focusing well on the words for reading's sake. A child's vision may be 20/20 and perfect, but he may still have difficulty with eye movement (ocular motor deficiencies).

If your child regularly complains of words jumping around on the page, rubs his eyes a lot when trying to read, has tearing of the eyes, complains of headaches while reading, or makes any similar complaint about eye fatigue, a developmental eye exam may be warranted. Additionally, if you notice your child frequently losing his place on a page, reading words on the line above or below where he was reading, skipping lines or words frequently, then you may want to seek a developmental eye exam.

Do not seek a developmental eye exam as a promised "cure" for dyslexia. It is crucial to be aware that developmental eye disorders are not the same thing as dyslexia. True dyslexia is neurological in origin, is a language-based phonemic awareness problem, and is likely to be diagnosed when a child has difficulty with phonemic awareness, working memory problems, and processing issues. Vision therapy will not cure true dyslexia.

Many people misspeak or misinterpret any kind of difficulty with reading as "dyslexia," but ocular motor (developmental vision) disorders are an entirely different area of treatment. Vision therapy will only make a meaningful difference if a child, in fact, has a developmental ocular motor issue.

Sometimes a child will have both an ocular motor issue and true dyslexia, which can make the diagnosis and treatment process more involved. Unfortunately, neuropsychologists diagnose true dyslexia, but they do not assess developmental eye issues. Similarly, Developmental Vision specialists do not test for the neurological processes that cause phonemic awareness-based dyslexia. The two are entirely different areas of specialty and may require assessments from both types of providers.

If your child has both ocular motor deficiencies and phonemic awareness-based dyslexia, it is generally better to address the physical (ocular motor) barrier to reading first. If a child can't focus on the words, learning to read them will be more difficult, so correcting vision-based issues first makes good sense.

— **Auditory Processing Disorder (APD or CAPD)** – (Central) Auditory Processing Disorder is not a hearing problem per se, but it is diagnosed by an audiologist. Children with APD don't process sounds, particularly in noisy environments, in a typical way.

Many times a child's hearing is perfectly normal and she can distinguish precise tones in a sound-proof, audiologist's testing booth. When processing or filtering sounds in a more natural environment, a child with APD will have difficulty separating sounds, processing all of the sound information coming in, and may find it very difficult to cope with noisy environments.

Auditory processing disorder can cause difficulty with sound discrimination while learning to read, spell, and speak. It can also cause sensory overload issues when the child is in a noisy environment. If your child seems to have difficulty with understanding spoken directions, is intolerant of noisy environments, or has difficulty with phonics, you may want to consider an APD evaluation with a qualified audiologist.

The list above is not a comprehensive list of all types of evaluations, but it covers the most commonly recommended and sought evaluations. Although your child may require multiple types of evaluations, your budget, time, and the stress levels of your child will dictate a priority order for which types of evaluations you should seek first. If there are physical or medical issues that put a barrier between your child and his learning, then it is best to address those physical or medical barriers first. Whether the barrier requires therapy, medication, assistive technology, or accommodation, after you break through any physical barrier, you can then connect with your child more easily in the teaching-learning process.

Overcoming neurologically based cognitive or learning difficulties will require a lot of time and specialized educational programming. Thankfully, there are many great programs available for addressing both cognitive and learning challenges. The key is to know what types of programs your child needs, and then to ferret out those programs that will best meet your child's needs.

How do I know when or if I should have my child evaluated?

I believe the best time to have a child evaluated is as soon as you realize there is a problem. Many studies have shown that early intervention is a significant factor in a child's ability to fully overcome areas of disability. If your child exhibits several areas of concern, having an early assessment for neurological difficulties can allow you to start therapies during your child's prime development years.

If your child's problems are not severe and his problems seem to be more directly related to learning and remembering, you might want to wait until your child has reached an age where educationally-based testing can be more comprehensive. A child is usually old enough to answer questions and respond well to the elements in a comprehensive evaluation around 7 or 8 years of age.

If your child has notable problems with crawling, sitting, walking, talking, speech-language, memory for every day objects, or similar areas of significant difficulty, obtaining an evaluation early can be of immense benefit. In many cases, there is a window of opportunity when the brain is neurologically more changeable, which is open when a child is young and developing rapidly. Although brain plasticity remains to a degree throughout life, it slows as a person becomes a young adult (early 20's).

Taking advantage of the early window of development is always beneficial and the success of early intervention is well established. "Studies show that prevention and early intervention and instruction will help most students avoid reading failure, says Victoria Molfese, Ph.D., who conducts research in the development of language and cognitive abilities in young children," (Langsford Learning Center, N.D.). The wisdom of providing early intervention in order to prevent failure applies to all academic areas.

If a child is demonstrating learning or memory difficulties at a very young age (4 or younger), then the origins of the child's difficulties may be difficult to pinpoint. When a child is very young he can't answer written questions, give writing or drawing samples, or even cognitively understand many of the probing questions that comprehensive evaluations include. Thus, a very young child must be "observed" in his interactions, speech, problem-solving skills, etc., but a young child often cannot directly communicate what he is thinking.

When a child is younger than five, he may have what is called an "arena evaluation." In this type of evaluation, there are several therapists—occupational, physical, speech-language—as well as a child psychologist who will "play with" the child in a room with toys and various problem-solving activities. The evaluators will note responses and behaviors to try to determine whether the child has difficulties that need immediate intervention. Sometimes a child will be evaluated by a single individual who plays with the child. The session may or may not be recorded and shown to other evaluators at a later time, or may be observed through a one-way window by multiple people.

I personally believe it is difficult to accurately pinpoint a child's learning-based difficulties at a very early age and it may not be beneficial to have a very early evaluation unless the child's disabilities are interfering with basic functioning and development, such as when a child has an autism spectrum disorder. Waiting until a child is a bit older can provide greater accuracy and specificity to an educational evaluation, but a trade off might be made in regard to early intervention initiatives. The key is not to wait too long before getting an evaluation when your intuition is telling you something isn't quite right with your child's cognitive or learning abilities.

The ideal age to have an in-depth educationally-based evaluation is around age 7 or 8, but having one a bit earlier might be advised if the child is struggling significantly with learning. Around eight years of age, the child can be administered many different types of evaluations which allow the exploration of a wide variety of possible areas of learning difficulty.

If your child is older than 8 and you think he may have a disability, and especially if you have suspected it for a while, I would urge you to schedule a comprehensive evaluation as soon as feasible because the window for brain plasticity and early intervention becomes more limited as time progresses. In regard to early intervention, research shows that plasticity (or the ability of the brain to change) varies with age and functional area of the brain.

There is a tendency among parents to want to "wait and see" if a child outgrows his difficulties. Please do not wait or do nothing in hopes of saving time, money, or avoiding a label, and simply hope your child outgrows his difficulties. Yes, some children do outgrow their difficulties, but the numbers show only about 15% of children who struggle early on eventually outgrow their delays. "The data from the studies are clear: Late bloomers are rare; skill deficits are almost always what prevent children from blooming as readers" (American Educator, 2004).

Thus, it makes little sense to withhold identification and learning help from your child based on a hope that he won't need any intervention in the long-term. Chances are much higher (85%) that your child will not outgrow his difficulties. Waiting wastes valuable time, all the while with your child experiencing educational frustration that leads your child to conclude he or she is not very intelligent or unable to learn.

If your child is highly intelligent, he will notice the learning gap quickly between what he is supposed to be able to learn versus what he is actually able to learn. This can lead to lowering of your child's self-esteem which he may never recover from. Issues with self-esteem are avoidable if your child gets the right kind of educational assistance early enough to prevent failure. Having an evaluation early on can help you place your child on a path to educational success at a younger age, thereby minimizing the loss of esteem from learning failures.

If your child is eight or older, it is not by any means too early for an evaluation. The sooner you obtain an evaluation, the sooner you can help your child. Having an evaluation every 3-5 years can be helpful for tracking progress and shifts in your child's disability.

If there is any possibility your child will want to attend college or a technical school, you will want to have an evaluation after the spring of his 10th grade year, or in 11th or 12th grade. Colleges and Universities require a comprehensive evaluation that is *less than* three years old for the purpose of establishing the presence of a learning disability. The colleges look at both current and historical evaluation information to determine what types of supports, services and academic accommodations a student will need in college. Having a current evaluation readily available will make the process of transitioning your child into college less of an ordeal.

In conclusion, evaluating sooner rather than later is preferable. The sooner you evaluate, the sooner you can provide appropriate learning support and find the right curriculum to meet your child's needs.

I have an evaluation; how do I figure out what my child needs?

Often, parents don't have a clue how to read and understand the first evaluation report they receive from their child's evaluator. A parent's ability to understand an evaluation report depends upon how adept the evaluator is in explaining the information with understandable terminology. A great evaluator will explain evaluation results in layman's terms, with clear explanations of what the results mean and how the results apply to meeting the child's educational needs. Unfortunately, more often than not, the evaluator uses professional jargon or does not take the time to fully explain his findings.

If your evaluator doesn't explain your child's results in easily understood terminology, you may have to figure out what the results mean on your own. The basic process I recommend for understanding your child's unique needs assumes you have a comprehensive evaluation which assesses different types of comprehension (auditory, reading), different types of memory (short-term, working, long term, etc.), attention functioning (focus, attention, interjections of thoughts), executive functioning (planning, organizing, sequencing), processing (speed, auditory and visual processing), etc.

If you only have an academic aptitude test (IQ) and academic achievement tests in subject areas (math, reading, science, etc.), you simply aren't going to be able to glean meaningful information about your child's individual learning disabilities or educational needs from the test data. If you only have IQ testing and achievement testing, all you will know is whether your child is ahead or behind of peers in each academic area, and whether your child is behind or ahead of his own cognitive ability in any given area. You probably already know whether your child is ahead or behind in any given area without the need for an evaluation. Thus, if you are going to understand your child's specific learning struggles and help him overcome them, you must obtain a more comprehensive evaluation, as explained in the prior Q&A.

In order to evaluate what your child needs, and given you have a comprehensive evaluation, you should make a copy of your child's evaluation report. Prepare to mark all over your copy. Save the original evaluation report "as is," so you always have the clean original. Having the original will allow you to copy it and provide a clean copy to anyone whom you may choose to work with your child in the future.

To mark your mark-up copy, get two highlighters of different colors—I like yellow and pink. Set aside some quiet time to sit and read your copy of your child's evaluation report in detail with highlighters in hand. As you read, highlight each score that is above the 75th percentile in one color (I chose yellow-a sunshine, bright spot). For every score that is below the 25th percentile, highlight that score in your second color

(I chose pink as a friendly alert color).

Some of your child's scores will not be expressed in terms of percentiles, so you will need to understand the test's rating scale to be able to highlight any score at the top end or bottom end of the rating scale. You may need to search on the Internet to determine the percentile distribution for the particular test used. Simply search for the test/subtest's name, scoring, and "percentile ranking". Example:
[<testname> scoring "percentile ranking"].

For scores with a mean (average) score of 100, scores above 120 would be highlighted in the same color as those above the 75th percentile. Scores below 80 would be highlighted in the same highlighter colors as those scores below the 25th percentile. Scores between 80 and 120 are 'average' on a scale of 100.

Some "scaled scores" are on a scale with 10 as the mean score, which is considered average. In the case of most scaled scores, those scores below 7 are "below average" and scores above 13 are "above average." The middle half of scores fall between 8 and 12.

There are other forms of scoring, so it is important to understand the scale being used in reporting the scores for any specific test. You can almost always find the scoring scales by searching for [<testname> scoring "percentile ranking"] online.

The best way to compare the scores is through percentile rankings because the rankings allow you to compare scores across different tests. No matter what scoring system is used, the equivalent percentile rankings are based upon the 50th percentile being exactly average, with the middle half of the population scoring between the 25th and 75th percentiles. Scores below the 25th percentile are quite low and scores above the 75th percentile are comparatively high.

When highlighting your child's scores, you can, broaden your rating selection for scores falling below the 35th and above the 65th percentiles if you wish. This would include selecting scores with a standard score below 90 for the low end, and above 110 at the high end. For scaled scores, you would select scores below 9 or above 11, with scores of 9, 10, and 11 being the middle average. Selecting your child's scores a bit more broadly allows you to include scores that are "borderline low" and "borderline high" while eliminating scores that are completely average.

The analysis process I use here is not an exact science and your intuition about any score being high or low for your child can be factored into your score selections. If you feel any particular score is significant, and it is close to one end of the spectrum, you will probably want to highlight that score, because you cannot possibly over-understand your child's needs.

Through your careful reading with highlighters in hand, you are highlighting information that will help you determine your child's learning strengths and relative learning weaknesses. These are the most important aspects of your child's learning profile for you to understand. Read your report through two or three times for optimum understanding and to be sure you don't miss any key strengths or difficulties when highlighting.

After you feel you've highlighted every strength and weakness, the difficult and time-consuming process of understanding your child's specific needs begins. Get a notepad or notebook to make notations in, or be sure you have plenty of paper ready. I would like to suggest you set aside separate sections on your pad or in your notebook when you are taking notes: one section for learning strengths, one for learning weaknesses, and another where you can jot down notes regarding things you want to research, as well as questions or ideas you think about. Having the sections separated and making notes of concern to yourself will make the next step of processing this information easier for you.

As you go through your child's report again for the purpose of making notes, label one page for each test/subtest that you have highlighted. Leave yourself plenty of room on the page for making notes about the test's purpose and for notes about how the specific skill or cognitive process should be used or addressed for your child.

For each score you have highlighted, you need to understand the purpose of the test/subtest. You will need to know what the test seeks to measure in a child's cognitive processes or academic skill set before you can figure out how to address any gaps.

You can search online for interpretive information about each individual test, or you can consult a resource book, such as "<u>The Special Educator's Comprehensive Guide to 301 Diagnostic Tests.</u>" Most test publishers have descriptions of their tests and subtests online, but sometimes it can be time-consuming to find the specific information you need. I like having the comprehensive guide handy because it allows me to finish the research process faster. In the beginning though, I found the test publishers' websites to be quite adequate even if it took time to locate the information I needed.

Read to understand what each specific subtest is measuring in your child's abilities and make notes on your page titled for that subtest. Look up each test that was administered and read its general description. Make notes for yourself, so you will know the specific skill(s) you need to address for your child. Making these notes can be a somewhat tedious process, but if you think of yourself as a learning detective on behalf of your child, you can enjoy the hunt for insight into the workings of your child's mind.

As an example of how this process will work and what types of notes you may want to make, let's look at the Analytic Learning Disability Assessment (ALDA). From the test provider's information, we see this test "matches the strengths and weaknesses of the student's underlying skills with that student's most appropriate learning method for each school subject - 11 reading methods, 23 spelling methods, 6 math computation methods, and 8 handwriting methods. The learning methods are ranked in order with the most effective and efficient being numbered one and the higher numbers being the most time consuming" (Slosson, N.D.). What does that mean?

On this evaluation's spelling scale, a score of "1" means the specified method is the best for your child and a score of "23" indicates the worst method for teaching your child. Since 23 different methods for teaching a child spelling are evaluated, knowing which methods work best can be invaluable in helping your child learn to spell well. If your child took this assessment, you would make a note in your notebook of the best method(s) in your strengths section, and the worst method(s) in your weaknesses section. You would make this notation for each subtest area-reading, spelling, math, and handwriting.

Whatever tests were used in evaluating your child, you will have to research to find out what the test is actually measuring and what the result means. Please, whatever you do, don't give up here because you feel like it is too much work to undertake the research. The only way to help your child overcome his or her learning disabilities is to fully understand your child's learning needs and abilities. Please trust that the process will go faster than it feels like it will in the beginning. You will get into a rhythm of searching for a provider, locating the test description, and making notes for yourself.

As you research, if you cannot understand what the subtests measure by reading about them, it should always be acceptable to call your evaluator for clarification and understanding, since you undoubtedly paid a good amount of money for the evaluator's services. Even if your evaluator doesn't fully explain what each of the scores mean, just having the scores, both high and low, along with whatever information you can find about the meaning of the scores can empower you with a certain level of understanding.

The key is for you to take the time to research and try to understand what each of the scores means to whatever extent you can. As you research, you will see patterns of strengths and weaknesses emerge. This information is priceless when you are working to address your child's learning needs. By understanding the most efficient way to teach your child, and the least efficient way to teach your child, you can structure your teaching around the needs of your child rather than guessing about what may work for him.

As an example, if you have identified several tests with 'visual' measurements in them such as picture sorting, visual processing, visual memory, you may notice your child scored well on many of the visually-based tests. This would indicate that your child has a strong ability to process visual information, and you would want to consider heavily that he may be a visual learner or benefit from visual presentation of his learning materials. Using visual presentations will make learning easier and more efficient for your child. You can confidently seek visual sources for teaching and learning as you now know your child learns well from pictures, charts, documentary films, graphs, etc.

The second piece of the instructional puzzle is to look for relative weaknesses for your child. Look for patterns within your child's low scoring tests. Does he have a pattern of weakness in memory, processing speed, attention, reading comprehension, math computation, etc?

For any specific area of weakness you can identify, acquire programs to help strengthen that learning process for your child. Identifying and addressing your child's learning weaknesses can bring about some of the greatest learning gains, if you tackle these problem areas directly. You can use brain training programs to tackle a lot of the underlying neurological processes such as memory and processing speed. You'll be able to find a variety of programs to help your child once you know his precise needs.

In overcoming learning disabilities, the key is to identify the weaknesses and then work on strengthening them. Keeping your child on track with content learning by using alternate means of instruction for all learning content is equally important. If you use audio/visual teaching tools, hands-on activities, audiobooks, etc, you can enable a child to learn about science, history, peoples of the world, great works of literature, etc., even if your child is not yet able to read or write well. By working on your child's weaknesses and keeping all other content learning moving forward, you can keep your child on track educationally and position him for a better academic future.

I can't afford to have my child evaluated; what should I do?

This question is difficult for me to answer well. I know there are many people who cannot afford to spend one to three thousand dollars on an evaluation for one child. After all, eating is essential! There was a time when I lived in government subsidized housing and faced hundreds of thousands of dollars in medical bills from my late husband's chemotherapy and his subsequent 3-month stay in intensive care. It was difficult just to keep a roof over my head and buy food. Having lived well below the poverty level for several years, I know the depth at which you may yearn to have your child evaluated for the sake of your child, but I also know that money can be mighty difficult to come by when you are living in dire circumstances.

Paying for a comprehensive evaluation eliminates much of the guesswork and legwork in figuring out how to meet your child's needs, but if you don't have any money for an evaluation, it doesn't help to know that. What does help is the knowledge that given time and your own drive and initiative, you will be able to narrow your focus to your child's specific needs to a significant degree. You will have to put on your detective hat and go on a mission to find all the information you can about your child's specific, observable difficulties and strengths, and that information alone will help you provide your child with a better education.

You basically have two no-cost routes you can take in assessing your child's needs:

Route One: The easiest route on you, given no flack from the school system, is to have your local public school provide an evaluation for your child. The school psychologists can perform evaluations and give you basic feedback about your child's learning strengths, difficulties, and needs. You may not get a thorough evaluation, but it will give you someplace to begin. You can use the measures in Route Two to further your understanding of your child's needs.

Under the IDEA laws in the U.S., schools are required to evaluate any child who is suspected of having learning disabilities within 60 days of receiving informed consent from the parent. The school system must evaluate your child at no cost to you when you give them a written request for an evaluation.

What you must do to obtain an evaluation through the school: You must give a letter to your local public school stating:

> *"I suspect my child may have a learning disability. As specified in IDEA's Child Find provisions, I am hereby requesting that the school psychologist evaluate my child, <name of child>, for learning disabilities. You may consider this letter consent to proceed with an evaluation. Please contact me at <phone number> to schedule an evaluation appointment sometime in the next 60 days.*
>
> *Sincerely, <your name>"*

Sign and date the letter, then hand deliver it to the school's office to the attention of the principal or mail it with tracking, so you will know when your letter arrived and will know when the sixty day window in which the school is legally required to evaluate begins.

Drawbacks: Public schools have a lot of children to evaluate and limited personnel on staff. Thus, they often perform evaluations that are limited in scope to determine if a child has a disability. When using the public school's services, you are likely to get an evaluation result that states your child has a disability in the area of reading, or writing, or math. The schools will perform some level of testing to determine if a reading problem is in decoding or comprehension, if a writing problem is in the area of grapho-motor skills or written expression, and if a math problem is due to issues with math computation or math reasoning.

Seldom will a school delve deeply into all aspects of reasoning, memory, comprehension, processing, attention, and executive functioning. At whatever level they explore and provide you with results, those results will be more information than you presently have, and that is a benefit.

Reports received from public schools are often lacking in clear, understandable explanations, thoroughness and broadness of the evaluation, and sometimes lacking in meaningful instructional suggestions. Results vary widely from state-to-state, district-to-district, and sometimes even from one school to another within the same district. Some districts do a fabulous job, so I pray you are in one of those districts. Generally speaking, my opinion is that evaluations done by public schools are better than no evaluation at all, but seldom is a school's evaluation better than a private evaluation performed by a highly qualified neuropsychologist.

Caution: When going through a public school for an evaluation, depending upon the evaluator's bias for or against homeschooling, poverty-stricken people, people of other races, etc., the school might attempt to make a judgment call on your worthiness to homeschool your child due to your child's specific needs. Even with a Master's Degree under way, one administrator laughed at the idea of me homeschooling my child. She called my home two months into our homeschool year and asked if I was "done playing school yet" followed by her comment that when I got tired of it, of course the school would be willing to take my boys back. Her tone of voice was condescending to me and it was a stupid comment, because they're a public school which is required to take any child. Needless to say, I was not the least bit interested in re-enrolling my boys in the belittling, educationally deficient school!

You should know ahead of time what your rights are in regard to homeschooling your child and what special requirements your state may have in place for homeschooling children with identified special needs. It is legal to homeschool any child in every U.S. state, whether the child has special needs or not, but some states have extra requirements a parent must fulfill in order to homeschool a child with special needs. Make sure you are in compliance with all homeschooling requirements for your state prior to seeking an evaluation; otherwise you could get yourself into legal trouble for lack of legal compliance. More likely than not, if you are out of compliance with homeschooling requirements the public school personnel will pursue efforts to prevent you from homeschooling.

See *"What services are public schools required to provide for homeschoolers?"* in the "Getting Started" Series, and *"Doesn't our local school have to provide testing for disabilities?"* in this "Testing and Evaluation" Series for more information about evaluations provided by public schools.

Route Two: Do it yourself evaluations can enable you to focus on the areas of learning your child is struggling with and allow you to narrow down the scope of possible remediation methods. However, a "do it yourself" evaluation will not enable you to assess all aspects of reasoning, memory, processing, comprehension, attention, and executive functioning. You will have an incomplete assessment of your child's needs, but as I have said, having some assessment is better than no assessment at all.

Some assessments can be as simple as playing a game of Memory Matching with your child using picture cards to see how your child performs. If your child has a difficult time with the task, his or her memory probably could use some strengthening. Thus, you can play the memory game with your child often or find memory enhancement programs online.

For any area of weakness you identify in your child, you can address it through tools and programs, whether or not you have identified the need with pinpoint accuracy. Working on any cognitive area or foundational learning skill will strengthen the skill whether it is the root cause of your child's learning struggles or not. Therefore, one approach to not having an evaluation can be to provide programs for every issue your child faces. You may end up using a wide variety of programs, and that can work favorably as a strategy although the broad-based approach usually takes longer to bring forth improvements in your child's educational functioning.

In order to assess your own child, you can search for online tools that will enable you to assess for various abilities and performance levels. For example, the University of Oregon has a tool which is available online to assess a child's functional reading and math levels called DIBELS (Visit: https://dibels.uoregon.edu/measures/). DIBELS is used by public schools to identify students who need additional instructional support, and it is free to use at home to determine if your child needs instructional support.

It is likely your child does need help if you are reading this series, but the DIBELS tools can also be used to help you track your child's functional level and progress as you work on enhancing her academic abilities. You would simply use the DIBELS tools at regular intervals (at least three months apart, preferably six months apart) to assess your child and see if there are any measurable improvements.

If you know your child needs help with reading, you can use tests such as the assessment included in the book "Reading Reflex". The book has an assessment which you can administer to your child to determine if your child specifically has an issue with phonemic awareness.

You are most likely to find free assessment tools associated with specific programs where the free assessments are designed to measure a child's placement into or need for the specific program. In order to find the free assessment tools, search online for the words "screening" and "free test" along with the cognitive skill you believe may be an area of weakness for your child. You can search for specific disabilities such as dyslexia, dysgraphia, dyscalculia, along with or as alternatives to specific skills such as reading decoding, reading comprehension, handwriting, written expression, etc. For example, your search terms might be "dyslexia free screening test."

Searching for viable assessment tools can be time-consuming, but when you find them, they are worth using to gain as much insight as you possibly can into your child's specific learning needs. If you find a good placement test, bookmark it and use it several months down the road to see if your child has made measurable progress.

Drawbacks: Not having training in neuro-psychological processes, your assessment of your child's learning needs will not be as comprehensive as an independent evaluation would provide. However, a purposeful attempt at assessment by you will be better than guesswork.

You may also have preconceived thoughts about your child's abilities or weaknesses which will limit your ability to accurately assess your child's needs. I think it is difficult for a parent to set aside beliefs about her child's disabilities in order to open the door to other thoughts and possibilities, so be on the lookout for your own limiting thoughts and be aware of alternate avenues to explore.

Be aware also, not having a robust evaluation will limit your ability to assess and meet your child's needs in some areas. As an example, you may accurately determine that your child has difficulty with phonemic awareness and you will be able to find programs to assist with teaching phonemic awareness. However, the process of teaching could be frustrated if your child also has difficulty with memory or comprehension that you have not been able to identify. You can minimize evaluation gaps by reading broadly about each area of learning difficulty you suspect your child has.

Caution: Attempting to undertake an evaluation as a solitary effort done solely by you is likely to leave unidentified areas of need and gaps in provisioning. A solo route through evaluation is more likely to lead you off target, if you are not thorough in your attempts to identify all learning difficulties your child may have. Failure to identify all areas of need can leave you and your child frustrated by a lack of meaningful educational progress, so it is important to be as thorough as possible in your research and evaluation of your child.

Given a thoughtful process for understanding your child's specific needs, you can come somewhere close to meeting your child's actual needs. The majority of parents waste a lot of time trying various programs without ever sitting down to thoughtfully and purposefully analyze their child's actual struggles, strengths, and specific needs. If you take the time to analyze in as much detail as you possibly can, you are much more likely to implement the right kind of program at the right time for your child.

Don't let a lack of funding for a professional evaluation stop you from helping your child; just be mindful of the need to evaluate your child's needs with openness to whatever those needs may be.

Even though your progress may be slower than it would be with an expensive evaluation, there is a high likelihood that your one-on-one help for your child will bring about better progress than he'd make in a traditional classroom anyway. Don't despair about not having the best; your efforts will pay off in the long run.

One last note on this topic: don't dismiss your child's bad behaviors as purposeful non-compliance with completion of schoolwork. When your child is resistant to doing his school work, look at each instance of obstinacy or defiance as a possible indicator of an area that potentially needs improvement.

By studying what subjects or tasks your child is trying to complete when he shuts down or has an angry outburst, you can figure out additional areas of difficulty or frustration within your child's learning. Look for environmental disturbances, what type of curricula is causing frustration (books, a computer program, etc.) and focus on determining what factors may be triggering your child's frustration.

Once you've identified the causes of meltdowns and angry outbursts, you can switch to a different teaching medium, learning presentation, program, etc. to help your child overcome his difficulties. Often, focusing on behavioral outbursts as a problem to be solved rather than as a discipline issue can help both you and your child have a better homeschooling experience.

It isn't easy to gain insight into your child's mind without a comprehensive evaluation. However, it is possible, if you are purposeful in your approach to problem-solving each of your child's educational difficulties. I pray my Lord will help you find great solutions for your child. Having been poor, I know what it is to yearn for your needs to be met—particularly when they involve the well-being of your child.

3 ADDRESSING YOUR CHILD'S SPECIFIC LEARNING NEEDS

This series of Q's & A's is perhaps the most important sequence for enabling you to help your child. Given a comprehensive evaluation and a clear understanding of your child's abilities and needs, you can use the information in this series to tailor a custom made educational program for your child.

The process we will undertake in this Analyzing Learning Needs section is the heart of what I have deemed to be "Individualized Instructional Design." My Master's Degree is in Instructional Design, which is a process for designing successful instructional initiatives. While the process is usually applied at an institutional level in corporations, universities, or anywhere there is a population of people who need to learn something, it can also be applied to a single learner. By narrowing the instructional design process down to focus on a single learner, your child, you can develop a viable learning program for your individual learner! So let's get started.

How do I determine my child's learning style?

Whether your child has been evaluated by a private evaluator, your school, or yourself, you will also need to analyze your child's learning style and preferences in order to provide the best learning environment and outcomes. Let's begin by walking through the process of determining how your child learns best, followed by Q&As to determine your child's specific learning needs, his learning strengths, and most importantly how to develop a program to allow your child to be successful in learning.

There are several different ways of analyzing learners and their learning styles. Each learning styles model has a different approach to categorizing a learner's strengths and learning needs. Each model contains valuable information for you as you try to determine the individual learning needs of your child.

Among the most popular learning style models are the VAKT (Visual, Auditory, and Kinesthetic/Tactile) model, Gardner's Multiple Intelligences, and the Dunn and Dunn Learning Styles Inventory. Each of these learning style models are discussed on the Learning Abled Kids' website in the "Learning Styles" section. Therefore, I will not reiterate all of the content explaining each of these styles here. Instead, I highly recommend you visit each individual section using the links here, or by going to the Learning Styles section and selecting each model from the menu at the bottom of the page.

After you have read about each of the three learning styles models, you will need to determine your child's individual learning style. Determining your child's style based upon the Dunn and Dunn model is probably the easiest because they have inexpensive, comprehensive assessments you can use which are tailored specifically to each of four different age groups. You can access your child's learning style using the age appropriate inventory at: http://www.learningstyles.net/en/our-assessments.

You will notice there are no assessments for a child six years of age or younger on learningstyles.net. Typically a child younger than six will not have enough cognition of his or her individual preferences to articulate them during an assessment. Thus, if your child is an "older" six, you might be able to get away with using an assessment for the 7-9 year old group, but I would not recommend using the assessment for younger children.

The Learning Styles Inventory based upon the Dunn and Dunn model, as provided by the assessment tool above, will provide you a detailed report with specific information you can use for designing an optimal learning environment for your child. The Dunn and Dunn model seeks to meet the physiological, emotional, and social needs of a learner better than any of the other models. I like to use the Dunn and Dunn learning style inventory as a basis for building the ideal learning environment for a learner.

Once a viable learning environment has been established for a child, including consideration of the entire range of physiological needs, we can focus on the cognitive aspects of learning. Both the VAKT model and Gardner's Multiple Intelligences focus on the personality and/or natural learning strengths of an individual (Gardner, 1998). By understanding your child's natural gifts and preferred ways of learning, you can tailor your instruction to capitalize on your child's learning strengths.

For Gardner's Multiple Intelligences, there are several tools out there you can use, but again—with a younger child it is more difficult to assess each of the "intelligence" areas. Even though your child may be young, given each of the areas of intelligence, you may be able to see where your child's main intelligences seem to be. You may be able to pinpoint the likely areas of intelligence depending upon the types of activities your child enjoys, how much he enjoys being around people or being alone, how much he talks, builds with blocks, sings, etc.

Researching the characteristics for each of the multiple intelligences by taking a couple of the assessments below will probably give you some direction if you can relate the characteristics to your young child's natural choices.

For an older child (middle school aged or older), this is my favorite Multiple Intelligence assessment: http://www.literacyworks.org/mi/assessment/findyourstrengths.html. The results provide the three most closely matched areas of intelligence, along with a rating scale. Each area's rating is provided at the bottom of the results. If you have a younger child, go ahead and take this free assessment yourself, then look at each of the rating areas and see which ones you believe apply to your individual child.

With any aged child, use the inventory at: http://www.edutopia.org/multiple-intelligences-learning-styles-quiz to determine which area(s) of intelligence seem to apply to your child most. Once you have made a determination about your child's specific areas of "intelligence," you can use this information to help structure your child's learning program around his strengths.

For example, if your child has "Musical Intelligence," he would have high learning engagement when you use jingles, rap songs, or other musical presentations of concept knowledge. You can search on Amazon for virtually any topic (math, spelling, grammar, etc) and the word "songs" and find a wide variety of musical presentations for various learning concepts.

If your child has a high level of "Int*ra*personal Intelligence," (self-intelligence) he may learn better when he is alone or working one-on-one with you. If your child has a high level of "Int*er*personal Intelligence," (social intelligence) he may learn best in a group situation where discussion and interaction are prominent. By considering your child's individual areas of intelligence, you can tailor instruction to your child's specific learning strength(s).

Lastly, and probably the most well-known of the learning style models, is the VAKT Learning Styles model. Virtually everyone I have worked with is familiar with the Visual, Auditory, and Kinesthetic/Tactile way of considering a learner's preferences. Be aware: seldom does any learner fall singularly into one of these categories. There is often a strongest learning channel, a middle channel, and a weak channel.

In traditional classrooms, the teaching style is definitively geared toward an auditory learning style—focused on hearing, reading, and language processing of all kinds. To a lesser degree, traditional classrooms utilize visual learning presentations with charts and images. To the least degree, teaching is provided in a kinesthetic/tactile manner using movement, hands-on projects, etc.

Thus, when considering "learning disabilities," those identified as having "learning disabilities" are, in my way of thinking, "learning disadvantaged." They have an ability to learn; they just don't learn well via the language-based methods commonly used. Children who struggle with language and/or language-based learning are virtually certain to be at a learning disadvantage in a typical lecture-based class, where reading is a major source of content, and writing or worksheets are used as a measure of understanding.

We all know that ADHD, particularly the hyperactive type, is a great nemesis to the traditional classroom teaching environment, but I believe it is because the kinesthetic/tactile learner is not being taught in a way that meets his needs. Many kids with ADHD, particularly with the hyperactivity component, need to get up and move around in order to process information effectively.

In traditional classrooms, kids are usually expected to sit in their desks without moving around, standing up, or fidgeting. Since a kinesthetic learner has a need to move in order to learn well, if you make learning experiences active and hands-on, suddenly a child who is diagnosed with ADHD is more engaged in learning activities, therefore he learns more easily. At home, you can create an active learning environment and let your active learner get up and move around at will.

Tip: Don't try to make your kinesthetic/tactile learner sit in a desk reading and doing worksheets for hours—it's not a functional way to school an active learner. An active learner will have difficulty focusing because he's more likely to be thinking about wanting to move around or will impulsively get up. For young, active learners, the requirement for them to sit still can become a serious point of contention that really isn't worth the battle when you can add movement to your child's learning.

I think it is very important for you to know that most children who struggle with traditional schooling either have a visual or a kinesthetic/tactile learning style as their primary way of processing information. Therefore, unless your child is an auditory learner, you will need to think outside of the traditional textbook-lecture style of teaching in order to effectively meet your child's individual learning needs.

To determine if your child is an Auditory, Visual, or Kinesthetic/Tactile learner, I like this quick and easy assessment: http://www.schoolfamily.com/school-family-articles/article/836-learning-styles-quiz.

The assessment is quick and the questions are easily understood by most children. The assessment provides a form of ranked results, letting you know your child's primary, secondary, and least favored learning styles.

There is also a fairly quick, easy, and free inventory which is a printable PDF at: http://www.njea.org/pdfs/LearningStyleInventory.pdf. This inventory is also easy to use and gives you a clear, singular result.

Similar inventories, with different questions, can be found at:

http://www.whatismylearningstyle.com/learning-style-test-1.html and http://www.whatismylearningstyle.com/learning-style-test-2.html. These two tests are both provided by Piedmont Education Services, but use different testing formats. Use whichever one you prefer, or use them both. For that matter, feel free to use all of the learning styles assessments, then compile your results.

By using the variety of tools I have suggested, you should be able to assess your child's learning style with fairly good accuracy. It is helpful if you make notes in your notebook regarding your child's learning preferences, main form of "intelligence," and the order of his preference for the VAKT learning styles. This information will be useful in your educational planning. Mistakes in setting up your child's learning program can be counterproductive, so you don't want to go solely from memory—please write your child's learning style preferences down or print the inventory results for your records.

I should also let you know that research shows the most effective means of teaching a child with learning difficulties is through multi-sensory teaching. Multi-sensory teaching seeks to provide instruction using all of the VAKT presentation forms simultaneously: auditory, visual, and kinesthetic/tactile. Note, this is an "AND," which means a teacher uses all three teaching styles for each lesson.

When using multi-sensory instruction, you can use books, but you should also use models, videos, experiments, etc. to reinforce learning across all of the learning channels. Your main goal is to provide the highest quantity of instruction using your child's primary channel, and reinforce that learning using the secondary and least preferred learning channels for your child. Study data shows learning retention is increased when multi-sensory instruction is provided.

What is multi-sensory teaching?

I touched briefly upon Multi-Sensory teaching in the previous question, but this teaching methodology merits an answer section all to itself. Multi-Sensory teaching is at the heart of the Orton-Gillingham method, which is used for teaching children with dyslexia to read. Multi-Sensory teaching is shown to help learning retention when used for teaching a child with any major learning disability.

While the question about multi-sensory teaching isn't directly related to analyzing your child's specific learning needs, examining this teaching methodology is a great way to meet your child's learning needs more effectively. I have a free, online tutorial about Multisensory Instruction which would be highly beneficial for you to go through. You can find it at:
http://learningabledkids.com/multi_sensory_training/page01-welcome.htm.

Multi-sensory teaching seeks to provide instruction simultaneously in an auditory, visual, and in a kinesthetic/tactile manner, but doing so can be difficult to do if you have a strong preference for any singular teaching style. In this Q&A we will discuss the need to analyze yourself in order to better teach your child.

It's important to know each person has a unique preference for learning and teaching. Thus as teachers, we tend to teach in our own learning style rather than in the learning style of our child. If your teaching style and your child's learning style are the same, it creates a great synergy for learning. However, if your styles are different, it will require thoughtfulness to meet your child's learning needs.

If you haven't done so already, reference the previous Q&A about learning styles and take the learning styles inventories yourself. Determine your learning preferences, your areas of intelligence, and your VAKT learning style. Knowing your own personal tendencies will help you understand the differences and similarities between your teaching style and your child's learning style. Understanding your differences is a key component for addressing areas where your styles are dramatically different and for taking advantage of areas where your styles are similar.

Briefly, as an example, my older son prefers a quiet, undistracted, direct-instruction form of learning. My younger son is a kinesthetic, on-the-move, music-loving child. My style is most like my older son, and my younger son's learning style is 'disruptive' to both my older son's learning and my teaching.

Does that make my younger son's learning style "wrong"? By NO MEANS! His style is perfect for him. It is my job as his teacher to meet his needs without belittling him, making him sit still, and without sacrificing his learning for my convenience in teaching. It would not be right to stifle my younger son's learning on behalf of my older son, so our schooling needs require me to creatively manage learning activities and learning times to best meet the needs of each of my boys.

I know a few "on-the-go" moms who love to go, go, go, and experience many field-trip learning opportunities, but they travel with a dragging, complaining children who "just want to go home." I sometimes think the moms don't understand their children prefer a quiet, structured, familiar environment for learning. The moms may think their children should love active learning because that is what they prefer. While doesn't mean a mom has to give up everything she enjoys, it is wise for her to be aware that her child's learning will be lessened if she is not meeting her child's individual learning needs.

Outings are always great educational activities when it comes to providing well-rounded, multisensory instruction, but on the go learning is not an optimal way to learn for every child. It pays to be in tune with your child's needs, not so the world can revolve around your child, but so your child can learn effectively and make adequate educational progress without a lot of stress and frustration.

The key to effective instruction is to understand your child's unique needs and not weigh any particular learning style as "bad" or "wrong". While your teaching style is neither bad nor wrong, if you want your child to learn effectively, you must meet his needs. It may be challenging for you to meet the learning needs of your child if his needs are dramatically different from your own style. However, if you transform your teaching to be what your child needs, then you will enhance your child's learning achievement. I hope that makes sense!

After completing the learning style inventories for yourself, look at your style(s) side-by-side with your child's. What is the same? What's different?

When your styles are exactly the same, you can experience greater progress in your child's learning. The teaching will be easy and fun for you and learning will be easier for your child. In areas of similarity, you can relax and do what comes naturally for both of you.

For those areas where there is a difference, particularly differences that are virtual opposites like intrapersonal (self) versus interpersonal (social), you will have to make purposeful changes to meet your child's needs. This is where the true measure of your sacrificial parenting and teaching comes into play. As a parent who is willing to homeschool, you likely already place your child's needs very high on your priority list, so hopefully meeting your child's learning needs in this way will be a natural choice for you.

Given your child's learning style is different from your own, you will struggle a bit to find the right methods for teaching your child. You will not gravitate naturally toward solutions that go against your own personal preferences.

In looking for viable solutions, you may want to search for "multi-sensory" or "experiential" learning programs. Using multi-sensory curricula will reinforce learning across each of the major learning channels. By using a wide variety of presentations via models, videos, experiments, books, activities, field trips, etc., your child will benefit from being taught in his individual learning style as well as through the other learning channels without suffering from a lack of learning retention. The key is to provide the majority of your child's direct instruction in his preferred mode of learning.

Given awareness of your child's learning preferences, it will be much easier for you to provide instruction of the type that benefits your child the most. Focusing on your child's learning needs will provide a high quality educational experience for your child.

Each of the next three Q&As will discuss the visual, auditory, or kinesthetic styles in detail. Although it would seem prudent to focus only on the learning style(s) that match your child's style, you will benefit from understanding each of the styles as a means for providing multisensory learning reinforcement for your child and variety in your teaching.

How do I teach a child with a visual learning style?

In the previous two Q&As we talked about how to determine your child's learning style and your teaching style. As we discussed, research shows the most effective means of teaching a child with learning difficulties is through multi-sensory teaching, but focused teaching through your child's preferred learning style can enhance learning outcomes.

In this Q&A we will discuss specifics for teaching your child if he prefers visual learning. Visual learners prefer learning through images, 3-

D (three dimensional) objects, graphs, charts, photographs, movies, etc. They prefer image-focused learning.

I want to clarify up front, that information preferred by visual learners is picture and image based, and it is processed in the visual center of the brain. Many people mistakenly think that reading is a visual activity, but it is not a picture or image based mode of learning.

When reading, the intake of the letters and words is a visual process, but the letters and words are transformed into language-based information which is processed in the language-processing center of the brain. When a book is read, the information is processed by the brain as if the book's author is "talking" to the reader. Thus, reading is primarily a language-based, auditory learning activity that is not ideal for a visual learner. With that said, visual learners may need to see the words on a page to process any information presented through text, but the text itself is not a highly effective *visual* learning activity for most visual learners.

Children with weak language skills often have difficulty learning to read as do children with visual processing deficits. Reading is a unique learning activity that requires both visual and verbal (auditory) processing capabilities. I feel this is why reading difficulties are ranked as the most frequent area of learning disability.

If your child prefers visual learning, you will want to look for highly visual instructional materials that are rich with photographs, drawings, diagrams, etc. Coffee table books on any topic are usually full of pictures as are many of the "visual" encyclopedias available on the market. For any topic your child needs to learn about, you can search for picture-rich encyclopedias, documentary DVDs, museums, hands-on activities or reenactments, etc. Highly visual books can effectively let your child "see" the scientific concepts or historical actions. I find that searching for "visual" along with the topic, such as "visual volcanoes," will bring up at least a couple of books that are visual guides to the topic.

Mathematics is more of a challenge for visual learners. There are math curricula that use manipulative blocks, templates, teaching DVDs, charts, graphs, etc., to convey mathematical concepts, and it is important to use these types of tools with a visual learner. Some of the best math curricula for visual learners include Math-U-See, Cuisenaire Rods, and Base Ten blocks. Often software-based programs have good visuals as well.

The key is not to rely solely upon printed numbers as they are not visual representations of quantities or processes. Having a visual image or graphic to depict each mathematical concept will enhance learning for your visual learner. Images of sticks, graphs, pie charts, etc. are a few illustrations of visual depictions of math concepts which will help your visual learner.

The difficulty of teaching reading and writing to a visual or kinesthetic-tactile learner depends upon the child's language processing skills. If your child has a lot of difficulty with language processing and struggles with making the sound-symbol connections required for reading, you will probably need an Orton-Gillingham based instructional program to effectively teach your child to read.

Orton-Gillingham programs provide explicit, direct instruction through multi-sensory techniques by incorporating visual, auditory, and kinesthetic/tactile activities simultaneously. For example, a child will trace a large letter on the carpet with her bare feet while saying the sound of the letter out loud. Tracings can take place via hand or foot, on traditional chalkboards, with finger on velvet, in a sand table, in a soapy pan, etc. Simultaneously moving, saying, and seeing helps the child store the sound-symbol relationship in her memory better than using any one of these methods in isolation.

When teaching your visual learner, you can use any of the following ideas for visual presentations of information:

Visual Learning Activities		
Bar Graphs	Flow Charts	Manipulatives
Charts	Concept Maps	Models
Demonstrations	Highlighter texts	Multimedia
Diagrams	Picture Flash Cards	Photographs
Drawings	Image-based Computer Programs	Pie Charts
Educational Videos	Highly Formatted texts with bold-faced section titles, outlines, and graphically pleasing layout.	Rainbow Writing

Graphic Organizers	Geographic Maps	Timelines
Hands-on Experiments	Color-coded worksheets	Webquests
Iconic Images	Field Trips	Visually Rich books
Illustrations	Picture Vocabulary	Visualization techniques

By incorporating various visual representations into your child's educational program, you will help your visual learner retain more of the information she learns.

How do I teach a child with an auditory learning style?

In the previous Q & A, we talked about teaching a child with a visual learning style. I briefly mentioned reading as a combination of a visual and auditory activity. We will discuss reading as a learning activity more in depth within this Q & A along with discussing specifics for teaching auditory learners. Auditory learners prefer learning through hearing an audio presentation where the information is presented via books-on-tape, lecture, audio-visual programs, etc.

Let's go ahead and discuss reading as both a visual and auditory learning activity. As mentioned in the previous Q & A, when a child is reading, the intake of the letters and words from the page is a visual process, but the letters and words are "interpreted" as language-based information and processed in the language-processing center of the brain. Reading is a unique activity requiring both visual and verbal (auditory) processing capabilities. That said, the visual aspect of reading is a relatively small portion of the reading process and learned content is not processed in the visual center of the brain at all. The content itself is processed in the language-center of the brain where meaning and understanding is applied to the words that have been read.

Thus, reading is more suitable to a verbal/auditory learner than it is to a visual learner. If a child has no visual difficulties, no other interfering learning difficulties, and he is an auditory learner, then reading is likely to be an easy skill for the child to acquire and use in his schooling. Since auditory learners have processing strengths in language, once they know how to read, reading is a good curriculum choice for them.

If your child is an auditory learner and does not have underlying neurological learning difficulties or other medically-based learning issues, he is likely to perform fairly well in a traditional classroom. Most schools use lecture, books, discussion, writing on the board, and other auditory means of conveying information. The majority of classroom teachers have an auditory teaching style, thus the traditional classroom favors auditory learners the most. If your child is an auditory learner, then you should have a relatively easy time finding instructional materials to use when schooling your child.

There are several mathematics programs that favor auditory learners. To teach your child, you can use any program that has an auditory component explaining the mathematical concepts. Math curricula that favor auditory learners include Teaching Textbooks, Math-U-See, Chalkdust DVDs, Thinkwell or Math Tutor DVDs. Each of these programs includes auditory explanations of mathematical concepts while an instructor is teaching the concept. Because most explanations in these programs use digits and symbols on a board rather than visuals, the programs are more effective for auditory learners than they are for visual or kinesthetic/tactile learners. The one exception is Math-U-See, which uses manipulatives to demonstrate concepts as the DVD instruction is explaining concepts.

Teaching reading and writing to an auditory learner can be easy if the child has no visual processing issues or underlying speech-language issues. If your child has a lot of difficulty learning to read, use an Orton-Gillingham based program to effectively teach your child to read. The multi-sensory nature of Orton-Gillingham based programs makes them effective for most learners. You can simply focus your teaching more heavily on those activities that match your child's learning style.

For all content learning, you will want to select an auditory activity for teaching your child. You can present information using the ideas listed in the table below or come up with your own ideas for auditory presentation of information.

Auditory Learning Activities		
Bees (Geography, Spelling)	Make your own "Walk and Talk" tapes for memorization	Rhythmic Clap and Tap Spelling
Audiobooks	Mnemonics	Role Playing
Debates	Mock Trials	Story Telling
Educational Videos	Music (Making songs or tunes for memorization)	Talking Books
Expressive Reading	Plays or Skits	Text-to-Speech software
Flash Card Drills	Poetry (Making rhymes for memorization)	Use background music or "white noise"
Interviewing	Read Alouds	Walk while listening to Audio Books
Lectures	Reading	Writing

By using the different, creative ways of presenting information to your auditory learner, you can keep your child engaged without becoming a droning, talking-head. Using a variety of methods and materials makes learning more fun.

How do I teach a child with a kinesthetic/tactile learning style?

Now we are going to talk about our most underserved learners—those with an active style of learning. Children who are kinesthetic/tactile learners require movement and hands-on learning to effectively process information. I feel kinesthetic/tactile children are the most likely to be identified as having Attention Deficit Hyperactivity Disorder in traditional schools because it is difficult for them to sit still for long periods of time, much less to learn by sitting at a desk listening to someone talk for an extended period of time.

Let me say up front that kinesthetic/tactile learners can be among the most fun and most challenging to teach. On one hand, undertaking hands-on projects, going on field trips, moving while memorizing, bouncing while reading, or otherwise being active while engaged in learning can create an energetic learning environment. On the other hand, aside from learning projects, mass market, and comprehensive curriculum programs designed specifically for kinesthetic/tactile learners are virtually non-existent. Although games and hands-on projects are used as instructional activities, they are not a large portion of any traditional curriculum. So, what can you do?

When looking for products and programs for teaching your child, it helps to know the industry buzzwords to search for when looking for teaching materials. The most common description will be either hands-on or "learning games." You can also search for "experiential" as a keyword in your searches, for example "experiential learning" or "experiential program". Also, brain-based learning activities incorporate movement which will meet the needs of kinesthetic learners.

For teaching mathematics, number concepts can be taught using claps or stomps for addition and subtraction. Using manipulatives and objects your child can handle will help solidify other math concepts. The hands-on programs that meet the needs of visual learners will be a better fit for your kinesthetic/tactile learner than text-only curricula. Programs that use hands-on manipulatives include Math-U-See, Cuisenaire Rods, and Base Ten blocks. Aside from these pre-made programs, math games are fun reinforcements to learning for kinesthetic/tactile learners, and you can use games in conjunction with any program; you just have to figure out when to include the extra activities.

For teaching reading, using large-body movements when teaching the sound-symbol correspondences will help your kinesthetic/tactile learner assimilate the information. Large-body movements can include making very large letters on a traditional chalkboard hung at an effective height for a child to use (we have our chalkboard hung about two feet above ground level). You can also have your child trace the letters on carpet or on any textured surface with his bare foot or finger. Your tactile child can fashion the letters out of clay as he recites the sound of the letter or he can trace the letters on a soapy baking sheet or in a pan of sand. There are any number of options for incorporating movement and a sense of touch into your daily teaching, but it will require creative thinking and planning on your part.

For Kinesthetic reading, kids may like to read in a rocking chair or while bouncing on a large exercise ball. With any workbook, reading, or audiobook, a child can rock and learn if a rocking chair provides sufficient movement for that particular child.

Most Kinesthetic activities work well for tactile learners. The table below contains ideas for kinesthetic teaching. These ideas use large body movements, so they are "kinesthetic." I have included an additional table of primarily hands-on, tactile types of activities in the tactile-learner portion of this Q&A. You can use the ideas listed in the kinesthetic table, the tactile activities table, or come up with your own ideas.

Kinesthetic Learning Activities		
Air Writing	Have child set up a "Shop" to practice math with money, the child is the cashier.	Rhythmic Clap and Tap for Spelling & memorization
Build Models		
CatchBall Drills - Play catch while reviewing facts	Interpretive Dance	Role Playing
Cooking or building for measurement studies	Jump Rope Recitation - Memorization while jumping	Scavenger Hunts
Field Trips	Large Arm writing on whiteboard or chalkboard	Science Experiments
Frequent activity breaks / Brain Gym	Letter Tiles	Walk while listening to Audio Books
Hands-on Experiments	Make your own "Walk and Talk" tapes for memorization	Walking Review - Walking while listening or reciting
Hands-On Museum Visits	Nature Hikes	Plays, Drama, or Skits

The tactile learning style is almost always joined with the kinesthetic learning. Both styles involve bodily movement, and are very similar, but the tactile style is more moderate. The tactile style is geared more toward the hands, the sense of touch, and fine motor movements, rather than the large, whole-body movements seen in the kinesthetic learning style. The Tactile Learning Style takes in information through the sense of touch and feeling, and generally a tactile learner has good eye-hand coordination.

People with a tactile learning style often have active hands. They fiddle with knobs and buttons, explore objects, examining and evaluating traits of objects. When in a store, persons with a tactile learning style may touch and explore many objects to 'understand' the characteristics of the object.

Hands-on learning is the primary method for teaching tactile learners. Tactile learners enjoy manipulatives, using different media such as finger-paints, art materials, building projects, drawing, blocks or objects for math, hands-on science experiments, lap-booking (making their own books), games, making models, dioramas, etc. If your child is a tactile-based learner, a project-oriented method of teaching will probably appeal to your child's learning needs.

Below, you will find a chart of tactile activities. These activities may or may not work well for kinesthetic learners, depending upon the level of activity your learner needs. Select any of these tactile means for teaching a concept to your child or come up with your own ideas.

Tactile Learning Activities	
Drawing	Modeling Clay or Playdoh
Felt Story Boards	Painting
Finger writing on velvet, textured cloth, sandpaper, sand table, rice table, in a pan with Vaseline, pan with oil, or pan with liquid soap, or any other textured surface	Foot writing - with bare feet, trace / write information on carpet, grass, sand, or other textured surface
Games	Project Kits
Lap Books	Sorting
Making Dioramas	Science Experiments
Making Models	Writing
Math Manipulatives	Cutting shapes with scissors

Having a kinesthetic/tactile learner can afford you a lot of active and fun learning in a homeschool environment. Unfortunately, it is more difficult to have the needs of a kinesthetic/tactile learner effectively met in a traditional classroom environment, because it is difficult for a teacher to manage a large number of kids who are simultaneously active. Additionally, having a single active learner in a classroom can be a distraction for other students, so I often think the needs of active learners are best met outside of a traditional, sit-at-your-desk type of classroom.

How do I use Gardner's Multiple Intelligences Theory for teaching my child?

In the previous Q & As, we talked about teaching children using the VAKT learning styles. Let's talk about another learning styles model, Gardner's Theory of Multiple Intelligences (Gardner, 1998), and learn how you can teach toward your child's specific area(s) of intelligence.

To begin with, let's clarify that the Multiple Intelligences theory is not related to IQ or intelligence as measured by any cognitive aptitude test. Rather, Gardner's Multiple Intelligences seek to identify unique strengths possessed by each individual. We all know children who are musically or artistically inclined; who are highly social, friendly and outgoing; or, who are quiet and self-reflective. Each of these unique ways of expressing one's self in the world can be used for teaching a child in a way that the child is naturally inclined. Thus, if you know your child's area(s) of personal intelligence, you can capitalize on your child's natural inclinations to make learning easier.

Gardner's Multiple Intelligences (MI) model includes nine areas of "intelligence" (Gardner, 1998), but I prefer to think of them as areas of ability or giftedness. By focusing on the natural abilities of your child, you will be able to more easily bring information into your child's memory where it can be processed at the point of your child's natural understanding.

Conversely, if your child is highly artistic or musical and you try to make your instruction logical and mathematical, it will be more difficult for your child to understand the concepts being taught. Math can be taught through singing, painting, or drawing. Drawing or singing can be taught using a step-by-step, logical approach relating to geometric shapes and/or rhythmic beats in music. Your approach to teaching any given subject will be understood more readily when presented to your child in her natural area of intelligence.

For the most part, Gardner's multiple areas of intelligence are relatively self-explanatory in regard to the area of strength a person has. It is usually less clear in regard to how you would use these areas of intelligence for teaching your child. For each area, I will list a few examples of how this area of intelligence should be considered when teaching. Some of the areas are more easily incorporated into instruction than others, but all can be utilized to some degree. The nine areas of intelligence identified by Gardner are:

- **Logical-Mathematical** - A person with this area of intelligence is skilled in logical reasoning. Thorough, step-by-step, explicit instructions for every area of learning, including the hows and whys, will help the Logical-Mathematical learner retain information more effectively.

- **Spatial** - Learners with this area of intelligence are most closely related to Visual learners in the VAKT model. Having spatial intelligence allows a person to think three-dimensionally about objects, activities, and information representations. Using hands-on projects, models, educational TV or DVDs, and visual depictions of information will help this learner retain information. Please refer to the Visual learning style information preceding this question for additional teaching ideas.

- **Linguistic** - Learners with this area of intelligence are most closely related to auditory learners in the VAKT model. Students who are linguistic like talking about concepts, discussions, audio-visuals, etc. They are language-based learners who are likely to learn well from lectures, audiobooks, educational TV or DVDs, and books. Please refer to the Auditory learning style information preceding this question for other suggested teaching activities.

- **Bodily-kinesthetic** - Learners with this area of intelligence are most closely related to kinesthetic/tactile learners in the VAKT model.

Children with a Bodily-kinesthetic intelligence learn well when they are active. They are generally good at sports, hands on activities, and prefer active learning. Please refer to the Kinesthetic/Tactile learning style information preceding this question for suggested teaching activities.

- **Musical** – Children with musical intelligence love singing, humming, and listening to music. Learners with a musical intelligence can be taught using poems, mnemonics, learning songs, rap, or other rhythmic presentations of information. Allowing your child to make up songs about any topic being studied is a great way to reinforce concept learning and have fun with his musical intelligence.

- **Existential** - Learners with an existential intelligence are spiritually centered. They like focusing on larger questions of existence and being in this world. While this area of intelligence is more difficult to incorporate into instruction, seeking to relate teaching and concepts to your religious faith, spiritual matters, or to the existence of the world, will help with learning retention.

- **Interpersonal** – This area of intelligence is a 'social intelligence.' Interpersonal individuals like interacting with other people, whether in pairs, small groups, or large groups. Learning in social settings will make learning more effective if your child has interpersonal intelligence, because it will provide your child an opportunity to connect concepts with other people's ideas, experiences, and information sharing.

- **Intrapersonal** - Learners with intrapersonal intelligence have a self-reflective focus on improving themselves. They want to know how specific information relates to themselves as individuals. When teaching your intrapersonal learner, provide explanations regarding how information relates to your child as an individual. Explain what concepts mean in terms of your child's lifelong needs and personal development to deepen his connection to the information being taught.

- **Naturalistic** - These learners love the outdoors, nature, the elements, plants, etc. Naturalists are focused on the sciences. Teaching information by explaining how each concept relates to the natural world will help your naturalistic learner understand how concepts relate to the universe through the eyes of nature. Studying history through the effects of events on people and their geographic area, the effect on nature, the climate, and the world relates historical events to naturalistic concerns. By focusing on nature-based math problems for math and books about nature-based topics for reading will help your child engage with subjects that are not typically naturalistic.

How do I use the Learning Styles Inventory for teaching my child?

If you haven't had your child take the Dunn & Dunn Learning Styles Inventory yet, you may want to visit the website to determine your child's learning preferences. Also, let me say that I do NOT receive any benefit whatsoever from readers taking the Dunn & Dunn Learning Styles Inventory (D&D LSI). It just happens to be the model I think is the most comprehensive and most useful for establishing an effective learning environment for your child. You can find the D&D LSI at: http://www.learningstyles.net/en/our-assessments.

What can you learn by having your child take the D&D LSI? The Dunn & Dunn model assesses physiology, psychology, sociology, environment, perception, and emotion as they relate to your child's learning. Each of these areas has an impact on a child's ability to learn. Failure to provide an environment that favors your child's preferred mode in any of these areas will affect learning to some degree. If you use the Dunn & Dunn assessment and meet your child's needs in each area, then you will establish an educational environment that helps your child learn more easily without being distracted by disagreeable learning conditions.

While creating an ideal environment will help learning, there is no learning environment that is perfect every moment of every day. However, if you can closely match your child's needs by establishing a comfortable environment, he will learn better than if you fail to meet his needs at all.

For analysis, look through your D&D LSI results. As you read through the report, take note of specific changes you can to make in your child's learning environment in order to better meet his needs. You will want to consider each domain area carefully. Below are some general questions to get you thinking about how your child's learning preferences relate to changes you may need to make:

1. **Learning environment: light, sound, temperature, and seating.**

Do you need to make your child's environment brighter, dimmer, natural, sunny or provide softer lighting?

Do you need to provide background music or noise reduction?

Do you need to make the environment warmer or cooler?

Does your child need a desk or a big comfy chair?

2. **Physiological learning needs: perceptual, intake, time of day, and mobility**

Is your child's primary learning preference auditory, visual, kinesthetic or tactile according to this model?

Does your child need to be well-fed or have drinks and snacks handy while studying?

Does your child learn best early in the day, mid-day, or late in the day?

Does your child prefer sitting still, moving around, or lying down while learning?

3. **Emotional learning needs: motivation, responsibility vs. conformity, task persistence, structure:**

Does your child have intrinsic motivation to learn, or does he need encouragement through incentives?

Does your child conform by following provided instructions, or does he prefer to be self-directed or exploratory in his learning?

Does your child drive forward and stay with a task, even when it is difficult, or does he give up fairly easily?

Does your child need a regimented routine to move through his studies effectively, or does he respond better to going with the flow of the moment?

4. **Sociological: self, pairs, peers, teams, adult directed, or social variety:**

Does your child prefer to do things by himself?

Does your child learn better when interacting with or being challenged by another child or a small group of children?

Does your child learn better when he's part of a team working together or when challenged by a group of peers?

Does your child learn best when instruction is provided one-on-one by an adult?

Does your child get bored with any one social scenario and prefer a variety of social settings for learning?

5. **Psychological: Analytical vs. Global, Reflective vs. Impulsive**

Does your child focus on the details and step-by-step learning, or is he a big-picture thinker?

Does your child do more thinking or is he an active doer?

By using the results from your D&D LSI, you can create what might be considered the ideal learning environment for your child. Because the focus of the D&D LSI is more physiologically-based than specific to cognition and learning, it is an entirely different type of learning styles model than most other models used. Therefore, the way in which you use the information gained through the D&D LSI is likewise different. By using each category's characteristics as a checklist in establishing your child's learning space, you can set up an environment that is optimized for his learning.

How do I know what to work on first?

After you've established a viable learning environment based upon your child's Learning Styles Inventory, determined your child's primary Intelligences, his VAKT Learning Style preferences, and have your child's comprehensive evaluation results, you can use the information to begin your quest for the best learning solutions for your child.

Because the entirety of meeting your child's needs can seem overwhelming, I suggest starting by focusing on one thing at a time initially. When addressing a child's specific learning needs, there is a hierarchy of needs to be considered. The order I use in determining which learning problems need to be addressed first is:

1) Physical barriers (vision, hearing, fine motor, etc.)
2) Cognitive processes (memory, attention, processing, etc.)
3) Foundational skills (reading decoding, math computation, basic writing)

The simplest place to begin meeting your child's needs is to start creating a physical learning space that suits your child's learning preferences. The space will be based largely upon the physiological aspects of the Dunn & Dunn inventory, but will include consideration of activity space, visual wall art, or listening stations depending upon your child's VAKT style. You will also want to consider your child's multiple intelligences when creating his learning environment.

The second area of physical barrier is in regard to your child's physical abilities and limitations. For example, a child who has difficulty learning to read may have vision problems, ocular motor deficiencies, phonemic awareness difficulties, scotopic sensitivity, or several other conditions which make it difficult to read. If a child is physically unable to focus on the words upon the page, she will be unable to learn to read regardless of any phonemic awareness training. Thus, your child's physical barriers to learning must be addressed early in the process of optimizing learning.

Again using the example of a reading difficulty, a child needs to be able to see and use his eyes effectively in order to read, so any physical barrier to reading must be addressed first. If vision can be corrected with glasses, then glasses should be obtained. If a child has difficulty with smooth eye-movement (ocular motor deficiencies), he needs vision therapy, so the words won't appear to "jump around on the page." If a child is blind or has low vision, reading must be addressed through Braille or audiobooks.

A child's physical needs in writing or math fall under similar hierarchies of need. Your child may need physical therapy or occupational therapy to enable him to grip a pencil correctly, to work with math manipulatives, etc. There are many young children who struggle with writing and pencil grip is a frequent area of difficulty. If a child doesn't need therapy, he may need special ergonomic pencil grips to position his fingers correctly and enable him to hold onto a pencil more effectively. The key is to work on addressing the physical needs of your child as a first order of need, but not at the expense of content-based learning.

While working on the physical needs of a child, learning does not need to be held back in any content area. Assistive technology can help a child learn while he or she gains the needed physical abilities for reading, writing, and doing math. For example, if a child cannot yet read, the child can still learn science, social studies, literature, etc. through audiobooks, audio-visual presentations, having material read aloud, etc. A child who cannot write yet can dictate into a speech-to-text program on a computer. Speech-to-text capabilities are excellent for teaching a child to express himself in writing, even if the child is not yet able to physically write by hand.

One of the best aspects of homeschooling a Learning Abled Kid is that you can provide accommodations from the very beginning of your schooling. Using accommodations will keep your child moving forward academically while you are still working on basic skill development through special therapies or programs. Unfortunately, public schools tend to be resistant to quick and prolific use of assistive technologies which can be used to keep a child on grade level while he is continuing to work on acquiring basic academic skills.

After your child's physical needs are identified and are being addressed by viable programs, any underlying cognitive processes for learning which have deficits must be addressed. The underlying neurological barriers to learning include processing speed, working memory, memory recall, attention functioning, organization and planning skills (executive functioning), sensory integration, etc. These neurological processes are used to process, understand, and store learned material into the child's long-term memory. If any of these cognitive processes are weak, they can interfere with your child's ability to learn.

Brain-based areas of cognitive processing can be improved through any number of games, tools, or brain training programs. For example, memory recall can be improved by playing daily memory games with cards or on a computer. Working memory can be improved by working on what is known as "digit spans" where a child is given a sequence of numbers and asked to give the numbers back in the same or a reverse order. The quantity of numbers in the sequences is increased as the child gains skill until the child can hold and manipulate about seven numbers in his mind.

For example, you would tell your child, "I will give you three numbers. Put them in reverse order in your mind and say them back to me. I will say 1--2--3 and you will reverse the numbers and respond back with 3--2--1. Let's begin." You would then give your child each three-digit sequences, allow your child time to manipulate the numbers in his mind, and then he can say the numbers back to you.

The skill is developed in a slow progression of advancement by practicing with three numbers for a period of weeks, then moving to four digits, then five digits, and so on. When your child has no errors for most trials with seven digits, his working memory skills should be viable for spelling, reading, writing, and performing math calculations in his mind. There are computer-based brain training programs that can be used to practice this skill, which may be preferable to practicing these drills with your child. Use whichever works best for you and your child.

There are programs like "Interactive Metronome" for attention functioning. "Dance, Dance Revolution" can be used to improve attention, processing speed and memory functioning at home and in a fun way. Brain Gym exercises can be used to improve planning and sequencing of bodily movement as well as to improve attention functioning. As mentioned, there is a wide variety of programming available, so you need to seek programs specific to improving any neurological deficits noted by your child's independent evaluator.

One of the better online brain enhancement programs with solid research behind it is BrainWare Safari (http://www.mybrainware.com/who-we-help/parent). You can read about research-based outcomes at: http://www.mybrainware.com/safari/research, and it is offered by the same, well-respected company that offers Fast ForWord.

BrainWare Safari is designed to enhance 41 cognitive skills in six different areas, including attention, memory, visual processing, auditory processing, sensory integration, and thinking skills. It specifically targets reception, perception, memory, and thinking skills in a videogame-like format that children generally find fun and engaging. If your child struggles with any of the underlying processes, I would highly recommend checking out this program as a foundational program for enhancing your child's learning.

When your child's physical needs are met and the enhancement of neurological processes is under way, you can effectively begin instruction in the core academic skills. The core skills include reading decoding, handwriting or writing using a keyboard, learning to spell, structuring sentences and paragraphs, and performing basic math computations (adding, subtracting, multiplying and dividing). Generally speaking, after a child can decode words effectively, she can begin reading for meaning. After a child can perform basic math calculations, he can begin learning more advanced math skills like solving word problems. After a child can construct sentences, he can begin working on forming persuasive essays.

These academic skills are the foundation for more advanced academic pursuits, but truth be told—they aren't "essential" for higher learning if your child can't master them. While each of the core academic skills are part of the foundation for more advanced instruction, no physical barrier, cognitive processing issue, nor core academic skill needs to interfere with presentation of scientific concepts, history, fine literature or other academic material to a child. Aside from comprehension difficulties, a child can watch educational programming, listen to audiobooks, go to museums, perform science experiments with help from an adult, and engage in numerous learning activities that do not require the core academic skills.

Therefore, I encourage you to provide viable opportunities to learn about scientific, historical, and literary works through a variety of presentations regardless of whether your child is able to read, write, or perform math calculations. Assistive technology and the wide variety of learning tools available today enable learning abled kids to master content-based learning regardless of difficulties with core academic skills.

Keep in mind, accommodations allow a child with a disability to access curricula even where profound physical disabilities exist. Children who are blind can access written content through audiobooks and text-to-speech technology. Children who have no hands can write through dictation software. Children who can't recall math facts or calculate math outcomes in their heads can use calculators. The root of learning centers on comprehension and understanding, which a child often has even without mastery of the specific academic skills. Therefore, you should not let your child's inability to read, physically write, or calculate be a barrier to content learning.

That said, often children are 'held back' from higher level instruction in schools until core academic skills are mastered. This causes what is known as "The Matthew Effect," which occurs when a child falls further behind in every subject area even though he only has a disability in one academic skill.

If a child is designated as "mildly mentally impaired," then it is more likely the child will be held back from learning broader content, particularly in traditional school environments. There is no need to hold any cognitively capable child back in such a manner.

It is important to note that every child with a specific learning disability is a learning abled kid. A child must be able to learn to be diagnosed with a specific learning disability. Therefore, you should never let anyone tell you your child cannot learn if he has a learning disability in reading, writing, or math.

Is my child really mentally impaired?

Through the years, there have been cases where a child with learning disabilities is measured as having a "borderline" IQ using common IQ tests. In some cases the child doesn't seem "mentally impaired," so the child's parents question the mentally impaired designation because their child hardly seems that impaired. A "Mildly Mentally Impaired" (MMI) diagnosis can be shocking, depressing, and bring a whole flood of emotions. If your child's diagnosis is followed by the thought, "I don't think he is mentally impaired," and you find yourself questioning the diagnosis, you could very well be CORRECT.

Granted, there are children who are quite limited in their cognitive learning abilities, and in those cases, a diagnosis of MMI usually does not come as a shock to that child's parents. Conversely, when a child shows ability to learn outside of school, is clever, verbally expressive, or has a high level of knowledge about topics of interest to him, he hardly seems mentally impaired; the parents are quite surprised by a mental impairment diagnosis.

There have been a number of cases where a child has multiple learning disabilities, the child is diagnosed as MMI, but later it is found the child actually has multiple learning disabilities. Deficits in subtest areas bring the child's composite IQ score down to a level that falls within a MMI range, but the child's overall cognitive ability is higher than his composite indicates.

If your child is such a child, do not despair! It has been proven repeatedly that intense remediation of a child's learning disabilities can improve a child's IQ score—sometimes by a significant quantity. In one study by Mary Emma Cleary of Loyola University Chicago (Cleary, 1945), students made significant gains in IQ when given intense remedial reading instruction.

Of the 34 students tested, 30 had significant increases in their IQ scores, with the median gain being 16 full-scale IQ points in one academic year. In the study, one student gained 26 IQ points during the academic year, which moved the child from borderline MMI to the upper end of the "average" range, just short of "superior" intelligence. I know that was one excited mom!

In the book, "Education As the Cultivation of Intelligence" by Michael E. Martinez, he says it's an established fact that IQ measurements can and DO change (Martinez, 2000). As such, I think it is important for you to focus on meeting your child's remedial education needs rather than concerning yourself about the limitations of your child's measured intelligence.

By focusing on the fact that your child CAN learn, his or her IQ can change over time. If you set to work on meeting your child's educational needs, then you are likely to have a better outcome than some professionals may lead you to believe. In our very case, those in charge at our school told us our son would probably never read well, but they were completely wrong. Our son achieved a college-level reading ability and his IQ has increased over the years, so I can also off this as personal evidence that measures of IQ can change over time as your child's learning needs are adequately met.

A small caution though: Your child's measured IQ can go down too. Years of educational 'neglect' by not teaching a child well, leaving a child in a school environment where his needs are not being met, or failing to provide sufficient intensity in instruction can lead to declines in measured intelligence as well.

Study information from Matt McMillen makes the point well, and parents are wise to stay alert to whether their child's educational needs are being adequately met or not, particularly when your child is in public school. Matt's article is on WebMD Health News, (2011) and is titled "IQ Scores of Teens May Change Over Time: Study Shows IQ Scores Can Fluctuate Over the Course of Several Years." I highly recommend you go read the article. You can find the article on WebMD Health News at: http://www.webmd.com/parenting/news/20111019/iq-scores-of-teens-may-change-over-time.

While innate learning ability is both nature and nurture, doing all you can to make sure your child's learning needs are nurtured can equate to a better outcome for your child. Study data indicates IQ is not fixed in measure, so do not despair—work on vigorous educational provisioning instead. Set your mind upon the possibilities and not on today's snapshot. You CAN make a difference by making sure your child's educational needs are met.

Can my child be gifted and have learning disabilities?

A child can absolutely be gifted and have learning disabilities. A child with specific learning disabilities is often measured as having a borderline IQ using common IQ tests. Yet, I frequently hear parents of children with learning disabilities describe their child as "really smart." People ask, "How can a child be both 'learning abled' and 'learning disabled' at the same time?"

"There are two basic misunderstandings here: that the learning disabled aren't smart and that giftedness means high achievement. If someone thinks learning disabled means 'dumb,' and that the gifted are 'smart,' you can't be smart and dumb at the same time. *However, federal and state definitions of learning disabilities specifically limit the term, 'learning disabled,' to children of at least average intelligence. So you have to be smart to be learning disabled!*' (From 'The two-edged sword of Compensation: how the gifted cope with learning disabilities,' by Silverman, Linda Kreger, Gifted Education International; 2009, Vol. 25 Issue 2, p115-130, 16p)," (NAGC, 2009).

That said, with a parent's intuition telling her a child is gifted added to the previous question where we talked about IQs changing over time, even if your child is not measuring as "gifted" today, he may very well be gifted in his cognitive ability. When looking at a broad spectrum of evaluations your child may have, always look toward those scores at the upper bounds of your child's testing as a possible measure of his actual learning potential.

For example, if your child has scores in a range from 72 to 130, the scores toward the 130-level abilities may indicate higher ability than the average or composite score in your child's score calculations. In our dramatic case for evidence, my older son scored at the 5th percentile on the Gray Oral Reading Test and at the 2nd percentile in spelling in elementary school, but he scored at the 99th percentile in Science abilities and the 92nd percentile in Problem Solving. The broad range of my son's scores, including on IQ test measures, resulted in a composite IQ score that was precisely average.

When my son was fully remediated for his dyslexia, all of his scores shifted to being well above average. He still scores at the 99th percentile in science, at the 93rd percentile for math, and at the 85th percentile for reading. As you see, his reading level is still below his other abilities, but it is much closer to what you would expect to see in a gifted thinker. My son's composite IQ score is now at the 95th percentile, but he has always been that smart—his abilities just didn't evidence well on paper and are still pulled downward a bit by his dyslexia-based cognitive processing. So, my son is both gifted and has a learning disability, as do a number of children like him.

As with my son's reading disability, your child is not likely to obtain across-the-board high achievement in all areas if he has a specific learning disability. However, teaching with your child's highest abilities in mind will improve your child's overall educational outcome. If your child scores well above average in some areas, there is a good chance your child has areas where he is gifted with intellectual ability. The key is to help your child overcome the specific areas of disability that are holding him back. Your child's ability to perform well in an academic setting can be enhanced significantly by using assistive technology and/or one-on-one remediation to work around areas of disability.

In researching giftedness in children with learning disabilities, I'll tell you that you should track your child's test scores from the very beginning—including any testing for kindergarten readiness, benchmark testing, or official evaluations. Keep a log of all testing and track the results over time. Why is this important?

The earliest testing on your child measures your child's overall learning ability prior to starting traditional schooling. Children with learning disabilities often learn concepts and ideas well in a natural setting, outside of a traditional classroom setting, because learning is based upon your child's innate ability to assimilate information from his environment. A child may seem perfectly normal or gifted, having met all of the typical developmental milestones at home, be able to identify colors, objects, and convey ideas well when speaking before he enters a traditional school.

It is important to document that learning has taken place before your child went to school, because failure to learn in a traditional academic setting does not make a child suddenly unable to learn. Your child may be unable to learn the needed academic skills of reading, writing, and math with ease, but those are artificial "requirements" for learning. Yes, learning those basic academic skills makes performing well in school easier, but struggling with the core skills doesn't make a child suddenly lose his cognitive abilities. It just means the child has learning disabilities in the specific areas in which he is struggling, and assistive technology can be used to keep a child on grade-level in all content-based subjects.

For example, a portion of my son's early testing placed his non-verbal learning abilities at the 95th percentile. That should have been an early indicator to everyone that he was quite smart. Over the next five years in public school, my son's testing performance grew steadily worse, but that was because he had dyslexia and his educational needs were NOT being met.

By the time we pulled our son out of public school all of my son's cognitive measures had dropped significantly, and his testing placed his composite learning at the 45th percentile. In fact, by time we pulled my son out of public school, his scores measured in the "low" range for every single area of testing except for science and "using information," in which he scored in the average range.

My son did not become less able to learn over time, he just wasn't being taught at all according to his academic aptitude. Our case is a perfect example of the Matthew Effect diminishing a child's educational achievement over time.

After a decade of homeschooling, my son's composite abilities measured at the 95th percentile when he took his college entrance exams. Clearly, my son was gifted all along, although the public school failed to recognize his abilities and tried to convince us we were off our rockers to think that he was gifted!

Focusing on your child's overall learning ability is an important element in setting learning expectations. You must note your child's ability to learn before starting school, so you are never convinced by school administrators that your child "can't" learn. If your child's school isn't meeting his learning needs, I can guarantee they will say it is because your child can't learn and they will not admit to providing an inadequate education. I've yet to meet any public school teacher or administrator that is willing to say, "Yes, you're right. We aren't educating your child very well," even when the evidence is as clear as ours.

Failure to learn single core academic skills is an entirely different matter than being "unable to learn". Reframing your thinking about learning disabilities to focus on learning *abilities* can make a significant difference in educational outcomes for your child.

Teaching children who are twice exceptional can be challenging. Consider this: Given that 3%-5% of students are thought to be "twice exceptional" and their needs have been poorly understood, studying this population is becoming of increasing interest to educators. In a report about Response to Intervention (RtI) for twice-exceptional students by the National Assoc. for Gifted Children (NAGC, 2009), they say:

> *"The major flaw in the RtI approach is immediately apparent and is related to two inaccurate assumptions. The first wrong assumption is that the "broadly appropriate" classroom curriculum is a good match for a gifted student. The second wrong assumption is that the definition of failure for a gifted child is the same as the definition of failure for a child with average or below-average cognitive ability.* **The gifted student with a learning disability often times goes unnoticed in the classroom because performance with a broadly appropriate curriculum appears satisfactory to most**

educators. *On the one hand, the "adequate" performance is the result of high cognitive ability, which allows for the student to compensate in a less-than-challenging curriculum. On the other hand, the high cognitive ability is not fully realized because the disability prevents the student from fully expressing his or her talents (National Education Association, 2006; Silverman, 2003)."*

There is a lot of interesting reading available about twice exceptional students. Here are a few resources you may find interesting to read:

http://2enewsletter.com/

http://www.hoagiesgifted.org/twice_exceptional.htm

http://www.gifteddevelopment.com/What_is_Gifted/2echildren.htm

http://www.gifted.uconn.edu/nrcgt/newsletter/spring98/sprng984.html

How you approach your child's education can make a significant difference in your child's educational outcome. If you believe your child is a capable learner based upon your observations, teaching him on a personal level with the underlying assumption that he *is* a capable learner is likely to serve your child well. If your child SEEMS quite smart or gifted, he probably IS smart or gifted. With what we know about the affect of educational provisioning on a child's IQ, given you know from the previous question that a child's IQ can go up or down by 20 points or more, don't let your child flounder in an educational environment that is preventing your child from realizing his full potential.

Find a way to homeschool if you can, because the one-on-one teaching is proven to bring forth better educational progress. If you question your ability to homeschool, please read: "Overcome Your Fear of Homeschooling" for an inside perspective of how homeschooling can meet your child's educational needs, regardless of your current level of patience or educational training. (Book link is: http://www.amazon.com/Overcome-Your-Homeschooling-Insider-Information/dp/1490921222/).

4 CHOOSING CURRICULUM

The number one question people ask when joining the Learning Abled Kids' support group is, "What curriculum should I use?" Some ask the generic question and others ask more specifically which curriculum they should use for their child's particular disability.

For the general question of what curriculum to use for your child, there are a whole host of questions that need to be answered prior to making a meaningful recommendation for a specific curriculum to you. Just as often people ask a more specific question such as, "My child has dyslexia (or any other disability). What curriculum should I use for my child?" The questions I have in response are fewer, but nevertheless I still would need a lot of answers before making a recommendation.

At the heart of deciding which curriculum to use is a need to determine your child's learning style, learning strengths, and learning deficits, all of which were covered earlier in this book. If you've read about the need for an evaluation and each of the learning style Q&As, then keep reading here; otherwise, you may want to go catch those sections to fully understand how those pieces of the learning puzzle can help you make a determination about which curricula would be best for your child.

Most specifically, it is important to have a comprehensive neuropsychological evaluation to determine precisely what the child's areas of disability are. Not all reading disabilities are dyslexia. Not all observable attention deficits are neurological—some stem from boredom, use of the wrong curriculum type for the child's learning style, or learning disabilities that have not yet been addressed.

Without a viable evaluation, you could very well apply the wrong solution to a perceived problem rather than to the actual problem. Thus, the information in the answers for the Q's & A's which follow assumes three things:

1) Your child has been evaluated by a highly qualified professional, and you have your evaluation results, so you know your child's specific disabilities,

2) You have gone through the learning styles evaluations and you have a good idea of whether you need an auditory, visual, or kinesthetic/tactile type of program, and

3) Your child's evaluation has verified he or she has the specific disability as an underlying neurological condition for which I'm recommending curriculum.

If you do not have the three pieces of needed information about your child, then the recommendations may very well not apply to your child at all. If you need information regarding why you should have your child tested or how to determine your child's specific learning needs, please refer to the earlier sections of this book about "Testing and Evaluation" and "Analyzing Learning Needs".

What curriculum would you recommend for dyslexia?

If you suspect or know your child has dyslexia, I would highly recommend reading ***The Dyslexia Help Handbook For Parents***(available on Amazon) for a comprehensive guide to helping your child overcome dyslexia. True dyslexia is a neurological disability that involves deficits in short-term working memory, deficits in phonological awareness, processing speed issues and/or deficits in the executive functions of planning, sequencing, organizing, etc.

True dyslexia is **not** a vision problem of any kind such as ocular motor developmental issues, scotopic sensitivity, visual acuity, or visual perception problems, but these conditions are also discussed in ***The***

Dyslexia Help Handbook For Parents. I'll give you my typical answer to parents asking this question in the Learning Abled Kids' support group. However, you will find much more comprehensive information in the Handbook.

Determining whether your child has true dyslexia or not can be tricky even if you have an evaluation because not all professionals call dyslexia what it is, and some professionals call conditions "dyslexia" when they are not the specific learning disability designated as dyslexia. If your child has been determined to have a "specific learning disability in reading" or in "reading decoding," then there is a high likelihood your child has the learning disability known as dyslexia.

A key indicator is to look at your child's scores for Phonemic Awareness (PA). If your child's PA scores are low, then your child can benefit from curricula designed specifically for teaching children with dyslexia to read.

Visually-based problems are physical disabilities requiring vision therapy, specialized glasses, or color overlays, etc., and are not directly addressed by phonemic awareness curricula designed for the remediation of true dyslexia. To put it another way, if your child cannot physically focus on and track his eyes along the words on a page, working on phonological awareness and reading decoding skills will be frustrating, and possibly unnecessary if your child's reading difficulties stem solely from a visual issue. Your child's physical needs must be addressed and correction should be under way before worrying about phonological decoding of phonemes and words in reading.

Visual perception difficulties are a bit different as visual perception issues are neurological in origin. Even so, visual perception difficulties require a different type of intervention to improve a child's visual perception. Visual perception problems will not be improved through phonemic awareness training, and a phonemic awareness program will only help if your child has true dyslexia.

That said, be aware your child may have both physical vision-based problems and true dyslexia, so physical problems must be addressed first. If your child complains about "words jumping on the page," has eyes that burn or tear up while trying to read, gets headaches or has other physical complaints about reading, you can safely assume you need to pursue an evaluation for developmental vision problems related reading or scotopic sensitivity. A developmental optometrist is a good place to begin. You can find doctors via the College of Optometrists in Vision Development at http://www.covd.org/.

That said, if your child has true dyslexia, the long-standing, proven methodology for teaching a child with dyslexia to read is the Orton-Gillingham Methodology (O-G). Created by Samuel Orton and Anna Gillingham, the O-G Method is a multi-sensory, sequential, explicit, comprehensive and direct instruction method of teaching a child with dyslexia to read. Let's take a minute to look at what each of those elements means:

— Multi-Sensory = instruction uses visual, auditory, and kinesthetic elements simultaneously when teaching phonemic awareness. As the teacher, you will most heavily use whichever component matches your child's learning style.

— Sequential = instruction follows a prescribed progression of teaching each aspect of reading, moving from vowel sounds to consonant sounds to blends and digraphs to syllables and attack skills for new words.

— Explicit = instruction teaches every aspect of how one reads without leaving any piece to guesswork, including individual sounds, blending, syllables, etc.

— Comprehensive = instruction covers everything from the smallest element of how to pronounce the sounds represented by letter symbols to advanced reading skills used to decode large, multi-syllable words.

— Direct = instruction is provided one-on-one to the student in an individually customized progression created as each day of instruction is completed. The direct instruction is designed to move forward only with the individual student's mastery of each concept as his reading abilities develop.

One child may spend a week working on mastering the five short vowel sounds, and another student may spend a month working on those same five sounds. Thus, the instruction itself is highly individualized and provided directly to the student rather than in a large class format.

There are several proven Orton-Gillingham (O-G) based programs for teaching a child with dyslexia to read. Most homeschooling families prefer a scripted or computer-based program, or a combination of these types of programs. Using the pre-scripted programs enables the teaching parent (you) to use the program without formal O-G training. O-G training, if you can acquire it, is well worth the time and money. It will enable you to understand how, why, and the application of the methodology as it pertains to your individual child.

Before we began homeschooling, I took a 56-hour O-G training course, which I believe was invaluable for enabling me to understand my son's learning needs and to better teach him across all subject areas. By using properly and intensely provided O-G instruction, my son was able to go from a non-reader to a college reading level in three years of instruction during his fifth, sixth, and seventh grade years of homeschooling.

Given a program provided properly with sufficient intensity on a daily basis, your child should likewise be able to make good reading progress. Below are the top six programs I recommend most for homeschoolers. My recommendations vary somewhat based upon price points and a family's budget, as well as the child's individual learning style:

> All About Reading & All About Spelling – This is my top choice because it is the least expensive, very comprehensive, and scripted. This program has manipulatives, teacher books, student books, and is straight-forward in its use. A parent can easily adjust this program to use multisensory teaching that matches her child's learning style.

This program, like the Barton and Wilson programs, will be easier for you to use if you have O-G training. Training will make the program more understandable and implementation will be easier for you, but training is not required for you to understand how to use the program.

The All About Reading manipulatives kit is around $50, and each of the reading levels is currently priced at $100. You can test your child to determine which level to begin instruction, so your costs will vary depending upon how many levels your child needs to complete.

> Barton Reading – This program is perhaps the most liked by parents because it is heavily scripted. It tells you exactly what to do, when to do it, what to say, and guides you through the process of teaching your child. However, it is also costly.

Each level currently runs more than $250 and there are ten levels with a total cost of $2900 at the time I am writing this book. It's a good program—it's just expensive. If your budget can afford the Barton program, you will appreciate knowing exactly what to do each step of the way, which is likely to result in better compliance in your use of the program, which can equate to better outcomes.

> Wilson Reading – This program is similar to Barton, but much more heavily used in schools. Wilson Reading is a tried and true program that has been on the market longer than any other program on this list. Wilson Reading is scripted and has twelve "steps" of instruction within.

The deluxe, comprehensive kit, which includes everything, is currently less than $500, making the full program relatively affordable. Wilson is a great program, but it will be easier for you to understand if you've had either Orton-Gillingham training or the Wilson Reading training before using the program. The program does include specific instructions, but it was designed primarily for classroom teachers who have had some amount of training.

> Earobics – If your child needs to begin reading instruction from the very foundation of reading, including proper pronunciation of individual letter sounds, blends, and digraphs, this is a great computer-based program to use.

We used this program as part of our daily reading remediation, and our boys liked the program fairly well. After my boys completed Earobics, they repeated the program in its entirety, and then we followed it with the Lexia SOS program.

Earobics is not a complete, stand-alone reading program solution, but using the program will provide a lot of the required, repetitive practice your child will need to master reading decoding. Using the program as a back-up reinforcement and extra practice tool for your child will speed up your child's reading skill acquisition. If you can shorten the number of months or years you spend teaching your child to read, this program is well worth the cost.

➤ <u>Lexia Reading's Strategies for Older Students</u> (SOS) – This program is very comprehensive and covers all reading instruction needed to bring a child to a proficient level of reading. Like Earobics, it is a computer-based program, which insures there are no gaps in your child's learning, and it is ideal as a review and reinforcement program to your child's multisensory reading instruction. We used SOS after our boys completed Earobics in order to provide ongoing reinforcement of their reading instruction and to insure 100% mastery of reading.

The SOS program begins at the foundational level with individual phonemes and progresses to a level of teaching Latin and Greek roots of words to give your child a better understanding of unfamiliar words. Our boys went through all five levels of the program, and then we had the boys repeat levels 4 and 5 for additional reinforcement of the more advanced reading skills.

➤ <u>ABeCeDarian Reading Program</u> – This is a research-based, explicit, comprehensive, multi-sensory reading program an increasing number of homeschooling families are choosing for reading remediation at home. I have not personally seen this program, nor worked with it, so I cannot attest to the level of scripting it provides, but a large number of the Learning Abled Kids' support group members are choosing this program and giving it strong recommendations as a quality and worthwhile program.

The program provides the depth and structure necessary to help the weakest readers make outstanding progress. The comprehensive and straightforward organization of the program make ABeCeDarian an excellent choice for homeschooling, and this is a similarly cost-effective solution like <u>All About Reading & All About Spelling</u>.

When helping my boys overcome their reading issues, I used the two computer-based programs, <u>Earobics</u> and <u>Lexia Reading</u> in conjunction with instruction using Orton-Gillingham methods in one-on-one teaching on a daily basis. You can read detailed specifics of the programming I used to help my sons overcome their dyslexia by visiting

my webpage at:
http://www.learningabledkids.com/reading/how_we_remediated_dyslexia.htm.

As you will see, we included several other elements in our reading remediation programming. Because your child may or may not have similar speech-language issues, the program we used may be overkill for your child, or you may require more in the way of speech-language or auditory processing focused instruction.

The programs we used met my boys' specific needs well. The specific programs we used may or may not meet your child's specific needs well. Only you can determine the precise type of instruction and level of provisioning your child requires.

What curriculum would you recommend for ADHD or attention difficulties?

At the neurological level, there are various causes for attention deficits. If a child is sleepy, hungry, bored, or doesn't understand what is being said, he may tune-out of instruction. An attention deficit caused by these types of situations is different than an imbalance in brain chemistry that causes the type of attention deficit commonly treated by medication. Since the root cause of your child's attention deficit will dictate the treatment, it is important to have your child evaluated to determine the cause of your child's attention deficit.

It is also important to determine the affect of the attention deficit on your child's learning and to determine the appropriate type of treatment, whether treatment needs to be medical, behavioral, or any need for treatment will be eliminated by remediating other learning disabilities. If your child's ADHD is caused by any factor that is not due to an imbalance in brain chemicals, you'll need to focus on environmental management, a change in curricula, and/or remediation of underlying learning disabilities that cause your child to have difficulty understanding the material being presented.

For example, one of my sons had "secondary ADHD" caused by his speech-language issues and dyslexia. When his teacher presented material to him by talking and writing on a board, or by having him look at words in a book, my son would "zone out" of instruction and focus his mind on something else because he had no ability to understand the words in front of him. In my older son's case, his attention deficits were *caused by* his dyslexia, and his ADHD was not the primary cause of his learning difficulties. Our neuropsychologist told us that once our son could read, his attention deficits would likely disappear, and they did.

If the ADHD is a neurological deficit caused by an imbalance in brain chemicals, then treatment of the chemical imbalance in the brain needs to be handled as a primary matter in order to enable your child to learn. For example, our younger son had a lot of difficulty with reading comprehension and attention. We thought maybe he had dyslexia like his older brother.

When we had our younger son evaluated, it was determined that although he had some issues with phonological awareness and mild dyslexia, he had diagnosable ADHD that was the primary cause of his learning difficulties. For our younger son, treating his ADHD as an imbalance in brain chemistry was recommended, and with treatment, many of his ADHD symptoms disappeared. We also used some of the methods and programs I discuss in **Reading Comprehension for Kids** to improve his reading comprehension.

Given that you have determined whether your child has primary or secondary ADHD, and assuming you are addressing core neurological needs, the curricula I would recommend for a child with ADHD depends heavily upon your child's individual physiological and psychological needs. If your child is prone to attention deficits, anything and everything that does not meet his needs can be a distraction.

For example, if a child desires a quiet environment for learning and it is noisy, he will not learn effectively. If a child desires white noise to tune out the environment, then total silence will have him distracted by every interjection of noise from any source.

If you haven't already, I would highly recommend going through the Dunn & Dunn Learning Styles assessment to determine how to establish the best learning environment for your child. Again, that website can be found at: http://www.learningstyles.net/. I'm in no way affiliated with the company, but believe they do have one of the best tools for assessing your child's environmental learning needs for a very low fee.

Thus, for a child who has attention deficits, figuring out the best learning environment is the first order of business you should undertake. Secondarily, figuring out how your child prefers his instruction—visually, auditorally, audio-visual, hands-on, in short sound-bites, or bigger chunks—will help you pick a curriculum and use it effectively. If you refer to the Q&As earlier in this book to determine your child's specific learning preferences, you will be able to create a program tailored more specifically to your child's needs.

If your child is diagnosed with the "active" or "hyperactive" component of attention deficit disorder, I will say that it is highly likely that your child is a kinesthetic, hands-on type of learner. Thus, your child is much more likely to learn from experiments, projects, trips to museums, re-enactments, etc. rather than from traditional written curricula. While books may be a foundational component of your curriculum, using them as references for projects and hands-on activities will likely work better than forcing your child to sit and read textbooks for any extended period of time. Refer to the earlier Q&A about teaching kinesthetic learners for more ideas on how to meet the needs of active learners.

Which curricula you choose to use will depend totally upon your child's preferences, which can be as varied as the number of children in the world. Thus, for children with ADHD, it is difficult to make any wholesale recommendations for a specific curriculum choice without knowing specifics about your child's preferred learning environment and style. In addition, there are relatively few programs available which are targeted specifically toward active learning styles, but looking for "experiential learning" programs will be helpful when seeking out curricula to meet your active child's learning needs.

If you'd like to check out the latest experiential learning sites, Rutgers University has a webpage that lists various experiential learning resource sites. You can visit them at: http://njaes.rutgers.edu/learnbydoing/weblinks.html.

What curriculum would you recommend when a child hates schoolwork?

I would recommend using curricula that he likes! The answer to this question requires the teaching parent to think outside of a traditional school box. Most often children who hate schoolwork are forced into using traditional workbooks and textbooks for their entire educational program. The hatred either stems from a mismatch in the child's personality or learning style with the curricula or from a sense of failure that comes from being forced to do school work at a level the child cannot yet successfully complete. Let's look at each of these problem areas to see if we can help your child overcome his hatred of schoolwork.

In the case where a mismatch of the curriculum with a child's learning style is the root cause, you can make changes fairly easily. This requires undertaking some of the learning styles assessments discussed earlier in this book, and then diligently seeking out educational programming that meets your child's preferences.

Finding materials for those who like books and reading is fairly easy. However, if you have a child who prefers visual learning, you will need to seek out audio-visual programming or highly illustrative books with lots of images and/or pictures.

If you have a child who is a hands-on, active learner, your job is hardest of all. There are few comprehensive, ready-made curricula that are geared specifically toward hands-on learners, so you will need to take an active role in finding projects, museums, hands-on classes, and other learning opportunities that will engage your child's attention.

Whichever type of learner your child is, if you are using materials that are either above his level of understanding (too difficult) or below his level of knowledge (too easy), you are likely to have problems with your child engaging with his school work. Regardless of whether the work is too easy or too difficult, a child will often say it is "boring," so you should not use the expression of boredom as an indication the work is easy. "Boring" simply means, "I don't like this," and the reason is often not readily evident.

In order for your child to be engaged in his learning, instruction has to be provided at your child's "point of optimal learning" (POL), which is just above your child's current level of educational ability. The key is to have the curriculum and study challenging enough to be engaging and give a sense of accomplishment when completed, yet not so challenging as to seem impossible to complete at all. Math and Reading afford themselves as easy examples.

In the case of reading, if your child can read at a fifth grade level, putting a heavy-weight college textbook with words he can't read into his hands would be pointless. The child's eyes would glaze over and he couldn't read the book at all. Likewise, if you gave him a first-grade reader, your child would think the book was dumb and likely not want to read it at all.

The key is to find books that are just above your child's current level of reading achievement, and as he reads and understands most of the text, he will gain skill with the slightly more advanced text. Once your child accomplishes reading at that level, you can again advance the reading level by a small margin in an ever-advancing progression of reading skill.

Similarly with math, if a child can add, subtract, multiply, and divide, he is ready to learn fractions and their associated concepts. If a child cannot yet add, subtract, multiply, or divide, he won't be able to work with fractions. Likewise, he won't be able to jump into doing trigonometry either. If he can already add, then working on addition further would seem like busy work. Math instruction needs to be at a level where the problems are somewhat challenging and require a bit of thinking to solve in order to be at your child's point of optimal learning.

While the point of optimal learning won't be as evident with science and social studies, you can provide curricula near your child's level of comprehension. Be attuned to your child's ability to understand content when selecting programming or curricula.

For example, there are books about the solar system at every level possible. There are early education picture books, middle-grade science books, high school level books, and college texts. If you are using books, select books most closely related to your child's current level of reading ability. If your child is not a reader, and is highly intelligent, select DVD programs or computer-based learning content based upon his level of understanding, or go visit a science center, planetarium, etc. Two great free resources for online learning content for children who need audio-visual content are WatchKnowLearn.org and KhanAcademy.org.

Keeping your child's schooling at a level that is challenging for him, but isn't too overwhelming or too difficult, is an art. You can take cues from your child, but also be aware of his present level of educational performance in each subject area. In order to maintain awareness of your child's educational performance levels in each subject, it is helpful to undertake standardized testing each year before you purchase the next year's curricula.

Just be aware, that scoring presented as "Grade Equivalents" doesn't mean your child is at the specified grade level, but rather that your child does the current grade level work as well as a child in the specified Grade Equivalent (GE). It's important to understand the grade equivalents in standardized testing as they differ from achievement level testing performed by a psychologist. Achievement level testing by a neuropsychologist often provides an actual grade level achievement equivalency, which can be used as a direct reference to select grade-level materials.

On the ITBS, Stanford tests, or other achievement tests commonly used by schools, the test results are based upon the grade level of the test itself as the reference point. For example, say a 5th grade child takes a 5th grade test and scores a Grade Equivalent at 1st grade, 9th month for reading and 8th grade, 8th month for math. This means the 5th grader can read 5th grade content as well as a 1st grader at the end of 1st grade—or not very well. This 5th grade child can do 5th grade math as well as an 8th grader in the 8th month of school can do 5th grade math. In other words, the child can do 5th grade math very well. She is not, however, ready to begin Algebra.

Whether your child takes the Stanford Achievement Test, Iowa Test of Basic Skills, Kaufmann Educational Achievement Test, or any other achievement test on an annual basis, tracking your child's level of educational achievement will enable you to better select curricula or learning programs that are neither too easy nor too difficult.

In fact, testing isn't even required if you are well in tune with your child's proficiency levels in each subject. If he's finishing up 5th grade math and doing very well, you can move him up to sixth grade math. If he's working on third grade reading and struggling mightily, drop the reading levels down to first or second grade. If you don't have testing to give you precise information about your child's ability, the next best thing is to make purposeful adjustments up or down when selecting instructional materials for your child.

Also, be aware that a child is seldom uniformly at the same grade level across all subject areas. A child is often stronger in one subject area and may be able to work a grade level or two ahead in that area. Conversely, he may be weak in another academic area and may need to work below chronological grade level in his area of weakness. Seldom is a boxed, single grade-level program ideal for a child. Feel free to vary the grade-levels of your curricula in each subject according to your child's individual needs.

What program should I use for handwriting?

For handwriting, a child must have decent grapho-motor integration to be able to form letters. Preliminary practice activities that are good for developing this skill include coloring, solving maze puzzles, drawing, playing with clay, making art with beads, etc. In particular, starting with large, easy-to-solve mazes and working toward more difficult and complex mazes can help a child learn precision in using a pen or pencil. Also, proper grip is important, so you may find that rubber pencil grips or mechanical pencils with grips formed around them are helpful for improving your child's grip on his pencil.

When your child is ready to begin learning to form letters, a favorite program to use is Handwriting Without Tears (HWT - http://www.hwtears.com/). This program is simple, uses manipulatives, and emphasizes simplicity in form rather than using an ornate style in the handwriting. There are no curly-Qs on the tips or ends of letters or other unnecessary decorations which complicate writing for a child who is already having difficulty. The HWT program is easy to use, encouraging, and most children like it well enough.

Although HWT is my favorite program to use, there is not enough practice in the workbooks for handwriting mastery, in my humble opinion. HWT does have an online tool you can use to generate practice sheets, which is helpful if your child requires additional practice, but printing a lot of worksheets can become tedious too. Thus, after completing the HWT program, we used the Italic Handwriting series by

Barbara Getty. The Italic Handwriting series uses a similar style of writing that is not ornate. There are six workbook levels which provide ample practice with handwriting.

That said, if your child has dysgraphia, his handwriting may remain difficult and moderately legible. We worked on handwriting for eight years before our neuropsychologist basically told us to give it up and consider our son's handwriting "as good as it's going to get." Instead, he recommended we teach our son keyboarding skills, which our son welcomed!

While handwriting is essential for being able to fill out forms, whether for school, work or otherwise, a lot of adults have poor handwriting. Once a person is able to fill out forms with basic information such as name, address, etc., or able to fill in the blanks on an exam, most other written work can be accomplished via keyboard.

Thus, if your child is past elementary age and still not adept with handwriting, you might find it beneficial to weigh the level of improvement your child will make if you continue working on handwriting. If your child has struggled with it ever since the beginning, then improvement is not likely to be significant with an additional year or two of practice. Therefore, it might be helpful to begin working on keyboarding skills, so your child is adept at using a keyboard when he starts writing high school or college essays. Aside from keyboarding, there is also speech-to-text dictation software (like Dragon Naturally Speaking) that can help anyone write a composition without needing to have legible handwriting.

What do you recommend for spelling?

My answer for this question depends upon whether your child has dyslexia, an auditory processing disorder, or any other language-based learning difficulty. For any child who does not have a learning difficulty related to language, there are many viable spelling programs available on the market. Many people like to use free online programs such as:

http://www.spellingcity.com/,
http://www.spellingstars.com/, or
http://www.homespellingwords.com/.

There are a number of good book-based programs as well. Spelling Power, Megawords, and Beyond the Code are very popular book-based spelling programs among homeschoolers.

If your child has a language-based learning disability such as dyslexia or auditory processing disorder, spelling can be one of the most difficult skills to teach. If your child has or may have aspirations toward higher education, it will be important for him to know how to dissect spoken words, to segment them into syllables, and to be able to spell them with some degree of accuracy. For a robust, comprehensive teaching of spelling ability, I recommend All About Spelling (AAS).

All About Spelling is a thorough, step-by-step, explicit, multisensory program designed to provide spelling success for every student. It begins with the first required skill for spelling (and reading)-- recognition and knowledge about what letter symbols represent each sound in our spoken words. For example, a child must know the sound of /s/ is represented by the letter 's'. For every sound we make in our speaking, there is a corresponding set of letter symbols which we must know before we can spell.

Likewise, children must know these symbols before they can begin reading. All About Spelling teaches the sound-symbol relationships prior to attempting to teach word construction for spelling. Mastery of sound-symbol relationships is critical for spelling success by children who have dyslexia or other language-based learning difficulties.

As far as online programming goes, one of the favorites among Learning Abled Kids support group members is ClickN SPELL. The program is interactive and works to insure mastery of the most commonly used words in the English language. There are only about 1200 words that account for a large majority of commonly written text. The list of 1200 most commonly used words is called the "Sitton List," named after its creator, Rebecca Sitton. ClickN SPELL works on mastery of 800 of the most commonly used words. Mastery of this subset of words will enable your child to write basic, grade-level essays.

Word Magic - this isn't "online," but it is an app that can be used anytime, anywhere and is a great program. Word Magic is ideal for kids between the ages 3 to 6, but I think the games would appeal to children as old as 10 or 11, depending upon your child. "It is an excellent application for kids to have fun with words and their spellings. Word

Magic is very ideal for parents since it engages kids while driving, in the airport or while waiting in the restaurants." It's a very inexpensive app well worth having available for your child's reading and spelling practice anytime, anywhere.

The following are all free programs available online. These programs won't provide progress tracking for you, if you need it for your homeschool records, so it may be beneficial to pay for a site that will provide tracking. Nevertheless, these are great sites your child can use anytime for fun, interactive spelling practice.

— Knowledge Adventure Spelling Games - Great site with the ability to select grade level and subject. Easy site to use.

— Homespellingwords.com - "Home Spelling Words provides an interesting mix of verbal and visual teaching that will help your child improve his or her spelling test scores. This program is fun and free."

— Spellingcity.com - There is a lot you can do for free on this site. Full access does carry a membership fee though.

— 1000 Sight Word Superhero App - AWESOME practice app that allows letter tracing and practice that can truly be multi-sensory. The program provides short lists and words are checked off as they are mastered.

— Cimo Spelling Sight (Lite) - Great app for teaching a combination of high frequency and sight words (from the Dolch Sight Word list). "The list of 50 words was selected to cover words that a child encounters most often when learning to read (high frequency)"

Given your child has had comprehensive spelling instruction, and continues to spell poorly, research shows that using a self-correction method is more effective for long-term spelling retention than weekly spelling tests. You would not use self-correction alone or in lieu of phonemic spelling instruction. Self-correction is used following comprehensive spelling instruction.

In order to use the self-correction method, you would use a highlighter or spell-checker to note your child's spelling errors. Your child then looks up and corrects the spelling of each word that is misspelled. If your child is like mine, then initially there will be a large number of errors, so you wouldn't want to note them all and make the self-correction task seem overwhelming to your child. Have him correct about 25-50 misspellings in a lengthy paper when first using this method. Over time, as there are fewer errors in your child's writings, your child will have less to correct anyway.

For more information regarding the specifics of using the self-correction method, visit:
http://learningabledkids.com/language_arts/what-works-self-correction-method-for-spelling.htm

The self-correction method worked very well for my son in correcting the long-term difficulties he had with phonemic spellings. He knew how to spell phonemically, but could not remember which phonemes occurred in specific words, like reely (really), rong (wrong), wat (what), etc. Using the self-correction method throughout high school enabled my son to be an excellent speller by time he went to college.

What should I use for hands-on math?

Because difficulty with math computation and mathematical reasoning is less pervasive than difficulty with reading, there are fewer remedial math programs available on the market. However, there are good programs that move away from straight textbook-based teaching. Some of the more popular programs for those who struggle with math include:

Math-U-See, ETA Hand2mind (formerly Cuisenaire Rods),
Base Ten Blocks,   Reflex Math,   TouchMath,
Teaching Textbooks, Thinkwell, and Times Tales.

<u>Math-U-See, ETA Hand2mind (formerly Cuisenaire Rods), and Base Ten Blocks</u> are programs that include manipulatives for hands-on learning and teaching. Math-U-See is a complete program that includes teaching DVDs for each daily lesson, workbooks, teacher books, blocks and manipulatives to help teach math concepts. For hands-on learning, it

is probably the most preferred of traditionally-based programs. Math-U-See provides math curriculum from the beginning number recognition math concepts up through Calculus.

Both ETA Hand2mind (formerly Cuisenaire Rods) and Base Ten Blocks are manipulatives that can be used with any math program for demonstration purposes. Each of these sets of manipulatives has workbooks, written by unassociated individuals, which can be purchased specifically for working with the manipulatives. These programs are excellent for children who are having difficulty understanding basic math concepts such as addition, subtraction, multiplication, and division. Hand2mind also has fraction manipulatives that help with fractions, decimals, and percents.

ReflexMath is an online program that provides "diverse, fast-paced games and rewards for effort and progress." In today's computer-based, video game oriented world, Reflex Math is rapidly becoming a favorite among parents and kids. ReflexMath provides a way for children to gain fluency with their math facts when they don't want to use flashcards for drilling. ReflexMath has an informational video on their website that will give you some insight into the program.

Times Tales is a program that works on math fact fluency through mnemonics as memory tools. Through creative presentation and practicing with the mnemonics, a child is able to remember and recall the multiplication and division facts more easily. Times Tales is limited to multiplication, but can be a great tool for children who prefer the clever mnemonics over other forms of learning.

For children who like to have everything explained to them auditorally, Teaching Textbooks is a great, detailed program with teaching CDs. While this isn't a "hands-on" program, it does incorporate auditory instruction with teaching video content. Students are able to work problems, enter their answers into the program and receive automatic grading. The instantaneous feedback can help a child realize quickly whether he or she understands how to work the problem.

Thinkwell is good for high school mathematics. Thinkwell is an Internet-based program which teaches using multimedia instructional videos and provides immediate feedback for answers. I really like their teaching videos because the video clips are highly focused and eliminate any unnecessary distractions. This is particularly helpful for any child with ADHD / ADD.

The videos show only the teacher's face while he's talking and hands and the white board when he's working the problem. The instructors talk directly to the student and there is no background class to serve as a distraction (as there is in the A Beka and Bob Jones DVD courses).

Thinkwell has online exercises, which are automatically graded for immediate feedback. The feedback gives an explanation for why the student was correct or incorrect. Each course also has books available, which are primarily the content taught in the video printed on paper for additional review. We found the workbooks helpful for working problems FIRST before working problems on the computer. Once you enter an answer on the computer, it is scored and permanent, so you would want to be sure your child understands the concepts before attempting the exams. For a child who does not need a lot of repetitive practice, but needs focused, undistracted teaching, the Thinkwell programs are an excellent choice.

TouchMath is a truly multisensory program for teaching math that is both award-winning and research proven. If your child struggles with basic math concepts and facts, you may find this multisensory program to be your best solution. I highly recommend it if your child is a tactile or kinesthetic learner.

For additional math learning and reinforcement, you may want to check out these free online audio-visual math resources:

— Knowledge Adventure Math Games - Great site with the ability to select grade level and subject. Easy site to use, fun for practicing math skills.

— PBSKids' Numbers Games - For basic math number skills; All KINDS of games, but they aren't organized in any particular format. It's a great place to visit and play around.

— Purple Math - for help with Algebra. The site has a narrow focus, but great content.

— MathTV - high school level math teaching videos that are well organized. MathTV could be used as part of your child's regular high school coursework. It is a great addition to any math program you may choose because it provides audio-visual teaching for math concepts in various high school math courses.

These are the main programs I would recommend for teaching a student who needs specialized instruction in math. Depending upon your child's unique needs, one of these programs may be a better fit than another, but they are all good programs. We used different programs with each of our boys to meet their individual learning needs.

How do I teach math if I don't understand it myself?

You are in luck! In today's world, with technology being widely available and free resources abounding on the Internet, there are many great ways for your child to learn math without you having to teach it to your child. There are several free websites with math lessons available across all of the high school math courses, and additional programs to help elementary kids with math. YouTube has great Math teaching channels that you can access for free. Other great online resources include the same programs as listed in the previous Q&A:

— Knowledge Adventure Math Games – Great site with the ability to select grade level and subject. Easy site to use.

— Purple Math – Primarily focused on providing help with Algebra.

— MathTV – High school level math teaching videos which are great for kids who prefer not to read text or who need audio-visual instruction.

— KhanAcademy.org – High school and college level math instruction that includes both teaching videos and text-based instruction. Khan also provides instruction in a wide variety of other subject areas such as chemistry, physics, etc.

— WolframMathWorld – An extensive math resource site which focuses on high school and college level math instruction, primarily text-based.

Even though we used a traditional math program, my sons accessed the sites listed above on an as needed basis. They watched some of the free teaching videos and read additional explanations whenever they were having difficulty understanding a concept. Usually, reading the content or watching a video or two would enable my guys to understand the difficult content, which allowed them to move forward.

My boys actually preferred to use these resources rather than come to mom for help. When they had a problem, it'd take me a few minutes to figure out where they were and what they needed to know even though I completed up through Calculus II in college. Sometimes I had to go to the math resource sites myself, so eventually my boys just cut out the middle-mom and went straight to the teaching videos themselves. It was more efficient for them to go find help on Purple Math, Khan, or YouTube than wait for me to figure out where they were and recall how to work the problem.

Aside from using the online sources, if you choose a curriculum that includes teaching DVDs, then you will have a built in "teacher" for your child. Teaching Textbooks, Thinkwell, Chalkdust, and Math-U-See are all math programs that provide teaching DVDs along with the workbooks. If your child uses one of these programs, the explanations and demonstrations accompany the lessons, so the program usually enables a child to understand the concepts. On those occasions when your child has difficulty understanding a concept, then resorting to the resource websites listed above can be very helpful.

If you think your child might have difficulty with some of the concepts, particularly if he struggles with math, then you can enroll your child in an online course that has an instructor. I would caution though; if your child struggles substantially, be sure to look for "at your own pace" courses. Many "at your own pace" courses are limited to a one year time span for completion, but having a full year to complete a course is a lot better than having specific chapters and exams due by a specific deadline date.

My younger son took Derek Owens' online Physics class. I know Physics is science, but Derek Owens also offers high school math courses. We also used Keystone High School for some individual courses. Keystone is a large, national program that enables students to take any individual course at the student's own pace. Each course has an instructor, so the student can ask questions any time he needs assistance.

Schools providing similar "at your own pace programs" include Lincoln Interactive, Alpha Omega Academy, and CompUHigh. Each of these allows a student to take courses and to receive help from an instructor. If accreditation is important to you, it is your responsibility to check to see if the program you select is accredited according to your personal needs as discussed in an earlier Q&A.

What foreign language is best for a child with dyslexia?

Foreign languages are difficult for any child with a language-based learning disability such as dyslexia or auditory processing disorder. Because learning to read and write in their native language is a struggle in itself, it helps to build a foundation of language understanding before attempting to teach a foreign language to a child who has a language-based learning disability.

Using an interactive program during the middle school years, such as Word Roots offered by The Critical Thinking Company, can help your child understand the roots of words and associated meanings. After your child has completed a word root study that enables him to recognize word meanings based on the core syllables in the words, he will be better prepared to study a foreign language.

As foreign languages go, the easiest language for a child who speaks English as his native language to study is Latin. This is because the English language is primarily built upon Latin roots. However, if your child has aspirations toward attending college, it is important to note that some colleges do not accept Latin as a foundational foreign language study, because it is not a spoken language. Therefore, although study of Latin is likely to be easiest, it is not necessarily the best choice.

The next easiest foreign languages for children with language-based learning disabilities to learn are Spanish or German. Both of these foreign languages have roots similar to English, making for an overlap in some of the vocabulary with similar spellings. Given that Spanish is more pervasive in the American culture, learning Spanish will afford the child more practice and exposure to the words in a written context in the community.

If your child is very oriented toward the possibility of going into a scientific career, it is good idea to weigh German more heavily as a foreign language. German was formerly known as a language of "science and scholarship" (Goethe Institute), and is beneficial in terms of studying early scientific findings. Although, in today's society, English is the most pervasively used scientific language, the German roots of scientific study prior to World War I lead to a foundational terminology in the sciences that stems from the German language.

According to our neuropsychologist, French is perhaps the most difficult language for a child with dyslexia or language-based learning disability to learn. The roots of French as a romance language are the furthest removed of the major English-based languages from the Anglo-Saxon roots.

Asian languages such as Chinese, Japanese, and Korean require learning everything from the basic symbols in the language up through structure, syntax, and pronunciation. Similarly, Arabic and Indian languages are not similar to English at all and may be more difficult for a child with a learning disability to master.

Regardless of the language to be studied, using an audio-visual, interactive approach to learning the language will work better than using a strictly print-based curriculum. Great programs for Immersion based language learning are Rosetta Stone, Pimsleur, and PowerSpeak foreign language programs. We have used these programs and had decent success with them, however neither of my boys enjoyed learning a foreign language.

For my boys, learning a foreign language was a necessity as part of their college prep curriculum, but foreign languages were not an area of study that either of them excelled at or liked very well. They both passed their foreign language study courses, but earning passable grades did require extra review, a lot of work, and both boys were most relieved when their foreign language studies ended.

How do I improve my child's memory skills?

Many children with learning difficulties have deficits in their memory functioning, particularly in the short-term working memory. Whether a child has difficulty with short-term working memory, long-term memory, or recall of information, having memory difficulties can dramatically affect your child's ability to learn, recall, and/or convey what he has learned. Improving memory and recall skills can dramatically improve your child's educational performance. Thus, as a foundational cognitive skill for learning, I recommend working on memory skills more robustly than any other area of need.

Short-term working memory is the ability to hold information in mind while manipulating or processing the information. Short-term working memory is of utmost importance for performing math calculations in one's head. It is essential for sounding out words when reading, for encoding words when writing, and for remembering a sentence long enough to write it on paper whether the child is taking notes or writing a composition.

Some children have difficulty holding the information in their minds, and others have difficulty with external stimuli interrupting their thinking, which causes the information to be "lost" for processing. Whatever issue exists with short-term working memory, if information cannot be held in a child's mind long enough to be processed, then a child misses many learning opportunities.

To strengthen short-term, working memory, there are many memory games that you can work on with your child. If your child struggles with short-term, working memory, I highly suggest engaging in some type of memory game play every single day to strengthen this critical cognitive ability. Because the memory games will be difficult for your child given a working memory deficit, he is unlikely to love playing the games, but please find a way to help your child understand the necessity of working on memory skills.

Games for working on short-term memory include reciting or manipulating digit spans, matching-games, problem solving through remembering clues, etc. Digit spans involve giving the child a sequence of numbers and having the child repeat the sequence back. A typical person can manipulate and respond with five or six digits and being able to hold seven digits in mind, to manipulate them, and respond is considered great memory functioning. Memory practice using digit spans, word lists, car types, business names, animals, or names of objects can easily be practiced in the car as a game to pass travel time.

As an example, you may say to your child, "I will give you four numbers. Give them back to me in order lowest to highest. 7, 3, 5, 1." Your child would then seek to manipulate the numbers in his mind and the correct response would be, "1, 3, 5, 7." To practice digit spans, you can have them given back in the same order provided, in order (lowest-to-highest or highest-to-lowest), or in the reverse order they were given. Similarly, you can say, "I'm going to name three vehicle types, give them back to me in reverse order.. car, van truck." Your child would respond, "truck, van, car." Use whatever appeals to your child.

To begin with, you will practice with two or three digits (letters, objects, etc.), and move to an increasing number of digits as your child masters each level. If your child can consistently and accurately manipulate three digits, then you should begin using four digits until your child can consistently and accurately manipulate four digits. Working on digit spans up to six or seven digits at a time is probably sufficient. Moving beyond that would provide some benefit, but isn't required.

For variety sake, I would highly recommend planning games with card-matching, picture matching, etc. or using memory-matching games online. You can use a standard deck of playing cards and have your child match Aces, 2's, 3's, etc. too. In a memory matching game, all cards are arranged face-down and the child turns two cards over to see what they are. The goal is to remember the location and number of those cards, flip them back face-down, and then flip over two more cards to see what they are. As the cards are revealed and remembered, when the child knows where two matching cards are, then those cards are picked up. The game continues until all matching pairs are gathered.

For building memory skills, you would begin with a small set of cards.. 4 or 5 matching pairs, mixed up, and arranged in neat rows. It is easier to remember positioning when it is patterned in rows and columns. As your child gains skill with 4 or 5 pairs (8-10 cards total), then you can add additional pairs. When your child can quickly and easily remember and match up 10 pairs (20 cards), then you may begin arranging the cards in a random fashion—not in neat rows, but in a scattered fashion. Begin again with a lower number of cards and work on building memory skills with randomly placed cards.

Aside from working with memory games and cards, you may find it easier to purchase and let your child use an online brain enhancement programs with solid research behind it, such as BrainWare Safari (http://www.mybrainware.com/who-we-help/parent). You can read about research-based outcomes at: http://www.mybrainware.com/safari/research. It is offered by the same, well-respected company that offers Fast ForWord.

BrainWare Safari is designed to enhance 41 cognitive skills in six different areas, including attention, memory, visual processing, auditory processing, sensory integration, and thinking skills. It specifically targets reception, perception, memory, and thinking skills in a videogame-like format that children generally find fun and engaging.

Similarly researched and available programs include Lexia's Cross Trainer (available at: http://www.literacyandmaths.co.nz/cross-trainer.html) and Lumosity (available at: http://www.lumosity.com/). Lumosity is written primarily for adults, but it is also viable for teens. I'd recommend Brainware Safari or Lexia Cross Trainer for younger children.

By playing memory games with your child or having him use a brain-training program diligently every day, you can improve your child's short-term working memory to some degree. Any amount of progress you can make in this area will be beneficial for learning.

Long-term memory, as an area of memory functioning, is entirely different than short-term working memory. A child may have difficulty working on math calculations, writing sentences, or other short-term memory skills, but may have a large general fund of information stored in his brain. Once information makes it into a child's long-term memory, the child will likely have the information at his disposal for years.

However, knowing what information a child has stored in his long-term memory can be difficult to determine if the child has a learning disability that makes it difficult for him to express what he knows orally or in written form. Additionally, if a child has difficulty with his memory recall, it can seem as if a child does not know the information, but in fact he may just not be able to recall the information at the moment of need. We will talk about memory recall next as a separate area to address, but first let's talk about long-term memory itself.

Long-term memory requires a person to store a unit of information in a "filing cabinet," of sorts, within his brain. Information can be categorized and stored in a variety of locations in the brain depending upon whether the information is visual in nature, logical, auditory, or a functional motor skill.

From the large number of comprehensive evaluation reports I have read, I can say with relative certainty that aside from a pervasive cognitive deficit that prevents the storage of information into long-term memory, the issues which affect the storage of information into long-term memory are widely varied. Long-term memory deficits may stem from attention deficits, interference by sensory stimuli, poor categorization abilities, and difficulty with comprehension, etc. The root cause of long-term memory issues is unlikely to be determinable by a parent through casual observation.

While the root cause of long-term memory difficulties is difficult for a parent to pinpoint, once the root cause is identified, the memory issues are usually able to be addressed by some means. Therefore, I highly recommend a comprehensive neuropsychological evaluation if your child has difficulty storing information in his long-term memory.

It is very difficult to teach content repeatedly, and doing so can lead to frustration and boredom for both you and your child. It can take up to 200-300 repetitions for some children to remember math facts, phonemes, spelling rules or other important pieces of information. Therefore, if your child has long-term memory processes that can be improved and eliminate the need for repetitive teaching, the time and money you spend on an evaluation will significantly enhance your child's learning outcomes.

Let's discuss a couple of common characteristics of long-term memory functioning, so you may be able to better meet your child's needs without having to wait for comprehensive evaluation results. The German psychologist, Hermann Ebbinghaus, in his studies of human memory, "found the rate of forgetting occurs most rapidly immediately after the learning period ends, and then the rate of forgetting slows as time goes on" (April 2013, http://blog.princetontutoring.com/2011/04/how-to-improve-your-long-term-memory/).

In other words, once information is stored in our long-term memory, the longer it remains there, the more likely we are to retain the information for a significant length of time. "Ebbinghaus found that he could dramatically improve memory retention by correctly spacing review sessions of the material. After each additional review session, the new rate of forgetting slows significantly. To improve retention, the new material should be reviewed at a very high frequency at first, and then at lower frequencies spaced out over time" (April 2013, http://blog.princetontutoring.com/2011/04/how-to-improve-your-long-term-memory/).

Another type of information retention issue occurs when the long-term memory process is easily interrupted by external stimuli or information interference from another source. When a child completes a lesson, simply going for a walk, rocking in a chair, quietly resting or taking a nap can help the child assimilate the newly learned content into her long-term memory more effectively.

For example, if a child is working on long division, seems to be doing well with the concept, but the next day it is as if the child has never seen the content before, the information may have been lost due to post-learning interference. Let me explain this concept to insure you understand how interference happens. If a child's memory processing is easily interrupted and she watches a TV show immediately after her math lessons, but before the math information is fully integrated into her memory, then the information from the math lesson will be lost. In such cases, avoiding interference for a period of time after lessons, can improve long-term memory storage.

Long-term memory problems also occur when a child's brain is neurologically taxed by a lack of sleep, illness, sensory processing overload, or significant attention deficit issues. Establishing optimal brain functioning through well-regulated bedtimes, providing omega-3 supplements, with vigorous exercise, and a calming, ideal learning environment can help memory processes by enabling the neurological processes to function effectively.

While the above three scenarios for addressing long-term memory deficits are common and manageable, there are frequently other causes for long-term memory difficulties and there are brain-training programs which may help with memory functioning. Please refer back to the short-term memory section of this Q&A for information on researched brain-training programs.

Aside from the information I've shared here, entire books have been written in regard to long-term memory functioning and improvement. Thus, it'd be unrealistic to try to give a comprehensive solution in the context of this question and answer. If your child has long-term memory difficulties, my best advice to you is to seek a comprehensive evaluation, look at memory enhancement methodologies based upon your child's specific memory issue, and work as much as is feasible upon improving your child's long-term memory.

Lastly, let's talk about memory recall. When information is stored in long-term memory, it must be recalled in order for a child to use the information or convey what he has learned. Recall pathways, just like short-term working memory, and long-term memory, can be affected in a way that makes it difficult to determine whether a child has learned the information he has been taught.

Unfortunately, if a child has recall issues, a parent or observer will not be able to determine whether the child has not stored the information in memory at all or if he can't find the needed information when requested. Determining whether an inability to recall a previously learned concept is due to a memory failure, due to an inability recall, or due to an inability to express what is known must be made by a qualified evaluator—usually a neuropsychologist. Again, a comprehensive evaluation is highly recommended.

I know I'm sounding like a broken record when it comes to pressing for an evaluation, but truly a good evaluation can help you provide carefully chosen, well-targeted programs for your child. If you don't get an evaluation, you will need to use a very broad-based approach and use programs liberally as if your child has every problem. Without an evaluation, you should work on every aspect of memory to be sure you've covered the specific issue affecting your child's memory.

We will explore recall-expression a little further, but as with long-term memory, the area of potential disability is broad and it is difficult to provide an answer that will be general enough to be of benefit to every reader. Some of this information may be of basic help though, so I will share a couple of tips.

Sometimes long-term memory and recall issues are created when a child's system for storing information is so disorganized that he cannot locate needed information when requested to do so. In such cases, the child may know the information, but appears highly inconsistent when asked to recall the information. One day he knows his colors, the next day he does not. Similarly, if a child repeatedly asks the same question, it may be that the answer is not stored in a "logical" or readily accessible location in his brain, so the child can't find the information when he wishes to answer a question.

In cases where the storage of information has taken place, but a child cannot readily recall it, here is a question-recall process that you can use to strengthen the recall pathways for your child. In this example, we'll use the simple question, "What's for dinner?"

If your child asks you, "What's for dinner?" then asks you the same question five minutes later, he may not recall that he asked you previously. To help strengthen his recall, you would say, "You asked me this question already. Can you remember what I said is for dinner?"

Your child is likely to say he doesn't remember. Tell him what is for dinner again and immediately ask him, "What's for dinner?" If you said, "Spaghetti is for dinner," he should be able to parrot back "spaghetti" using immediate recall.

Five minutes later, your son asks you, "What's for dinner?" You would again respond with, "You asked me this question already. Can you remember what I said is for dinner?" He may or may not be able to recall it's spaghetti.

If he cannot recall, tell him what is for dinner and again immediately ask him, "What's for dinner?" He should be able to tell you the answer again with immediate recall.

Five minutes later, your son may again ask you, "What's for dinner?" In such a case, you would continue to respond with "You asked me this question already. Can you remember what I said is for dinner?" Supply him with the answer only if he cannot recall when you've given him a minute of thinking time.

Whenever you answer a question for a second time, immediately ask your child to repeat the answer back to you. The point is to help your child exercise his recall pathways. Do your best not to get annoyed with the repetitive questioning because your child honestly can't remember at that second or he wouldn't be asking. Sometimes it is a case where your child can immediately engage the recall pathway, so using this process over time will enable him to recall quickly by himself.

The repetitive question—response cycle will help strengthen your child's recall pathways. Although you will not see any immediate results, over a longer period of time using this technique, you should see a reduction in the repetitive asking of questions. This process aids with recall of any information stored in memory, and is a recommended technique for addressing memory-recall issues. It is far better than getting irritated with a child and yelling at him for repeatedly asking the same question.

Simply asking your child a question in response to the child's question causes him to search his brain to see if he can find the answer. Given ample thinking time, particularly if he has a slow processing speed, sooner or later he will be able to recall the information he already knows as his memory recall pathways strengthen.

Memory and recall problems are issues that pervasively affect your child's learning and/or ability to convey what he has learned. Thus, having memory problems evaluated and working to overcome the issues can bring about excellent improvement in educational progress. This may be one of the most pervasive areas of learning difficulty, but tackling it head-on can also bring some of the most rewarding educational improvements and great strides in learning.

How do I improve my child's processing speed?

Engaging in speed-based drills and tasks can help improve your child's processing speed and build your child's neuronet within his brain. In a brain study, "Effects of Training of Processing Speed on Neural Systems," data shows that processing speed can be significantly improved with daily training (Hikaru, T., et al, 2011). Additionally, functional MRIs (fMRI) showed statistically significant increases in the associated brain matter relating to processing speed (Hikaru, T., et al, 2011).

What does this mean to you? It means you should work on increasing your child's processing speed if it is slow. You can choose your approach based upon what best meets your child's specific needs. There are computer-based programs that enhance processing speed, some studies show that video-gaming can improve processing speed, and there are hands-on games that can help improve processing speed.

There are both physical and mental undertakings that can enhance your child's brain performance. In the physical realm, Omega-3 oils and healthy fatty acids as well as antioxidants can help improve brain chemistry. Eating a healthy diet, getting ample sleep in regulated sleeping cycles, and spending time outdoors each weather-appropriate day can help prepare your child's brain for cognitive enhancement.

Video games where timing is a component, like the Wii Baseball or Tennis, could possibly help improve your child's processing speed to a mild degree because the child must repeatedly recognize and react to stimuli within a specific period of time. These are not necessarily "speed-based" drills and they would not be intense, but if your child has a very slow processing speed, Wii Sports can be a fun way to exercise the speed-reaction pathway without overwhelming your child from the beginning.

Similarly, Dance-Dance Revolution (DDR), as a game, requires your child to exercise his working memory and reaction time in order to keep up with the dancing. DDR is a more complex game and it requires more neurological processing than Wii Sports, so the processing improvements from engaging in regular DDR time would be more noticeable.

As far as video games go, one study found that playing games such as BrainAge and Tetris "improves executive functions, working memory, and processing speed in young adults. Moreover, the popular puzzle game can engender improvement in attention and visuo-spatial ability compared to playing the brain training game." (Nouchi, R., et al, 2013).

For a well-regulated, measurable program to improve processing speed, you may want to consider computer-based programs that are designed specifically for the purpose of enhancing a child's processing speed. The main issue you may encounter with these programs is that your child may not really understand the need to undertake the speed-based drills for the sake of his brain performance, so he may be more likely to balk at daily practice. If, however, your child is compliant, you can help your child make the most of his brain in the shortest amount of time by utilizing researched and proven brain training programs already mentioned in this section. Below, I will list a few more options for your consideration.

Compublox, from the makers of Audioblox, is a computer-based program designed to enhance processing speed as well as other cognitive processes (see http://www.audiblox2000.com/compublox-brain-games.htm).

From their website: "Compublox is a brain-training program that improves concentration, processing speed, visual and auditory memory, and logical thinking. Compublox is suitable for children aged 9 up to adults. Unlike Audiblox, it is not suitable for children younger than 9, and also not for children of any age with low abilities. For children with reading and learning difficulties, Compublox is best used as a supplement to Audiblox."

Another computer program is MyBrainTrainer (MBT), which is Internet based and allows your child to practice anytime, anywhere via the website and it can be accessed at http://www.mybraintrainer.com/. Unlike most subscription types of services, MBT has in their policy that they will NOT automatically renew a membership, so you don't have to cancel it when you're done (but please do double-check that policy remains in effect before going on that assumption). They assume you will purchase the program, use it, and then not need it again. I like that because you don't end up with charges you don't want. That said, if you are going to use MyBrainTrainer, I'd highly recommend a single annual subscription (virtually the same cost as three months paid one month at a time), so you will be able to use the program longer-term and it will be inexpensive.

ALSO, IMPORTANT: In order to know how to operate the brain training exercises, your child will either need you to initially tell him the goal of each task or be able to read the instructions independently. Responses are fairly simple, such as pressing a single key when an event happens on the screen, but knowing what the response should be before starting an exercise is essential. The program is fabulous for tweens, teens, and young adults, but elementary aged kids would need assistance until they know the program well.

If you prefer a face-to-face program, LearningRx is a company that has been around for many years and they provide brain training in their learning centers. From their website: "The training is built from a tested and proven set of cognitive skills training exercises that improve Processing Speed, Visual Processing, Logic and Reasoning, Working Memory, Long-term Memory, Attention, and basic Auditory Processing skills." You can use their tool to find out if they have a location near you.

As with almost any face-to-face program, it is more expensive to receive services from a provider like LearningRx, so you may need to weigh cost with your family's resources. A program that is similar to LearningRx is PACE (Processing and Cognitive Enhancement, http://www.processingskills.com), and it has been around for a number of years and has a good reputation too. Either of these programs has a good track record.

Whether you choose a formal program like Audiblox or Interactive Metronome, or a casual game of speed and skill such as "Splash Attack" by Fundex, or a table game such as air hockey or ping pong, can all exercise your child's processing speed. The key to making good progress will be to use some sort of program each day.

My best recommendation is to try to make cognitive enhancement easy for your child by using the programs that are the most fun or easiest for him. Since cognitive enhancement is an area that requires regular daily exercise for meaningful improvement, you do not want processing speed exercises to become a torturous activity. Use a variety of programs if it helps keep your child engaged.

Studies by LearningRx, Gemm Learning, and other companies have found undertaking cognitive enhancements can bring about some of the biggest gains in learning. As far as priorities go, I would recommend putting cognitive enhancement and processing speed toward the top of your list of daily undertakings for the entirety of a summer (or two) or the equivalent of a year. By making processing speed improvement a priority, you can help your child's overall academic performance. Improving processing speed also leads to a much shorter school homeschool day.

What is unschooling and does it work?

Unschooling is a form of homeschooling wherein the parents do not have an advanced directive educational plan. They do not schedule and present their children with daily lessons. Unschooling is a form of child-led learning wherein the child decides what he wants to learn at any given point in time. The premise is that the child is naturally curious and will, at some time, want to know how to read, write, and do math, study algebra, biology, or any variety of other subjects. Children are encouraged to follow their passions and pursue learning for learning's sake, not because of some predetermined standards of learning.

As for whether unschooling works, I'd have to say yes and no, and some of the answer lies within your own views of educational outcomes and whether you take a total unschooling approach, or whether you fall somewhere on the spectrum of providing lessons in some academic areas. As with any form of schooling philosophy, there is a broad range of ways people use any given method, so your individual success with unschooling will depend upon the broader spectrum of how you pursue each lesson or academic skill.

If you believe it is okay for your child avoid pursuit of any avenue of learning he has no interest in, then you are likely to be okay with the educational outcomes of unschooling no matter what it brings. As an example, one mom describes her educational model as "radical unschooling." Her high school aged child can't perform basic math calculations with multi-digit numbers. The mom is confident her child can (and will) learn how to add and subtract multi-digit numbers when he gets out into the world of work and figures out he needs to know this skill.

It is true—given her son is an intelligent guy, he can probably learn the math skills at any point in time when he decides to study math. For me personally—I'd have difficulty being that laid back about my child not knowing how to add and subtract multi-digit numbers as a teenager.

I believe unschooling is fabulous for children who are self-motivated toward learning and research, and who are driven by a need to know. I also think unschooling is better applied to content learning areas such as science, social studies, and literature than it is to reading, writing, and math. I personally feel it is a disservice to any child not to insure he has the core skills of reading, writing, and being able to perform math calculations. Most unschooling parents I know do, at a minimum, insure their children know how to read, write, and perform basic math calculations, and I do think that is a wise foundation to establish for any child.

Notably, some children aren't all that curious about the world around them. They aren't driven to seek out information about a broad range of topics, and so they don't broaden their education voluntarily. In the case of "radical unschooling," when left totally to his own desires, a child may not desire to learn to read or write or do math.

In the case of learning disabilities, where learning core academic skills can be extremely difficult, I would say it is unlikely the child would be able to teach himself those skills. For example, a child with severe dyslexia who is not a highly motivated learner would likely need an intervention program that is pre-planned, sequential, and provided at a sufficient level of direct instruction in order to learn how to read.

Among the children I've known who have unschooled, the outcomes are very mixed. I've seen highly motivated, successful college students emerge from an unschooling background, and I've seen some resentful young people who are angry about the lack of what the child considers an adequate education. I feel the highly variable outcomes stem from the personalities of the children and the expectations of the parents. A laid back, unconcerned parent with a laid back, uninterested child is more likely to result in poor educational achievement through unschooling.

If an unschooled child doesn't have a strong learning foundation, becomes a young adult, and begins seeking a job or develops a desire to go to college, it becomes very difficult to move forward without playing catch-up. Sure, the young adult can enroll in a high school completion program and might be self-motivated enough to move forward, but it is far more difficult to complete high school as a young adult. A young adult who is still working on high school completion at age 20 or 21 can become very discouraged indeed.

Thus, I think a parent has to weigh factors carefully before deciding whether to unschool or not. The first major factor should be your child's personality and level of inquisitiveness. If your child is always curious, wanting to know why or how, and devours educational TV, non-fiction books, loves learning, and eagerly explores new avenues of knowledge, then your child could easily have a great unschooling outcome. If your child wants to lay back on the couch and watch pointless TV shows, play video games, or just play all the time, you would have to weigh more carefully whether unschooling would provide a viable educational outcome for your child. As children, unmotivated unschoolers don't have the ability to understand the ramifications of having a poor or no education.

The second factor to weigh is whether you are thinking of unschooling as a way to not have to teach, not have to worry about educational progress, or a way of not forcing your reluctant child to do school work. Properly done, unschooling is as much work for a mom as traditional schooling because the unschooling mom needs to assist her child in finding resources for the child's current area of interest, has to help guide the child into how to do research, clarify things the child doesn't quite understand, and depending upon the state—the mom may also have to find creative ways to document the child's wandering path of learning.

Thus, if you think unschooling would be cool because you "won't have to do anything," (and I have heard this before) then you probably ought NOT to unschool. The outcomes I've seen from those situations are generally not good, especially when unschooling was more of a lackadaisical approach to life than an educational path.

The third factor in deciding whether you should unschool would be whether your child has any special educational needs. A child with dyslexia is going to have a very difficult time teaching his or her self to read. A child with dysgraphia or a written expression disability will have difficulty learning to write. And a child with dyscalculia or math reasoning difficulties will not be able to teach himself math very well.

In fact, I'd go as far as saying it's highly unlikely a child with a learning disability will be able to master academic skills in his area of disability without explicit instruction. Thus, if a child has a learning disability, I think it is exceptionally difficult to unschool entirely and still have a viable educational outcome, except in the case where the child is driven to learn a skill in spite of his disability.

In the case of a child with a disability, and where you think unschooling is a viable path for your child, I think it is beneficial to have regular instruction in the core academic skills while letting your child's content learning take place along a natural path. Schooling would involve lessons in reading, writing, and in math computation, and the rest of the time your child would be encouraged to learn about whatever is of interest.

Unschooling is particularly effective for highly motivated, gifted learners. Students who learn easily and naturally can excel along many avenues of curiosity, which allows them to broaden their knowledge further than a traditional curricula-based program might allow. Einstein and Edison were educated through unbridled avenues of exploration. Truthfully, I think some children are just made to be unschoolers and they will pursue learning with a passion even outside of required academics. Such children do very well when unleashed from the constraints of any form of traditional schooling.

So, my main point to you is: chose wisely. Don't unschool just because it sounds fun or easy. Carefully consider your child's natural inclinations, disabilities, and gifts. Most people who unschool do so in a form of hybrid fashion with the foundational academic skills being taught if they don't develop naturally, and many unschoolers require their children to be working on some topic of academic study throughout the year.

Unschooling can definitely work well when you have the right parental mindset, when your child likes learning new things, and when you insure your child's basic academic foundation is in place. If your child is driven by his need to learn, then your outcome is likely to be fabulous.

What is a unit study?

A Unit Study is a subject-based study that is often designed to include each of the major academic areas of study—reading, writing, math, science, and social studies. While many homeschoolers study subjects similar to those taught in traditional schools such as 5th grade literature, 7th grade history, physical science, or algebra, a lot of homeschooling families prefer studying single topics in depth while including broader areas of academic learning. Unit studies are simply concentrated studies about a single subject, such as whales, and the unit includes many, if not each of the areas basic academic study.

Using the example of whales, <u>Sea World has great educational study units</u>, including one which is the study of whales. We used this excellent unit study. It includes vocabulary (language arts), whale anatomy (science), comparisons of the lengths of various whale species through measurement exercises (math), and information about whale knowledge "Then and Now" (history). The children write short answers to questions and the teaching guide includes suggested books that children can read for further understanding of whales.

Using unit studies can be a great way to engage your child in learning about subjects he otherwise would object to. For example, if your child hates math, but is interested in whales, he may not object at all to measuring out the lengths of various whales on the driveway and then visually comparing them. He might be totally oblivious to the math skills being learned through the unit study about whales. Given a wide variety of unit studies, particularly those that are designed to include every academic area, you can cover a broad spectrum of learning without having your child sit down with books and worksheets like traditional curricula requires.

The main difficulties with unit studies, in my opinion, is lesson planning, locating good unit studies, and pursuing the activities within each unit. Launching a unit study can be difficult if the study requires materials that you do not already have on hand. I like studies that have a listing at the front or back of "supplies you will need." With a list, you can carefully go down the list, note the items you need to locate or acquire, and can begin the unit study after you are equipped and ready to go.

We used unit studies as a way of studying topics of deep interest to our sons. We undertook unit studies on whales, electricity, videography, photography, computers, botany, rocks and minerals, and microscopy. I desired to have my sons follow a more traditional educational path, so I didn't use unit studies as the basis for our educational programming. However, I loved engaging in unit studies as fun alternatives to our texts once in a while. I highly recommend using unit studies for any topic that is of deep interest to your child, no matter what grade he is in.

We know families who use unit studies exclusively, and they are very happy with their chosen route to learning. They have dynamic and fun studies going all of the time and I think hands-on unit studies are ideal for visual or kinesthetic/tactile learners.

If you are inclined to engage exclusively in unit studies, I'm sure you'll find it a fulfilling route to take. It's not an easy route because of the various resources you have to gather for each unit study, but unit studies are definitely the most engaging way to teach across all of the subject areas on a regular basis.

To find unit studies, simply search for the topic you wish to study along with the words "unit study" in quotes. For example, you might search for: butterflies "unit study." You will find any number of unit studies on a wide variety of topics. If you don't find a ready-made unit study, you can always create your own unit study and share it with the homeschooling community.

SANDRA K. COOK

5 ASSISTIVE TECHNOLOGY AND TEACHING ALTERNATIVES

Won't using accommodations become a crutch for my child?

The purpose of providing an education to your child is to enable him to function in life and enter into whatever chosen field of work he'd like. The better your child can learn, the more capable he or she will be of entering into any field chosen in the future. As such, I'm a firm believer in providing robust accommodations and assistive technology for content-area learning. Using assistive technology allows your child to learn at the level of his ability to understand a topic and prevents withholding content unnecessarily.

For learning to read, write, and perform math calculations, I believe a child needs intense remedial until he can master those skills. However, a child's inability to read, write by hand, or perform math calculations off the top of his head should never be a hindrance to his or her ability to access learning content in broad subject areas.

If your child cannot (yet) read, providing audiobooks, text-to-speech capability with content on computers, etc. for science, social studies, literature, and other subjects that are content-based just makes sense. Providing accommodations for reading difficulties keeps your child learning the same general content as peers.

Similarly, when writing compositions your child should be able to use speech-to-text tools like Dragon Naturally Speaking, dictation, or have a scribe to enable your child to create compositions about scientific, historical, or literary topics. There is no reason to prevent your child from creating a composition simply because his handwriting skills are slow and not (yet) developed.

Children with written expression disabilities commonly write far less than they are capable of expressing if they are required to write by hand. Their compositions use simple words they know how to spell and are easy to write, so they don't go into much detail in their writing. Writings seldom reflect the level of thought a child has about any given topic. However, if you provide the child with assistive technology to allow her to dictate her stories and other compositions, she continues to develop the ability to compose good writing at her cognitive level rather than being limited by physical handwriting skills.

For math, there are those on both sides of the calculator versus no calculator argument. As one person who had trouble doing math in his head said to me, "That's what calculators are for." Given he can apply mathematical concepts just FINE and understands the application of higher level math, it really makes little sense to prevent him from working in higher math by withholding a calculator when he can't remember simple math facts. Memorization of math facts is difficult for many people, and is typically an issue with memory-recall functioning where the inability to remember math facts should not be a barrier to further math education.

The aim in providing robust accommodations using assistive technology is to avoid the "Matthew Effect," which is a phenomenon where children with disabilities in limited areas tend to fall behind in ALL areas because of the impact of their disability across all areas of learning. By using the accommodations and assistive technology, your child can remain on grade level with a performance level near your child's actual academic aptitude.

When accommodations are put in place, a child with disabilities needs ongoing intense remediation in reading, writing, and math computation or other specific areas of disability, so that the child will eventually not require assistive technology. If a child is receiving remedial instruction, the accommodations don't hamper the student's ability to function, but rather support the student until he or she gains needed skills in areas of disability. Accommodations actually enable a child to perform at his or her own level of cognitive ability in all subject areas the child is capable of understanding.

Given the goal of education, I think accommodations should never be about being "fair," as many educrats argue. Accommodations should support your child in learning at or near his or her level of cognitive ability. Each child deserves to be able to learn as much as he can, by whatever means can be provided. Why hold any child back from meeting his potential?

This difference between the "fairness" mindset and supporting a child at his or her own ability level is very important. This is especially true in the case of children who are twice exceptional (gifted with learning disabilities) because they can understand content at a very high level and it is a great disservice to hold them back by not providing needed accommodations. Again, why hold any child back from meeting his potential?

I would even argue that if your child is in public school and the school refuses to provide your child with accommodations to circumvent his area(s) of disability in content-based subjects like science, social studies, and literature, then the school is withholding educational progress from your child. To me, that is an abuse of power and denial of a viable education to your child.

Fairness should never be a cause for withholding educational provisioning, supports, and services from any child, much less from one who is unfairly disadvantaged by having a learning disability. Accommodations are a tool for enabling learning, not a "crutch" as some people say. Would you withhold crutches or a wheelchair from a child who lost a leg because it'd be unfair for that child to have assistance when no one else does? No—that would be ridiculous. Withholding tools for learning from a child with a learning disability is just as ridiculous.

Just because you can't see a learning disability doesn't make it right to withhold needed accommodations because you or someone else is afraid your child may come to depend upon the tools. Does a child without a leg depend upon his crutches throughout life?—You bet he does! Similarly, a learning disability is for life. Thus, your child should be taught to use assistive technology well, so he can use it for effective learning and peak job performance throughout his life.

In conclusion, don't ever let anyone talk you into withholding accommodations based upon some misguided concept of fairness to other students. The other students don't have learning disabilities. Additionally, your goal is to be certain your child is able to progress educationally according to his cognitive abilities and to equip him with skills for peak performance throughout his life.

Should I have my child use a computer? If so, how much is too much?

Whether or not to use a computer in providing education to your child is more directly a question of whether using a computer suits your child's learning style, learning needs, and other family concerns that may be eased by the use of the computer such as schooling multiple children. When considering computers educationally, I think there are three areas of use that need to be examined, prioritized, and then implemented with the goal of providing the best educational opportunity for your child.

The three primary ways which computers are used educationally include use as assistive technology, for remedial practice and instruction, and for serving up curriculum either by subject or as a comprehensive platform. Let's look at each of these areas independently, so we can consider the scope and benefits of using computers with your learning abled child.

First, I believe the use of computers as assistive technology is essential for any child with a learning disability to enable him to remain on grade level in subjects such as science, social studies, and literature. Assistive technology includes using text-to-speech and speech-to-text functions, audio books, CD, DVD-based, or online audio-visual programming, and calculators. All of these enable a child to access instruction, to express himself in writing, or perform math calculations even before he has the capability of recalling math facts, of reading and/or writing.

Given the goal of education is to enable a child to become a contributing member of society as an adult, it makes sense to provide instructional supports and services to any extent a child needs assistance in order to facilitate his learning. Therefore, using computers to provide learning assistance to a child just makes good sense. Since I discussed assistive technology in depth in the previous question, I will not repeat myself here, but if you haven't read the answer to the immediately preceding question, you may want to do so.

The second major area of computer use, as it relates to students with learning disabilities, is to provide remedial instruction. As a manual undertaking, a parent or teacher must regularly assess a child's level of skill mastery and repetitively provide instruction until mastery is achieved. The level of detail in providing remedial instruction can present challenges in both planning and provisioning. Because of the repetitive nature of the instruction and the large degree of required practice, software programs can be used for ongoing practice to enhance your child's progress. It can, over time, shorten the amount of time it takes your child to master the needed skills.

Additionally, the computer never becomes impatient when repeatedly going over the same set of instructions, and a computer doesn't forget or skip steps. Many remedial programs have mastery-based checkpoints built into them, so they can automatically review skills that have been forgotten or are not yet solidified.

Even when your child is receiving one-on-one, face-to-face instruction, using remedial programs is beneficial. These computer programs provide reinforcement of learning, provide assurance there are no learning gaps, and help your child achieve mastery in a shorter period of time by providing high-quality, repetitive practice. Additionally, the audio-visual nature of such instruction is an added form of multi-sensory instruction that will tap into the audio-visual learning pathways for your child.

The specific type of instruction required to teach a child with dyslexia how to read and write is repetitive, needs to be comprehensive and explicit to ensure there are no learning gaps, and requires many hours of practice. Using a remedial software program can speed the remediation process, add variety to your child's instruction, and give you a break from the level of repetition required. Similarly, if your child has dyscalculia, he requires numerous, repetitive drills using math facts in order to master math computation skills.

Programs that work on remedial skills can help with learning progress without requiring you to be the repetitive drill person. As with the use of computers on an assistive technology basis, I also strongly believe the usage of remedial computer programs can enhances your child's learning outcomes when the programs are used daily.

The third area of major computer use, which is often the kind that parents are actually concerned about, is the use of a computer to provide a child's daily content learning. For some children who absolutely love the computer, who learn the best from intensive audio-visual instruction, and to do not learn well through other avenues, using a computer to provide comprehensive curriculum can be of benefit. However, I think a parent has to carefully weigh the amount of time a child will spend on the computer when using it for assistive technology purposes, for remedial instruction, and for the provisioning of comprehensive curriculum.

I think it's clear to most parents that it wouldn't be beneficial for a child to spend the entirety of every day on a computer. Thus, as to the question of how much I would use a computer with the child, I would prioritize remedial instruction first, the use of the computer for assistive technology second until a child's learning difficulties are remediated, and then I would rank the provisioning of general content learning third.

Content learning is more easily achieved through a wider variety of learning activities. Therefore if your child is receiving remedial instruction via the computer and using a computer as an assistive device, I would recommend seeking other ways to provide general content learning until the remedial phase of your child's education has ended.

For example, when my older son was receiving remedial instruction in order to learn to read, he spent time every day on the computer practicing with software programs for the purposes of cognitive enhancement and remedial reading instruction. He also used the computer as assistive technology that enabled him to express himself in writing.

Because my son could not yet read, we spent many days cuddled up on the couch with me reading his school books to him. Not only was this an awesome bonding time for mom and son, but it also got my son away from the computer for extended periods of time. My younger son, who has ADHD, was able to bounce all over the place in the living room while I read aloud, which was an effective learning environment for meeting his needs. While we could have used audio books or curriculum with a text-to-speech function on the computer, because we were using the computer for remedial instruction and as assistive technology in our early years, we did not use the computer to serve up any content-based instruction.

After both of my sons could read and we were no longer using the computer to provide remedial instruction, we began shifting toward the use of the computer to provide content-based curriculum. This was somewhat a function of my boys' ages as they got older and wanted to work more independently, and it was a function of their ability to work independently. Additionally, using the computer to serve up general curriculum allowed my boys to use the built in text-to-speech function when they encountered a new word they were unsure about. This function allowed them to have the word pronounced aloud, so they could verify they were reading the word correctly.

When my younger son was in fifth grade he requested to have his schoolwork served up via the Switched on Schoolhouse (SOS) program, which seemed like a good idea to him at the time. Since we were no longer using the computer for any remedial programming, I conceded to let my son use SOS. It was not my top pick, but it was beneficial to provide him instruction in a manner which would keep my young son academically engaged and feeling like he had a say in his education.

For the entirety of his fifth-grade year, for every single subject, my son used SOS. However as the year progressed, even my computer loving son grew weary of being at the computer for all of his schoolwork. Therefore, the following year we used SOS for math and English grammar content and other programs for science and history.

The computer was able to provide immediate feedback about the correctness of any given math problem. The immediate feedback was beneficial for letting my son know whether he understood each math concept before he spent too much time working incorrectly on problems and enabled my son to seek my assistance quickly when he was having trouble. Completing math assignments and English grammar lessons on the computer each day, as well as using the computer for written assignments, provided more than enough time on the computer for each of my boys on a daily basis.

If your child will be using the computer as assistive technology, I would recommend only using computer-based curriculum for a couple of subjects unless your child needs interactive, audio-visual content for all of the subject areas. Also, I think the amount of time spent on the computer should be more limited for young children, and computer usage can be expanded as the child grows in maturity and in his ability to work independently grows.

Carefully selecting computer-based curriculum based upon your child's individual needs for assistive technology can help him be successful. If your child has dysgraphia, using a computer program in conjunction with dictation software could make completing assignments with compositions easier. If your child has dyscalculia, using a computer-based math program could help your child have immediate feedback on the correctness of his answers as well as providing an easily accessible, built-in calculator. For a child with dyslexia, using a computer for subjects with a heavy reading component can help by teaching with a heavy audio-visual component.

My sons both continued to use the computer with its assistive technology capabilities throughout middle school and high school, and are continuing to use it in college. Early on I had assumed once my boys could adequately read and write they would no longer use assistive technology, however when my older son went to college the Student Disability Services Director explained that although my son could read, because he has dyslexia, reading is still very labor intensive for him. At the college level, due to the sheer quantity of required reading and writing, the University actually insisted on providing audio books and speech-to-text accommodations to enable my son to access the learning content in a timely fashion and to respond in writing without undue burden.

Accommodations at the university level are provided as supports to enable learning without interference from a disability. Additionally, assistive technology is commonly used in workplaces. My husband, who also has dyslexia, boldly states that no one should be denied the use of a word processor because people use them every day in real workplaces and spelling need never be an issue because "that's what spell-checker is for." It is true! In the workplace, people always use word processors and technology, so there really is no benefit in withholding the use of such technology from students during their educational years. The use of computers as assistive technology will likely always be present in the adult life of a person with a learning disability, so using it in school just makes sense.

In summary, I advocate heavily for the use of computers to assist a child with his learning and to make the remediation process as efficient as possible. Whether or not you use computer-based curriculum by the subject or as a complete school package is your judgment call based upon your child's love of computers, his learning needs, and the amount of time you find acceptable for your child to spend on the computer.

Should I let my child use audiobooks?

I would highly recommend letting your child use audiobooks for all content subject areas that are not directly related to receiving instruction in reading decoding or reading comprehension. Effective learning in subjects like science, history, great literature, social sciences, etc., can be dramatically affected by a child's inability to read fluently. Thus, if your child cannot read yet, he will get further behind in all other subject areas unless he has access to the content he needs to learn.

Audiobooks serve as assistive technology in helping your child gain access to general learning curriculum. There is no reason to penalize your child for his inability to read when it comes to learning other subjects. Many children who struggle with reading have normal or above average IQ levels, which enable them to understand concepts and content in a wide variety of areas even though they can't read yet. Continuing to feed your child's learning abilities through audiobooks just makes good sense.

Even though you may use audiobooks, it's important to continue providing your child adequate direct reading instruction on a daily basis in order to develop his ability as an independent reader. In learning to read, your child must actually attempt decoding of words, therefore when your child is practicing his reading skills, you would not use audiobooks.

I should also let you know that highly intelligent students who have difficulty with reading are capable of memorizing any book that is read to them. Therefore, if you wish to assess your child's true reading ability, you must present a book or text he has not previously heard or had read to him in order to determine your child's true ability to read independently. That's just a word to the wise as I've known several highly intelligent children with dyslexia who quickly memorize the precise wording of a book, then parrot back the words, page-for-page as they simulate what they observed the reader doing when they read. Since the child isn't actually reading the text, it is a highly sophisticated coping skill which I admire, but also which must be avoided in order to insure your child can actually read.

Similarly if your child has difficulty with reading comprehension, programs must be used to address your child's inability to understand what he reads. I've written a book called **Reading Comprehension for Kids** which provides information about how to teach reading comprehension skills. We used some of the proven methods discussed in the book to improve our son's comprehension.

You would not want to use audiobooks to practice reading comprehension because audiobooks utilize oral or verbal comprehension, not reading comprehension. In other words, when your child is listening to an audiobook he is processing spoken language rather than content that he has read. Listening to an audiobook does not directly involve reading, so there can be no reading comprehension.

It should be noted that having a book in hand accompanied by an audiobook version can be a useful tool for increasing reading fluency and reading decoding skills. Simultaneous input, where your child sees the printed words and hears the words simultaneously, has an impact on his ability to process what he is seeing for the purposes of decoding and comprehension. There have been studies that show this type of practice can enhance a student's abilities. It is important to note this type of practice should not be used in lieu of direct instruction and practice with printed texts alone. Using audiobooks with a printed text is supplemental practice, not a means of remediation.

We used a lot of audiobooks throughout our schooling and I feel the use of audiobooks is essential for maintaining good academic progress across subject areas for any child with dyslexia. The wide availability of audio versions of books makes the use of audiobooks very easy to implement and to help keep your child's content-based learning moving forward.

Should I give up on handwriting and teach keyboarding?

This is a difficult call to make. It is certainly beneficial for any person to be able to write legibly. For adults who need to fill out job applications, complete forms for driver's licenses, medical forms, and other documents, having decent handwriting will serve them well throughout their lives. That said, handwriting is extremely difficult for individuals with severe fine motor dysgraphia issues.

At the other end of the spectrum, computers and word processors have become so prevalent in the workplace and our daily lives that keyboarding is probably just as essential for proficiency in the workplace and otherwise. Whether or not your child has difficulty with handwriting, I think it is a good idea to teach every student keyboarding skills. It is also best to be able to handwrite to a degree of minimal legibility in order to fill out forms as needed throughout life.

There are excellent programs available for teaching young children keyboarding skills, so I believe keyboarding can begin at the point in time in which your child recognizes words and letters on his computer screen. The typing programs targeted toward children typically flash a letter on the screen and expect the student to respond by typing the same letter on the keyboard. Thus, your child must have a minimal level of letter and word recognition to be successful with the keyboarding programs.

Handwriting skills can be undertaken with daily practice throughout elementary school and into middle school. Making handwriting practice a requirement in elementary school makes sense because children are developing their fine motor skills throughout this developmental period in their life.

Once your child reaches middle school, the degree of further development of fine motor skill will be much less than it was in elementary school. Therefore as long as your child is willing and able to work on improving his or her handwriting on a daily basis, I would recommend continuing with at least one practice page daily.

How do you know when to stop working on handwriting? If you reach a point when your child is in middle school and truly dislikes handwriting practice, is showing no meaningful improvement, and expresses a preference for writing using the computer, then it is probably best to cease practicing handwriting and allow your child to become proficient with keyboarding. Further handwriting practice is unlikely to yield big benefits which would make continued practice worthwhile.

I hear some parents objecting already saying, "but I can't even read my child's handwriting!" That is how I felt about my youngest child's handwriting when our neuropsychologist told me it was unlikely I would see any further improvement in handwriting and recommended we give up handwriting practice.

The truth of the matter is that my son's handwriting is difficult to read and requires concentration, but it is not illegible. We gave up handwriting practice as recommended, but that was a difficult choice on my part. You know what? It's fine. My son has had outside instructors and his handwriting doesn't seem to affect his ability to convey his thoughts. His handwriting isn't lovely, but it's decipherable.

I have seen some pretty bad handwriting, which I really could not read at all, but there again—the adults with really bad handwriting seem to get along just fine in life too. Thus, if your child is in middle school or beyond and he is balking at continued handwriting practice, giving up handwriting practice for keyboarding is certainly an acceptable choice to make.

Is there a good program to drill math facts?

Using computer-based technology is a great way to practice math facts when repetitive drills are necessary. With today's technology, there are several options available for use with handheld devices, PCs, or as apps on tablets.

A great online program that many Learning Abled Kids' members love and recommend is Reflex Math. You can find this program online at: http://www.reflexmath.com/. The Reflex Math website says this program provides major gains in math fact fluency for students of all ability levels. It includes diverse, fast-paced games and provides rewards for effort and progress. The program includes progress monitoring and data-based decisions based upon your child's progress. This means your child will review math facts until he has mastered them. Reflex Math's data reporting allows you to track and see your child's improvement in math fact fluency.

The "FlashMaster" is a handheld computer for mastering multiplication tables, and it is the highest rated, standalone device on Amazon for practicing math facts. The FlashMaster is about the same size as a calculator and allows your child to practice math facts anytime, anywhere. Reviewers give very high praise for this device, saying it has brought success to their child when other programs have failed to do so. The FlashMaster has programming for mastering addition, subtraction, multiplication, & division math facts to point of automaticity. Users describe it as fun and easy to understand and operate. Minimal supervision is required because of automatic prompts and the "see results" key.

As handheld devices become more proliferated throughout our society, I expect many top-notch apps for practicing math facts will be developed. As far as current math apps go, I really like <u>Math Magic by Anusen, Inc.</u> Math Magic uses a combination of vibrant colors, has a simple interface and incorporates a reward system to encourage kids to practice their math facts.

Also on the market, two highly rated apps are "CardDroid Math Flash Cards" and "Mad Minute: Mastering Number Facts." There are other apps which you may want to check out, but the ones mentioned here are the main apps with a large number of positive reviews at the time of this book's publication. I would recommend trying one of these if you have a handheld device, or you may want to search for "math fact apps" in an App Store to see if you can find a new app that may appeal directly to your child's interests.

For a laptop or PC, a great math fact game is "Treasure Cove" by The Learning Company. This game is a newer version of what was formerly Treasure Math Storm. My boys both loved Treasure Math Storm and it was an excellent way to get them to practice their math facts without realizing they were practicing. Treasure Cove is a software program for Windows and Mac PCs that is presented in a game-like format that is appealing to most children.

We also used Quarter Mile Math (<u>http://www.thequartermile.com/</u>), which my boys didn't like quite as well as Treasure Math Storm, but it was easy for them to use and see their progress. Quarter Mile Math is based upon a horse racing theme, so if your child likes racing or horses, the program might appeal to him.

As with the apps, you can search on Amazon for math fact practice, PC-based programs. There are new programs being created on an ongoing basis, so searching for the most current programs, reading the reviews, and searching based upon your child's individual needs will give you several worthwhile options.

What software do you recommend for reading instruction?

We have used several reading programs to help reinforce our direct reading instruction. Programs we have used include Simon Sounds It Out (Simon S.I.O.) (http://www.donjohnston.com/products/simon_sio/), Earobics (http://www.earobics.com/), and Lexia Learning's Strategies for Older Students (S.O.S.) (http://www.lexiaforhome.com/).

We used Simon S.I.O. for early reading practice, Earobics was used in the middle of our remediation period, and Lexia's S.O.S. was used in mid-late remediation.

We purchased each of these software programs, installed them on our computer, setup learning profiles for each of our boys, and then had our boys work in the programs for a designated period of time each and every school day. Lexia's S.O.S. was a software program that we purchased, but it is now only available as an online program.

The combination of these programs worked very well for us as supplemental reading instruction. Our boys also received daily direct, one-on-one reading instruction provided by me using the methods I learned in a two-week Orton Gillingham training program.

People sometimes ask me how much of my boys great progress was due to the computer programs, but it is impossible for me to differentiate the amount of progress that was brought about by my one-on-one instruction versus progress created by each of the computer programs we used. It is most likely that each element of our learning program worked together to provide the ultimate progress.

It may be helpful to recap and let you know the combination of reading instruction and reading programs we used, along with 20 to 30 min. of direct reading practice each day, took my son with severe dyslexia from a non-reader to a sixth-grade reading equivalent during his fifth-grade year. That year was our first year of homeschooling, and my goal at the beginning was solely to "do better than the school." Little did I know he would soar on reading wings and advance multiple grade levels in one academic year.

During our second year of homeschooling, continuing with the Lexia program along with continued one-on-one instruction and daily reading practice, my son advanced from the sixth grade equivalent to a tenth grade equivalent. In our third year of homeschooling, my son's seventh grade year, my son reached a 13+ grade equivalent for reading decoding. After our third year of homeschooling, we no longer had to spend time learning to read and began focusing on reading to learn. Within three years' time, my son's reading ability advanced to a level that has allowed him to read well throughout the remainder of high school and college.

Similar programs which could provide additional practice include: Starfall at http://www.starfall.com/, Ultimate Phonics at http://spencerlearning.com/, "My Virtual Tutor" for the Ninetendo DS, or ClickN READ Phonics at http://www.clicknkids.com/Affiliate.asp?PID=Learning&adname=none.

These programs are not specifically Orton-Gillingham based, but they do provide practice in a fun, game play format. Using a game-play format can be an effective avenue for tapping into your child's willingness to practice his reading decoding skills on a daily basis, and willingness to work on reading skills is helpful for any child with a reading disability.

Programs which are not specifically created for students with clinically diagnosed dyslexia are more likely to work for students who simply need a lot of reading practice to develop better reading skills. If you want a stand-alone learning solution for your child with a clinical diagnosis of dyslexia or who if your child lacks phonemic awareness, then you will probably have better results if you opt for a program specifically designed for improving reading skills in children with reading disabilities.

I recommend Fast ForWord (provided online by BrainPro at http://www.brainsparklearning.com/), or Lexercise (http://www.lexercise.com/) as programs you can use at home and which include professional assistance. Both of these are programs your child can use online in conjunction with a trained provider. The provider will direct your child's practice and instruction and make sure your child is on track with the software. If there are any issues or problems with learning, the provider will assist you with problem solving, instruction, and will make sure your child continues to make forward progress in his reading ability.

Because there is a provider involved, the BrainPro and Lexercise solutions are a bit more costly than standalone computer-based software products that you install and use independently at home. However, there is a benefit in paying for a provider, especially if you do not personally feel capable of directing and teaching your child.

Using software for reading instruction is highly beneficial as a reinforcement exercise. However I think most students, particularly those with severe dyslexia, also require explicit, direct, one-on-one instruction in reading decoding.

Since students with severe dyslexia require numerous repetitions of review and practice, using software for the repetitious practice can provide the student with variety in the instruction, can ensure that no learning gaps exist, and can provide a level of patience on a repetitive basis that is often difficult for a human teacher to maintain when teaching the same concept for the 100th or 200th time. A computer never gets impatient even with the 300th repetition of instruction. Therefore I highly recommend using a remedial software program on a daily basis to provide your child with ample practice in reading decoding and to advance his reading skills with improved mastery.

6 HOMESCHOOL MANAGEMENT

There are many issues involved in managing your homeschool. No doubt, there are many more issues than will be covered here, but the questions I answer here are some of the more commonly expressed concerns of parents when they begin homeschooling.

Management of your homeschool environment becomes easier over time. In the beginning, everything may feel overwhelming. You may find yourself questioning your sanity and wonder what made you think homeschooling was a good idea. However, most parents I know adjust well to the homeschooling lifestyle in about six months' time. Some parents require longer, but if a parent has the underlying abilities to manage and cope with the demands of the lifestyle, then she will almost certainly develop coping mechanisms during the first year or two of homeschooling.

That said, let's further explore some of the concerns that parents have when they are new to homeschooling.

How can I get my child to stay on task and work faster?

Ah, the meandering school day that seems to go on forever… That's an issue for you? It was for us too! A lack of focus, getting off task, and taking forever to complete schoolwork are all strong irritation points for homeschooling moms who are trying to complete each day sometime before bedtime.

With learning abled kids, there can be any number of issues that cause a lack of forward progress, so I'll address several different problem points. You'll want to refer to specific questions about ADHD, processing speed, working independently, and other issues as needed for working with your child in addition to this section.

First let's talk about wandering minds and lack of attention to the school work. There are three primary issues that come into play when a child can't keep his mind on his school work.

The most common problem is that the work is boring to the child and it fails to meet his specific learning needs. Critical areas of consideration include making sure you've evaluated your child's learning style and are teaching him in a mode that is easy for him to process. If your child learns through hands-on activity and you're forcing him to read everything out of a book, the reading is going to be much more tiring and time consuming for your child. He'll end up exhausted and tired. He'll probably say he's "bored," but the truth is your child is not engaged in the learning. Check the Q&As about learning styles and try to match instruction with your child's learning preferences so he will be able to benefit from the instruction more easily.

Another common problem is schoolwork that is too difficult for a child to complete independently. If your child doesn't have a solid reading skill foundation, it will be difficult for him to finish any work presented through text. If your child is not fluent with his math facts, completing math assignments will require a lot of cognitive energy and working each problem will be slow. Similarly, if your child has difficulty with handwriting or written expression, writing will be quite challenging.

If the work is too difficult for your child, then it is usually best to back up and work on mastery of the foundational skills. You'll also want to make sure your child's work is at his level of optimal learning. Reference the question, "What curriculum would you recommend when a child hates schoolwork?" and the section about assistive technology for a better understanding of the point of optimal learning and ways to support your child when he complains the work is too difficult.

Lastly, for the issue of a wandering mind and lack of attention, there is always the possibility of an attention deficit issue, whether it is temporary (caused by a poor night of sleep, stress, etc.) or has officially been diagnosed in your child. If you're having difficulty keeping your child on task during most school days, then you'll want to look at factors you can control or change to help improve your child's attention. Look at the strategies for managing ADHD without medication at: http://learningabledkids.com/learning_disability_ld/adhd_medication_alternatives.htm to see what changes may be of help to your child.

As an immediate solution to difficulties with focus, I highly recommend going outside for a while. Whether you go for a walk, play catch, tag or engage in some other activity, getting your child's heart pumping will get more oxygen to his brain. The increased oxygen will help with learning and focus for a temporary period of time. You may need frequent activity breaks (lasting 5-10 minutes every hour or two) to help your child concentrate throughout the day.

Getting off task can be an avoidance behavior for school work a child doesn't understand or for school work that is inherently difficult for a child. If you take time to calmly and compassionately discuss an assignment with your child, and you are certain your child understands what he is supposed to do, then it is more likely your child is finding the work too hard.

Seldom is a child defiant about finishing assignments unless there is an issue or problem with the assignment, yet parents often assume the child is just not doing the work because he doesn't want to. Most kids want to be successful with learning and they want to please their parents, so avoiding completion of schoolwork frequently lifts a red flag for deeper issues. Unfortunately, your child can't tell you exactly what the issue is with the assignment because he won't know if he's having processing problems, comprehension problems, attention problems, etc.

If your child frequently avoids doing his work, makes excuses, dawdles by doing other things, etc., you might find there are underlying learning challenges that are not as obvious as dyslexia, dysgraphia or dyscalculia. A child can have perception, memory, processing or comprehension problems that will only be identified through comprehensive neuropsychological testing. Until your child has had a comprehensive evaluation by a highly qualified evaluator, please do not assume your child is being outwardly defiant.

Punishing a child for failing to do things that he can't do does more harm to your child than you can imagine, so please assume your child can't stay on task until you know for certain your child just doesn't want to do the work. Truthfully, I have not yet met a child who was frequently off task who was just being defiant. So far, every child with difficulties, when evaluated, was found to have significant deficits in processing, perception, executive functioning, ADHD, or other significant learning disabilities. For the sake of your child's well-being, assume underlying challenges and find creative ways to engage your child before punishing him for a behavior he can't really avoid.

Lastly, taking all day to complete school work, especially when a child has been working with his lessons all day, is often an indicator of a very slow working or processing speed. A child's processing speed is often assessed at a comprehensive evaluation.

Where an average person's processing speed is at the 50th percentile, many kids with learning disabilities have processing speeds below the 10th percentile. Thinking slowly is not the same thing as not being able to think. Often kids with slow processing speeds are very smart, but it takes them much longer to process all of the information needed to solve a problem.

If your child seems to stay on task, for the most part, when completing his assignments, but it takes him forever to get the work done, then you might want to consider two avenues of approach to solve the problem.

First, consider speeding up the work by using audiobooks instead of having your child read, use dictation software for writing, and a calculator for math computations. If your child lacks fluency in reading, handwriting, or math facts, then building fluency in those areas can improve your child's overall working speed.

Second, you may need to build efficiency into your school day by having your child read and write about science and social studies so that your have fewer independent subjects to teach each day. Rather than have your child read typical literature, have him read historical narratives or great books about science concepts or scientists. Similarly, have your child write about science and social studies topics he has read about. By doubling up on the topics you can cut the work load so your child can finish his school day in a reasonable amount of time. That will be a relief to both you and your child!

How can I get my child to work more independently?

Many moms ask this question. Sometimes the heart of the question is a mom wanting to have less demanded of her and other times she is concerned about the working independence of her child. For learning abled kids, the ability to work independently is often an issue.

The cold, hard truth is that working independently is much more difficult for many kids with learning disabilities, so to a certain degree—you have to resolve yourself to the necessity of spending more time guiding and working directly with your child. There is often no way around the matter of your child needing your assistance.

With that said, the best way to enable your child to work more independently is through great assistive technology and multimedia-based learning. MANY textbook providers now produce audiobook editions of their books which you can purchase, or you can acquire audiobooks free of charge through http://www.learningally.org/ with appropriate documentation of a reading disability.

Also, most up-to-date computers have a built in screen-reading function your child can use to select text which the computer will then read aloud. Text-to-speech functionality works well if you use a computer-based program such as Switched On Schoolhouse, or any online school program that provides most of their learning content as text on the screen.

There are also products called "Reading Pens" which look a lot like a highlighter. As the person scans the tip of the pen over text, the pen captures the text and reads it aloud (for example, the Wizcom ReadingPen). Some pens require the person to plug the pen into their computer, and the computer reads the text aloud. The reading pens are cool gadgets because they can be carried anywhere and be used for reading virtually anything. For home education use, a reading pen can help your child work independently rather than constantly having to ask, "What's this word?"

For writing, we use Dragon Naturally Speaking software. This dictation software allows your child to talk in order to create written compositions. Using Dragon Naturally Speaking, or any other dictation-based software program helps build your child's writing skills because the program allows them to experience writing as a form of communication just like speaking. For many children with disabilities, saying what they think is far easier than writing their sophisticated thoughts on paper. Using this software enables students with dysgraphia to become fluent writers and allows them to share their advanced thinking easily.

We also have Ginger Software, which is an excellent spell-checker and corrector for people with spelling disabilities. It really works well for children with dyslexia because it uses phonemic prediction algorithms to determine which words a child might have meant to use. It works far better for children with pervasive difficulty in spelling than traditional word processors' spell check functions.

For hand-written work and correcting spelling when spell-checking software is not an available option, we use a speaking Franklin Speller. This is a gadget about the size of a calculator that has phoneme-based spelling logic similar to Ginger Software's capability which helps your child figure out how to spell words he has difficulty spelling.

For math calculations, if a child has a known math calculation disability and is unable to memorize math facts, but is able to understand the concepts of addition, subtraction, multiplication, and division, then allowing the child to use a calculator is not an unreasonable accommodation. Basic calculators are allowed for all students taking college entrance exams, and use of a basic calculator is a common accommodation in college. If your child struggles with memorizing math facts, use a program like ReflexMath to enhance your child's math fact recall, but let your child use a calculator for word problems and all higher level math. If your child is likely to go to college, you will want to have documentation of a disability to get use of a calculator as an accommodation in college.

By using these assistive technologies, you can provide ways for your child to access written text (text-to-speech) and to create written text (speech-to-text), and to work independently most of the time. Given accessing and creating printed words is the biggest issue for people with dyslexia or dysgraphia, these technologies let them work a LOT more independently! Of course, these are great tools for helping any student work independently, and they are common accommodations in college, so there is actually a benefit in having your child learn how to use these tools.

The biggest drawback for using assistive technology is cost, but it can be well worth the money to enable your child to work independently. Not only will it help you feel less chained to helping your child every minute, working independently will increase your child's self-esteem if he's able to complete his work without needing constant assistance from mom. This is increasingly important as a child moves through middle school and into high school. The middle school years are the ideal time to begin using the assistive technologies, particularly if your child is still struggling to learn reading, writing, or math calculations.

Using technology-based tools went a long way in helping my guys become independently successful students. They have taken online, joint enrollment courses during their junior and senior years of high school and did well with the courses. Taking courses online lets them use the text-to-speech tools and they don't have to take lecture notes.

Aside from assistive technology, using forms of educational programming other than textbooks will encourage your child's independent learning too. Any of the comprehensive programs provided via computer, whether online or via CD/DVD, can enable your child to work more independently. Good programs to consider include Time4Learning, Khan Academy, Alpha Omega's Monarch or Switched On Schoolhouse programming, BJU Press Homeschool DVD curriculum, and A Beka Academy Virtual Homeschool.

Can I homeschool while working?

If you happen to be one of those families where working is a requirement, and you need to homeschool your child, it can be done, but you will need extra support and assistance. There is a "Work and Homeschool" Yahoo! Group that provides support, creative ideas for managing challenging situations, and ideas for daily management for working parents who are also trying to homeschool. You can join that group at:
http://groups.yahoo.com/neo/groups/WORKandHOMESCHOOL/info?y guid=91500295.

There are various ways for families to homeschool while both parents are working. The most common way is for the two parents to work different shifts. Often the father will work a typical 9-to-5 workday and the mother will work either an evening shift or night shift. While this is functional for homeschooling the child it can be dysfunctional from a family unit standpoint, especially since the parents don't get to spend very much time with each other. In cases where families have set up this type of work schedule, the mother usually homeschools the child(ren) during the day and then goes to work while the father stays home with the child(ren).

Families with older children tend to have one parent work part-time during the day. Typical jobs include delivering newspapers early in the morning, driving a school bus in the morning and the afternoon, working as a retail distribution a representative, marketing a home sales-based product, or running any kind business from home. With older children, it is possible for you to give your child assignments to work on, and then tend to business while your child completes assignments. When you've finished your work, then you can work with your child answering questions she may have about her assignments. When working from home, you may also have the freedom to transport your child to and from activities she participates in.

Another common arrangement, if you have good personal support nearby, is for your child to stay with a grandparent, some other relative during the day, or a close family friend, while both you and your spouse work. You can give your child assignments to work on during the day and the caregiver will act as a supervisor who ensures your child completes her work. A caregiver isn't usually in charge of the assignments given, but is a facilitator to keep your child on task. When you finish working, then you can check your child's assignments and decide upon the next day's schoolwork. During the day, a caregiver can take your child to various activities, on field trips, to events that may or may not be specifically for homeschoolers, and can work on projects such as cooking, completing science experiments, and making lap books of topics that are of interest or spend time engaged in activities with your child.

In my opinion, the caregiver arrangement with two full-time working parents works best. This arrangement allows the child to be supervised throughout his or her day, provides your child with opportunities to get involved in activities with other homeschoolers, and provides a bonding relationship with the extended family members or the caregiver. While you are working, you don't have to worry about your child's care, and she most likely won't have the negative family affects seen when two parents are on two entirely different schedules.

One of the most common ways parents handle the need for a dual income is for the homeschooling parent to offer a service to the homeschool community, such as teaching other people's children, child care, or for the homeschooling parent to engage in some type of home-based business. Working from home while homeschooling can be easy or difficult, depending upon a person's individual ability to juggle different activities. How well this option would work for you will depend on your abilities, your child's age, and your child's ability to work independently. In our case, it definitely got easier to complete work-based tasks as my children got older and required less one-on-one attention.

I'm sure there are other creative ways of managing to homeschool while working, and the best place to find creative solutions is probably the Yahoo group I shared with you. That group has existed for many years and I'm sure there are a lot of great solutions in their archives. Homeschooling while working is undoubtedly a challenge, but I know it can be done because many people have done it.

How do I homeschool for little money or free?

Although there aren't a large number of comprehensive curricula available online for free, there are countless learning tools, programs, and subject-based units available for free online, through libraries, and at reduced prices through used book sales.

Perhaps the most popular, free, comprehensive curriculum guide available is Amblesideonline.org. Within AmblesideOnline "each year/grade has a list of books to lay out what resources will need to be collected or purchased, and an optional weekly schedule based on a 36-week school year to break the resources into smaller increments to help with pacing the books throughout the year. There is no fee to use the curriculum or website. Parents may use as much or as little of the booklists and schedules as they like." The schedule itself is free, and there are some free resource books you can download through the website, but you might prefer to find used books at reduced prices, so your child can read without being on the computer.

"Easy Peasy All-In-One Homeschool" is available at http://allinonehomeschool.com/. This website provides the personal schedules and information which one mom is using with her children and putting online, so that her program can be a resource for others. Her program is a Christian program, and it is specific to her children, so it is not really designed for children with learning challenges. Thus, you are more likely to find this site to be a good resource and guide for developing your child's general education program rather than as a comprehensive, ready-to-go learning program that perfectly fits your child's needs.

For interactive, online programming, check out: Interactive Sites for Education, which provides K-5 online, interactive, educational games and simulations in one place. The interactive, audio-visual lessons are organized in broad subject areas such as Language Arts, Science, Math, and Social Studies. Each broad area is then segmented into specific topics with multiple interactive educational choices. The Interactive programs linked to by Interactive Sites for Education are of very high quality and likely to be engaging for any student.

If your child is in K-12, WatchKnowLearn.org is an awesome place to start. You begin by putting in your child's age, then the topic you want. For example, if you type in "Fractions" for age 12, you can watch the Introduction to Fractions Song, Mr. Duey – Fractions Rap, Basic Math: Lesson 6 – Video Clip #3 – Equivalent Fractions or choose from a wide variety of other lessons on the topic. WatchKnowLearn can be extremely helpful if you need to find an audio-visual means of teaching your child a specific concept. Some of the videos will be helpful for kinesthetic/tactile learners if they get up and move along with the videos.

Khan Academy is a highly popular and robust educational site with teaching videos and interactive practice tools on a wide variety of high school math, science, and social studies topics geared toward high school or college aged children. It's ideal if your child has an audiovisual learning style. The academy provides a "knowledge map" which enables your child to follow a planned progression through lessons in an appropriate sequence. You can watch the Khan informational video at: http://www.khanacademy.org/video/overview-of-khanacademy-org.
Khan also provides teacher tools which allow you to set up a "class" and

plan out the sequence of learning activities for your child.

Also at the high school-college level, there are great courses available through Coursera.org. The courses are offered by a consortium of universities, so they would be best suited for advanced learners. The courses run in specified timeframes for a varied number of weeks, but the descriptions say the courses are "at your own pace." This would be a good option for advanced students who are able to finish within the specified timeframe, and want to focus on just a couple of courses at a time.

Both AcademicEarth.org and edX.org offer free online courses from some of the top universities in the world. Courses are free, online, include teaching videos and interactive exercises. Learning is at your own pace, but does require you to carefully consider whether your child is prepared to study at the high level of teaching provided through these videos. These courses are ideal for gifted learners who want to independently advance their learning.

MIT's Open Course initiative - http://ocw.mit.edu/index.htm, Open Yale - http://oyc.yale.edu/courses, and the Harvard Open Learning Initiative - http://www.extension.harvard.edu/open-learning-initiative, are open courses available for free online. Open University opportunities are great for advanced studies and several universities offer their course content online. Each of these open universities put their lecture materials, notes, and videos online, allowing open access to anyone, providing great opportunities for anyone who wants to take advantage of the courses. All you have to do is acquire the associated textbook and follow the teaching syllabus provided with the course materials. Purchasing the associated textbook on eBay or Amazon is the best way to purchase the needed textbooks for little money.

You can help your child gain a lot of knowledge at any level without worrying about the cost, location, grades, etc. if you are willing to delve into the free online programs, to plan a viable progression of lessons, and help your child progress through the content systematically. Given your child is in high school and a self-driven learner, the Open University initiatives, Coursera, and Khan Academy are among the best educational opportunities available for advanced learning.

Aside from the programs above, you can find individual learning units on just about any topic you'd like. For example, SpellCity is a free online program where parents can make spelling lists for their child to practice and allow the children to practice. Starfall and Progressive Phonics are free online phonics programs designed to teach early literacy skills. You can find free online lessons, apps, and games in reading, spelling, math, and virtually any other subject with a simple web search.

How do I meet the needs of multiple kids?

Meeting the needs of multiple kids is a challenge for any parent. Depending on the ages of your children, how you approach teaching management across your multiple age groups can vary quite a bit, and the variety of personalities involved can introduce all kinds of challenges.

If your children are close in age and academic ability, then you can opt to work with your children simultaneously—same subject, same level of instruction for more than one child. If the children are using the same or similar curricula, and the assignments can be given so that each child works at his or her own level of ability, then teaching your children simultaneously can be very beneficial to you. Teaching your children together reduces the length of your school day, which in turn allows more time for activities and fun.

Some parents have concerns about group instruction holding one child back or advancing another, but each child gains an understanding of the material equivalent to his cognitive ability. This type of group instruction works best for science, social studies, and literature where the children are relatively close in age. It also only tends to work for content-based subjects, not for skills based subjects like reading, writing, and math computation.

To teach to children simultaneously, parents often select a robust, multilevel curriculum that allows their children to work together. As an example, Sonlight curriculum includes a lot of reading of books that fall between two or three grade levels of readability and interest. For example, if you have a third grader and a fifth grader, then you could purchase a fourth grade level Sonlight curriculum package. The program is easily used with both students. Differentiation of instruction comes in your child's responses to portions of the program. For example, in writing essays or in response to the books being read, the third grader would be permitted to write a less detailed response than the fifth-grader.

You may wonder if teaching both grades together in such a manner would demand too much from the third grader or hold back the fifth-grader. I would say this depends totally upon your individual students and your selection of curriculum. Some curricula, such as Sonlight or Barefoot Books, have such robust learning content that it easily meets the needs of advanced grades, and it's likely to meet the needs of lower grades at the child's level of understanding. For lower level students, some of the more complex concepts might go over the child's head, but overall the child will gain a general understanding of what is being taught.

In the beginning of our homeschool years, I did just this—I purchased a single grade level package to use in teaching my boys' simultaneously. I did this because my fifth-grader was behind after being in public school for five years, and my third grader was advanced in his ability to comprehend information. I purchased third grade curriculum package. Using the single grade-level package for my boys added efficiency to our days and worked fabulously.

The following year, when my older son had reached a sixth grade reading level, we jumped from the third grade package to a fifth grade curriculum package. My older son was still not a fluent reader, so I used the grade level just below his sixth grade decoding skill level. Since my primary goal for the school year was to improve my son's reading fluency, I was not focused on advancing his decoding skills like I was the previous year. Using books at a slightly lower grade level gave my son great practice for improving his reading speed because the words were fairly easy for him to decode.

If you have multiple children at widely varied ability levels and grades, then it is unlikely that you would be able to work from a single curricula package. It would probably work better to purchase multiple levels of the same publisher's curricula and group your kids as much as possible in relation to their abilities and/or grade levels.

For example, if you use the A Beka curricula, then you would buy the subject levels for your children, or pairs of children, at their respective grade levels. Say you have a second grader, a fifth grader, an advanced eighth-grader, and ninth-grader, then you would purchase a second, fifth, and ninth grade language arts, math, science, and social studies from A Beka.

The A Beka books are very similar across subjects and grade levels in regard to the format and teaching requirements. Therefore, you can have each child working in chapter 3 of their science book at the same time. Although the subject matter will be different, and the questions and answers will all be different, everything will be laid out in similar formats where each of your children will read about the topic in his or her book and then answer true false and fill in the blank questions about what they just read. You can answer the questions for each of them as questions come up. Your eighth and ninth grader can help each other to a degree also.

If your children have difficulty working independently, have significant learning needs, have difficulty working in the same room with each other, or have other learning challenges, then you will have to plan very carefully how you manage your day. You can lay out a schedule where your children play learning games online, listen to audiobooks or watch teaching DVDs at various times while you spend one-on-one time with a single child. By rotating each child through a "work with mom" time and through other independent learning activities, you can spend time with each child working on lessons.

In the case of my boys, when we were working on reading remediation, I had to lay out a very detailed schedule that allowed me to work one-on-one with one child while the other was working independently on a computer-based learning program, watching an educational DVD, or spending time quietly reading or writing. I had alternating periods of about 30 min. each where each of the boys would work with me and then work independently. For the most part this worked well for us, although there were days when the independent worker had difficulty and our planned schedule was somewhat disrupted.

Of course, the more children you add to the equation, and especially if you have very small children at home, then managing traditional types of schooling among all of your children will be a challenge. Some moms get older siblings to help the younger siblings, or they tend toward a less traditional approach in regards to the actual schoolwork. Juggling multiple children is definitely a challenge, but it is one many families have successfully figured out how to balance.

While scheduling is often challenging and sometimes difficult in the beginning, I feel most parents figure out a workable flow in their weekly schedule within the first year of homeschooling. Parents sometimes question their decision to homeschool when they're having difficulty juggling the needs of all of their children, but then creative thinking and tenacity kick in and the parents almost always figure out a viable way to meet all of the needs of their children. Once that rhythm sets in and the homeschooling synergy builds, great learning begins to take place.

How long do you homeschool each day?

Homeschooling regulations vary widely from state to state in regard to the length of a home instruction day, but even where there are regulations, the length of an instructional day varies widely from family to family. The length of our school day in Georgia is required to be the equivalent of 4 1/2 hours of instruction per day, but some states don't have any required length of time spent in home instruction each day. What is a reasonable number of hours to spend on schooling?

Because of the high efficiency of the homeschool environment, many people experience shorter school days. For example, we can often get our work done in close to the required amount of time—4.5 hours. Like most homeschoolers, we don't actually have a schedule for how long our homeschool day is, but we are mindful of schooling for the required amount of time. I have a schedule laid out where I give each of my boys their assignments for the day. When they complete the assignments adequately their school day is done unless they have not yet put in 4.5 hours. In such cases, I simply have my child read a book, watch educational TV, or engage in some other meaningful educational activity for the remainder of the required amount of time.

There were some days when one or the other of my sons was highly distracted, couldn't keep his mind on his work, and his school work dragged on for hours. When that happened, our school day usually lasted until the work was done. If my son objected, we pointed out that kids in public school have homework just about every day and often on the weekend. We always let our boys know it is a requirement to get the work done, no matter how long it takes, with the thought that they would have to be willing to get it done—no matter what—when they go to college. Given a few school days that lasted 6 to 8 hours, our sons became diligent students and virtually always completed their school work in a 4-6 hour time frame. On average, we spent about five hours on school work each day, with slightly longer days for my slower worker and slightly shorter days for my speedy worker.

One factor that tended to stretch out our school days a bit longer was my husband's and my personal standards for learning. Because we don't school for schooling's sake, but rather to learn, we did not consider any lesson complete unless our sons could achieve an A or B grade on assignments, quizzes, worksheets etc. required in the curriculum that we used. A grade of C or D required my child to review the lesson and redo that particular assignment. A failing grade on a unit or chapter exam required the child to go back and start at the beginning of that learning unit or chapter in its entirety.

Truly, our method was not driven by perfectionism. Our thinking was that if a child fails to understand the concepts being taught, then the child failed to understand a good deal of the instruction and review was obviously needed. We sought good, solid learning, not merely a progression through lessons.

Very few families I know follow school day for a specified length, other than as dictated by the homeschooling laws of their state. Because homeschoolers can sit down and complete their school work without taking time for questions that they don't have (from other students) and have the ability to get immediate answers for questions they do have, a homeschooled child's work can be completed in a shorter period of time.

Additionally if a homeschooled child wants a snack, needs to go to the restroom, needs to stand up or wiggle a little bit, his needs can often be met instantaneously. This allows him to get back to learning quicker. Your homeschooled child need not be distracted by biological needs that take his mind off of learning as often happens when children in school are hungry or need to use the restroom at the 'wrong' time. Homeschooling tends to be very efficient when it comes to teaching and learning, therefore homeschooling days are usually shorter than public schooling days.

How can I get my housework done when I'm homeschooling?

Every homeschooler I know includes chores as part of their homeschooling day. We adopted the mantra: "this is a working co-op, not a country club." Therefore we had chore charts with each child's name, the day of the week, and their chore(s) of the day. Engaging your children in helping you with the completion of the household chores teaches your children valuable life skills.

As our boys got older, we gave them increasingly sophisticated responsibilities that included doing their own laundry and cooking a meal for the family. Initially the meal cooking was once a month and guided, but by the end of their junior and senior years of high school, cooking a meal was an independent activity our boys could complete with little assistance. Our boys know how to read recipes, determine whether or not we have the ingredients on hand, decide what needs to be on the grocery shopping list, follow the recipe, cook the item, and serve up their delicious creations. Following the progression of chores we used enabled our boys to easily transition to independent living as young adults at college.

When you are trying to run a home and homeschool your children, it is very difficult to get all of the cleaning, the laundry, the cooking, the shopping, the doctor's appointments, the errands, and the teaching of the children done single-handedly during reasonable waking hours. I do know a few moms who try to do it all, and they are frequently stressed out. Thus, I never recommend a mom try to do everything herself.

I highly recommend you look at the assignment and completion of chores as part of your regular homeschool day because it does teach your children highly valuable life skills. Generally speaking, our homeschool day was not finished until the chores were done, after which playing and social activities could take place. Simply put, engaging your children in helping with household chores helps everybody since your house can be kept in decent order and the household can run relatively smoothly.

How do I Maintain Learning Momentum During Summer Break?

Whether or not your child has a learning disability, your child can experience "learning regression" during the summer time. Regression occurs when a child forgets some of the academic skills or abilities that he had previously learned during the school year. Some families choose year-round schooling so they won't experience regression, but many families like having a summer break wherein regression becomes a concern. If your child has a learning disability, summer regression can become a significant concern.

Given that a summer break is desired or needed, as it was for our family, I recommend the ongoing use of my "Power Hour," as I called it. Use the Power Hour on weekdays during the summer and for any lengthy holiday breaks such as Christmas time.

A Power Hour eliminates regression because it keeps a child at the same level of academic proficiency, if not moving forward by an incremental measure throughout a school break. Additionally, having a Power Hour helps your child retain a mindset toward completing academic work each day. As a child gets older and understands the purpose behind having a Power Hour, he may even choose to engage in academic activities longer than the required amount of time. This can lead to additional progress, which is always great.

What is a Power Hour? A Power Hour consists of 20 minutes of reading, 20 minutes of writing, and 20 minutes of math. The 20 minute timeframes are approximations and don't require rigid adherence.

In our case, the reading material was 100% my child's choice in order to help instill a willingness to read, but you can assign reading if you wish. We went to the library and let each child pick out several books for the next week or two. Each child was free to pick out picture books with few words or full-length novels. The child could choose whatever he wanted for his reading books, but the books had to have words.

During our reading time, each child read as much of the book as he could in 20 minutes, but he was required to read at least 3 pages of a novel, 10 pages of a large-print book, or the entirety of a picture book that had relatively few words.

Depending upon reading speed, your child may read only a few pages of a novel, or the entirety of a smaller book. You will have to use your own gauge as to an acceptable amount of reading each day. The reading practice is what truly matters, so monitoring is accomplished by asking questions to be sure your child actually read the book. Alternately, you can have your child write about his reading for the day.

For our writing portion of the Power Hour, I allowed my boys to journal about anything, to write a short story, or write about their reading for the day. I required one half page of writing in elementary school and a full page of writing in middle school. Since my boys were relatively slow with their writing, a half page to full page generally took somewhere close to 20 minutes once the child actually started to write.

Using a strict number of minutes for writing was not functional because my boys would sometimes write as little as possible in such cases. One son chose creative story writing most days, while the other typically chose to write about his reading, and less frequently to write about recent events in his life.

None of the Power Hour writing is critiqued for perfection or skill because the goal is to continue the practice of having your child convey his thoughts through writing. I would read over my boys' entries, make occasional observations or comments, but not assess the quality of their writing to any meaningful degree.

Preventing regression in math was accomplished using McGraw-Hill Spectrum workbooks. I obtained the current grade-level book for each son. For the math portion of our Power Hour, my boys would work two pages of math problems from anywhere in the book. Because the workbooks were for the grade-level just completed, the work was primarily review with an occasional concept occurring that had not previously been encountered.

Selecting the just completed grade level workbooks enabled my sons to work independently and helped them feel the math was easy. The point was for them to engage in concept review, which helped them master the concepts more thoroughly, and it did not take very long for my boys to complete since it was all review.

Completing two pages of problems per day amounted to approximately 20 minutes (or slightly more) for my boys, but here again, you can adjust the amount of work as it fits your child's needs. I did not have my boys merely work math problems for 20 minutes because one of my sons may only complete two or three problems in that time if left to fiddle, procrastinate, scribble, or do anything else other than actually work math problems. Therefore, I required they complete two pages of math each day, but if you have a diligent worker, you may be able to specify a straightforward 20 minutes of math.

Some days the math would be completed in 15-20 minutes and other days it might take more than 30 minutes if my child was not focused on his work. By having a set quantity of pages to complete, each of my boys was more likely to remain focused in order to complete the required pages in the shortest amount of time possible.

Having easy review work in all subjects let our boys feel like Power Hour was quick and easy, so we never had issues with resistance to the Power Hour. Our Power Hour was a great tool for retaining learned skills over the summer and Christmas breaks.

If you are going to implement a Power Hour, use materials as close to your child's present level of academic performance as possible. You do not want Power Hour to be an overbearing, time-consuming practice. Given that the main goal of a break in the school year is for rejuvenation, and the Power Hour is simply to prevent regression, the Power Hour should be kept as light-hearted and simple as possible.

Typically, I also gave my boys one week completely free of any school work, with no Power Hour, for the first and last week of the summer break. They had the week between Christmas and New Year's completely off with no Power Hour. During vacation weeks, while traveling, the Power Hour was a perfect way to kill time in the car. While we were at our vacation destination, my boys were completely free from all school work, so they could enjoy the vacation too.

Whether your child is in public school, private school, or homeschooled, and whether your child has a learning disability or not, using the Learning Abled Kids' Power Hour can be an excellent tool for maximizing your child's educational progress. If no ground is lost during the summer, then your child can pick up from the end of the prior school year and continue moving forward without the need for six to eight weeks of review to refresh his memory.

7 RECORD KEEPING

Record-keeping is one thing I don't think any homeschooling parent likes to do. Unfortunately, it is a necessary requirement on some level in virtually every state with the state's goal of ensuring that every child is receiving an appropriate education. The variation from state-to-state is significant, so you must seek out your state's legal record-keeping requirements before embarking on your homeschool journey. Additionally, record-keeping for the purpose of ensuring your child can transfer schools or enter college is well-advised whether your state requires record keeping or not.

The level of record-keeping for college entry is seldom at the same level required by state law for homeschooling itself. Thus, it is wise for you to consider if your child has any inclination whatsoever toward attending college after high school, and you should keep records with college in mind as a possibility. This section will discuss the types of records that you should keep or consider keeping, and will provide information and resources for you.

What Do I Need to Do To Comply with State Reporting Requirements?

The number one rule for record-keeping is to follow all of your state-mandated documentation requirements for your homeschool. If you fail to document your homeschooling as required by your state, you may very well lose the privilege to homeschool should anyone ever call into question your ability to homeschool your children. This should go without saying, but if you fail to follow the legal requirements of homeschooling, then you are asking for trouble. If your child ever needs state or government provided services, if you face a divorce situation, or if anyone in your family feels you are doing an inadequate job and reports to the department of children's services, you won't be able to defend your homeschooling choice if you haven't complied with the legal requirements.

Additionally, if you have failed to follow the legal requirements, the local school system may determine that your child is truant from school, and will seek punitive measures toward your child or you as the parent. These scenarios have been known to happen, and outcomes are always better if you can prove you are legally homeschooling your child. Do the paperwork, however unpleasant it may be.

Homeschooling laws vary widely from state to state. Some states require invasive oversight through the public school system, where parents must submit lesson plans, the curriculum they are using, and meet regularly with the school to ensure that the child is being adequately educated. Other states require virtually no reporting at all, which of course makes homeschooling a lot easier on families.

Just a short note: Research by Dr. Brian Ray at NHERI.org found that the level of government regulation in homeschooling doesn't make any difference in educational outcomes for homeschooled students (Ray, 2010). All of the heavy-handed supervision by some states doesn't equal better outcomes for the students—It's just more paperwork for you.

Given varied regulations, the very first step you need to take to begin homeschooling is to locate your state laws and requirements for legal homeschooling. Details about finding and following state documentation requirements are covered in the "Getting Started" section, "What steps do I need to take to legally start homeschooling?" Q&A of this book, so I will not repeat them here. Please refer back to the first section of this book for detailed "getting started" information.

In Georgia, we were required to submit a letter of intent to homeschool and report monthly attendance. These were the only reports we had to submit to the state, but homeschoolers are required to keep other records to be provided when legally requested.

Whatever your state specifies in the way of legal requirements for reporting while homeschooling are the reports you need to generate in order to comply with your state's reporting requirements. Some of the types of reports which may be required are covered in the next few Q&As.

Do You Give Report Cards or Progress Reports?

Homeschooling parents don't usually give report cards to their children. Grades are a way for schools, whether public or private, to report a student's performance to the child's parents. These grades are necessary because parents are not directly educating their child, so the parents don't really know how well the child is performing academically without grades as feedback from the school.

With homeschooling, parents know how each child is performing in his school work, so the parents don't really need to assign grades to their child. However, in some states there are portfolios or other reporting requirements which may require a parent to assign her child a grade. In this case, assignment of grades is a way of letting the school system know how well your child is performing academically.

Thus, grades are a communication tool which are not typically needed when homeschooling. One notable exception to the grading requirement in homeschooling comes with high school. If your child is going to college or needs to present a school transcript showing completion of his high school education for employment purposes, you will have to assign grades for all high school coursework whether or not your state laws specifically require grades. It is easiest to assign your child a grade at the completion of each course when you have graded assignments available. Assigning grades in elementary or middle school is not necessary unless your state laws require grades.

Some children want report cards when they have previously been in public school, and some parents simply desire to have a report card. There is nothing wrong with making a report card if you wish to have one. In cases where a report card is required or desired, there are templates you can use, or you can make your own. You can find templates by searching on the internet for "sample report card template image" or by accessing one of the free printable templates at:

Donna Young's free printables:
http://donnayoung.org/forms/planners/grade.htm
   Or
Flanders' Family's free printables:
http://www.flandersfamily.info/web/2012/10/05/home-school-report-cards-free-printable/

Alternatively, you can make a simple Word document that has the name of your homeschool, the academic year, your child's current academic grade, the date of the grade reporting, a list of the subjects being taken, and the grades your child has received. In elementary school, it is common to give performance level grades such as "exceeds expectations," satisfactory, and unsatisfactory.

While some elementary schools use an A, B, C, D, F grading scale, virtually all middle schools and high schools use letter grades for their grading scale. In high school it is common to report a letter grade in conjunction with the numeric grade. For example, a report card may report that a student has the letter grade A and a numeric grade of 93 in an English class.

If you are making your own report card, keep in mind that report cards are usually one page or less, and often the size of a 5 x 7 card. If you are making a report card because your child wants one and you don't really need one for reporting purposes, you can always handwrite a report card on a 5 x 7 card for your child. If you need a report card in order to report your child's progress to your local school system or your state Department of Education, then you will want to make sure the report card is professional looking in appearance.

Most school years consist of a period of 36 weeks. Thus, reporting periods are typically nine weeks in length, but some high schools report grades on a semester system—at the end of the fall semester and the end of the spring semester—each of which are 18 weeks in length. In order to determine your grading periods, first count the number of weeks your child will actually be attending school. In weeks where there are fewer than five days you can add up the number of days within the incomplete weeks, counting one week for every five days total. If you are going to report your child's progress four times per year, then simply divide the total number of weeks by four and each reporting period will be that number of weeks. Similarly, if you are going to report your child's progress twice per year, then simply divide the total number of weeks by two, and your reporting period will be that number of weeks.

For example, if you are schooling your child year-round, you may take a little more than a month off between Thanksgiving and New Year's, and you may take a couple of weeks off during the summer for a family vacation, so your school year length would be 52 weeks minus 8 weeks of holiday and vacation time, giving a total school year length of 44 weeks. If you are reporting your child's progress four times per year, then each grading period would be 11 weeks in length (44/4). If you are reporting your child's progress twice per year, then each grading period would be 22 weeks in length (44/2).

A simple report card might look similar to this:

Report Card for:		(student name)					**Academic Year:** 2013-2014		
	1st Grading Period		2nd Grading Period		3rd Grading Period		4th Grading Period		Course Average
Subject	Letter	Numeric	Letter	Numeric	Letter	Numeric	Letter	Numeric	
English	A	93	A	94	A	95			94
Algebra	B	89	A	93	B	89			90
History	A	90	B	88	B	88			89
Biology	C	78	B	88	B	83			83
Art	A	95	A	94	A	93			94
P.E.	A	100	A	95	A	90			95
Grading Scale: 100-90 = A, 89-80 = B, 79-70 = C, 69-60 = D, 59-0 = F, I = Incomplete									

In our state, we aren't required to issue report cards, but we are required to keep annual progress reports for each child. While these progress reports can contain letter and/or numeric grades, guidelines do not specify the format for our progress reporting. Your state may be different. If you are required to create a progress report, you may be given a specific format to use; in which case you should generate a report that meets your state's reporting requirements.

Along a slightly different line of requirement, but similar to report cards, let's talk about "Progress Reports." Given that your state is like ours and you are required to keep progress reports, your reporting format can be more variable. We aren't given specific guidelines for the progress reports required by our state laws. If you have no guidelines, you can create a progress report that contains whatever information you feel like reporting, which may or may not include grades.

When I created our progress reports, I wrote about half of a page for each subject, which contained information about my child's skill level at the beginning of the school year, his skill level at the end of the school year, any challenges or issues we faced, our triumphs, and specifics about the resources we used including books, DVDs, specific curricula, related field trips or Museum visits, and other learning resources specifically related to the individual subject.

Aside from documenting progress in each individual subject area studied each year, we also documented all of our extracurricular activities, our field trips, any community classes taken, achievements or awards earned, enrichment opportunities such as the Duke Talent Identification Program (Duke TIP) or Stanford University's Educational Program for Gifted Youth (EPGY) participation, and documentation of our goals for the following school year. Our progress reports were typically 5 to 6 pages long for each child. The reports provided a comprehensive view of the child's academic achievement for the previous school year and provided a benchmark as a starting point for the upcoming school year.

Many people, including ourselves, create a simple Word document. I made our progress reports look "official" by making headers for each section and formatting the document into a nice, easy-to-read table. Here again, you can search on the Internet for "sample academic progress report" to see examples of various types of progress reports. You will find formats for progress reporting vary widely.

I don't think there is really a wrong way to create a progress report unless your state specifies specific requirements for information which must be contained in your child's progress report. If you are free to create your own progress report, you can let your report take whatever format you prefer.

What is a Portfolio and What Do I Put In It?

Many states require the keeping and/or submission of annual portfolios for each homeschooled child. Depending upon your state, you may or may not have specific requirements as to what information must be included in your child's portfolio. When a state requires a portfolio, they usually require that you specify all curricula, teaching materials, as well as all resources used for teaching each subject to your child. Typically, you're required to include samples of your child's work from different points throughout the school year showing typical academic performance, provide grades, and states often require you to include standardized testing results for each academic year.

A portfolio is more extensive than a report card or progress report. Making a portfolio requires consistent tracking of your child's schoolwork throughout the year and requires you to organize your documentation. In preparing to write your portfolio, review the preceding sections about report cards and progress reports. You will want to include similar information in your portfolio along with specifics about your teaching materials, student work samples, standardized testing, and the specific additional information that is required by your state or local school system.

While creating a portfolio can seem like an overwhelming task, if you keep everything for your school year together in a box, plastic tote, or file folder, including receipts for the purchase of your curriculum at the beginning of the school year, your child's work throughout the school year, and any other documentation you have, then to creating a portfolio is much easier at the end of the academic school year.

It also helps to create forms for yourself which will enable you to uniformly track each subject for each child from year-to-year. For example, we had "Course Reporting" sheets for each subject. At the beginning of the school year, I would print one of these sheets for each subject, for each child. Additionally, I purchased a large, 3-ring binder for each child, along with subject divider tabs, for organizing our course reporting efforts.

At the top of our course reporting form there is a section to specify resources used. In this section, I list the name of our curriculum, textbooks, trade books, DVDs, outside courses, projects, and any field trips or activities we would take or took that are related to the subject.

The middle section of the form is for recording grades for all major assignments and exams. I retain copies of the assignments and exams until the grades have been logged on the "Course Reporting" sheet and keep a few as examples in the portfolio itself.

The lower section and back of the page are used for notes regarding the child's struggles or ease of learning, his future interests in the topic, particularly keen insights or observations he may share about his studies, or any other notes that I felt were pertinent to our documentation.

During the school year, these "Course Reporting" sheets are kept in our handy 3-ring notebooks for each child, which I can grab and make notes whenever needed. I have dividers in the notebook separating it by subject, and I have a 3-hole punch I use to punch holes in assignment sheets and file them in the appropriate section of each child's notebook.

By being thorough in creating your portfolio, you can meet or exceed your school district's reporting requirements. Although we were not required to keep a portfolio in our state, I kept one because I knew it could be important when my sons began applying to colleges. If you make it a practice to keep a portfolio, whether you are required to keep one or not, then you will have a much easier time providing documentation of your child's learning if or when you are requested to do so.

If there is no portfolio requirement in your state, just be as thorough as you possibly can in your record keeping, especially during high school. By documenting each subject with grading criteria, grades, test scores, the curricula used, and activities your child participates in, you will have a much easier time if you have to produce a portfolio as part of your child's college application. Finalizing your child's record each year is relatively easy if you have documented heavily in your early planning, and if you have a system (like my 3-ring binder) for collecting your child's schoolwork in one easy location throughout the school year.

Even if you are not required to create a portfolio, it is wise to keep these records. Many parents fail to keep documentation throughout their child's homeschooling, and then they struggle when they are asked for a portfolio by a college admissions office or by a court in the cases of divorce or other legal issues. If you haven't kept a portfolio throughout your child's schooling, it is very difficult to recall the details of your schooling three, four, or more years after the fact. You may not need to keep overly strong documentation throughout elementary and middle school, but I highly recommend you document everything while your child is in high school.

As with report cards and progress reports, you can search for "homeschool portfolio sample" to see what other parents include in their portfolios and how they format each section. Making your child's homeschool portfolio as comprehensive as possible is beneficial because it is easier to remove excess information than it is to recall information years later.

The most important aspect of a portfolio is that it needs to include all information required by requesting entities, whether a request comes from your public school system, a college, or some other source. Since you don't know ahead of time which information the requestor will want to see, it's best to document everything you can. If you're thorough in creating your portfolio, it becomes fairly easy to produce the correct documentation whenever it is required.

How Do I Make A Transcript or Where Do I Obtain A Transcript?

Creating a transcript is often a do-it-yourself project for the homeschooling parent. There are two common formats used for high school transcripts. The first format arranges the student's coursework by grade level and lists everything a child completed in ninth grade under a section titled "Ninth Grade," everything a child completed in tenth grade under a section titled "Tenth Grade," and so on. It is easy to create a chronological transcript, adding a new section as the child completes each grade level. This is often the easiest method for the parent, but it is more difficult for colleges or employers to quickly see what courses the student took in each subject.

The second way transcripts are arranged is in subject-based coursework sections. In this case, there would be a section titled "Language Arts" where courses in Composition, World Literature, and American Literature are listed. Another section would list "Math" courses such as Algebra I, Geometry, and Pre-calculus, etc. Subject-based transcripts usually include Language Arts, Mathematics, Social Studies, Science, Foreign Language, Arts, and an Electives section. This format makes it easy for anyone to quickly see which courses the student completed in each subject area. Given the completion of specific courses in each subject area is the main focus for college admissions, this format is the best choice if your child wants to go to college.

For either transcript format, you need to determine the specific coursework that is required for college entrance at your child's chosen college or for your state's high school graduation requirements. You can then format your child's transcript to contain each required course, whether you format by academic year or by subject.

For graduation, our state requires four math courses, four English courses, four science courses, two history courses, economics, American Government, a Physical education course, a health course, two levels of the same foreign language and electives. Therefore, our transcripts were sectioned by subject area, so that anyone looking at our transcript could quickly see if our boys had taken the required number of courses in each section.

You can create your own transcript using Word, Excel, or any other document producing program you'd like. You may wish to purchase a program with pre-made transcript templates, which would make your life easier. The transcript solutions I am aware of include:

Lee Binz's <u>Total Transcript Solution</u> – This is a computer-based program that many use because the transcripts are pre-formatted, easy to update and change, and you can print copies whenever you need them. Generally speaking, it is easier to track on your computer and print transcript copies when needed. If you use a handwritten transcript, you have to re-write the grades and GPA calculations if you need to make any changes, but the computer information is easy to change and reprint.

Donna Young's free printables:
http://donnayoung.org/forms/planners/grade.htm

Flanders' Family's free printables:
http://www.flandersfamily.info/web/2012/10/05/home-school-report-cards-free-printable/

Any of these transcript resources will meet your needs. The only caveat I'd issue with the printable transcripts is that hand-written course names and grades don't tend to look as high in quality as a typed transcript. Typed transcripts are used by public schools, and colleges usually expect typed transcripts. Thus, if you want to present a transcript that looks "official," then you may prefer to go with Lee Binz's Total Transcript Solution or create your own using any word processing or spreadsheet program.

If you make your own transcript form, be sure your transcript contains all of the required or expected information such as student name, home address, birth date, graduation date, GPA, courses, both numeric and letter grades, and any other information the receiving institution expects to receive. We used an Excel spreadsheet that would automatically calculate GPA whenever a new grade was entered. Since I did not create that spreadsheet, I'm not permitted to give it away, but I can say the Total Transcript Solution will provide all of the functionality you will need.

Do you or should I give grades?

While this question is very similar to the question about giving report cards, parents have an underlying concern about tracking academic progress that has a slightly different focus than the question about report cards. Thus, this question will be similar to the report card question answered previously, but the answer here gives additional information. You may want to read the answer to "What About Report Cards and Progress Reports?" earlier in this section for a full understanding of grading and reporting grades.

Giving grades for school work is largely a practice used to communicate the academic progress of a child. As a homeschooling parent, you will know whether your child knows the content being taught or not by asking your child questions, by discussing the topic, or by having your child complete some sort of assignment that conveys how much he understands. Grading isn't really necessary, particularly at the elementary and middle school level. High school is somewhat different since high school grades are required for college and by some employers.

For elementary and middle school, it is helpful to look over your child's work, make note of the answers he missed and repeat instruction where necessary, but it isn't necessary to assign a grade to your child's paper. It is more helpful for you to look for gaps in your child's understanding and to consider errors as an indication that you need to review or re-teach the concept, so your child can learn the content well.

In regard to the specifics of how to grade your child's work, it is easier for kids to be "right" if they are graded on the understanding of the bigger picture rather than trivial facts. In my way of thinking, it is more important for a child to understand what happened, why it happened, and how the events of history unfolded rather than force your child to memorize trivial facts such as specific names, dates, and cities. Memorizing facts does not equate with understanding the historical significance of a person, event, or shift in society.

While many curricula have tests containing names, dates, and specific places, I never cared to grade my boys on trivia when they can look those facts up at any time they may actually need the information. When is the last time you needed to know George Washington's birth date, the names of all of the signers of the Declaration of Independence, or recite the specific capitals of all fifty states without any ability to look up the information? It is more important (to me) for students to understand the social implications of historical events by focusing on the interactions that caused wars or societal shifts in different eras.

Math, science, and structured writing rules (punctuation and spelling) need to be more precisely measured because it's essential for your child to understand the foundational concepts and laws. Thus, most of the time, math rules, laws of science, punctuation and spelling rules, and other foundational bits of knowledge must be memorized to support higher level learning in those subject areas. However, again, grading is not necessary for you to know whether your child has a concept memorized or not. Either a child knows how to apply a rule with ease or he doesn't.

In our homeschool, we continued reviewing rules and concepts until mastery took hold. With mastery being the goal, I would tell my sons we need to work on a concept some more and we practiced until my son could respond quickly and easily. Our goal wasn't perfection, but proficiency. Thus, as a matter of education, it isn't necessary to tell a child he "failed" when it comes to learning, but rather to let your child know "we still need to work on this."

That said, high school is different, particularly if your child has any inclination toward attending college. In such cases, you will need a high school transcript and you will be required to assign grades. Thus, we considered "grading" to be a high school requirement and my sons understood their learning performance would be assessed throughout high school. You can lay the foundation for this expectation during middle school by beginning to talk about the need to assign grades to a child's quality of work, so he must make every effort to do his best.

When proficiency is the goal, and working hard is the key to success, a child can learn to appreciate the progress he can make with his learning. Grading can be an incentive for a child to "show off" what he knows through his assignments. Once a child understands that success in education is the same as "showing off" what he knows, a child can really begin to embrace the learning process as he attempts to earn high grades.

For our high school grading during the freshman and sophomore years, I graded my sons' work by fairly traditional means. For history, I looked for my boys to have understanding of the why's and how's in regard to the societal dynamics that were in play for various historical events. They conveyed their understanding through papers, conversations, projects, and some via traditional school work. For history, we loved using the History Channel's Classroom DVD series. It wasn't a traditional curriculum, but it helped history come alive and was far more interesting to see the movie portrayals of events rather than read about them in a book. Grading for history was more subjective than objective, and definitely more difficult without a focus on fact memorization. For history, grades were assigned based upon my sons' ability to convey their depth of understanding, showing they had fully grasped the historical events, rather than upon any strict set of factual information.

For math, I used the automatic grading that accompanied our curricula. My boys used Switched on Schoolhouse for mathematics, which automatically graded their work. The work was either right or wrong because it was math! When they got an answer wrong, I would reset the particular question and they got a second chance at figuring out the answer. Switched on Schoolhouse allowed me to assign a fraction of the credit (usually 75%) if they had to re-work the question.

If one of my sons got a D or F on a unit, I reset the entire unit, which cleared all responses completely and my son had to re-do the unit in its entirety. Resetting was always done with compassion and understanding—as in, "I see you didn't quite understand this unit, so I'll reset it and let you go through it again. That way you'll be better equipped to pass the next unit."

Resetting entire units was not meant to be punitive, but rather to insure subject mastery and to instill an understanding of the need to study and pay attention to detail. My goal was to insure my sons actually mastered each concept because math knowledge builds upon itself and requires proficiency at each level.

With the exception of Chemistry, which each son took with an outside teacher, and the Physics course my son took through DerekOwens.com, we used Apologia for our science curricula. Apologia has questions the student answers at the end of each section and exams for each chapter. I used the provided answer keys to grade completed work and to assign grades. Given my goal has always been proficiency and understanding, if my sons got a question wrong, they did get a second chance to answer those incorrect questions for 75% of the question's points. As with the Math, if my sons failed an exam, they had to re-do the entire chapter.

Thankfully, we never had to re-do any chapter more than once, and usually we only had to re-do one or two chapters per child before the child would understand the level of attention he must give to his high school coursework. Because we used a proficiency-based focus in our schooling, my sons' course grades were always A's, B's or C's, never a D nor an F.

I do know homeschooling moms who give their children all A's, but I think that is a disservice when the child gets to college and reality bites. I've always wanted my sons to have a realistic view of their abilities and a good understanding of how grades are assigned in the collegiate world. The strong work ethic we established in high school has enabled my boys to consistently earn A's and B's in college.

In grading English coursework, clarity in expression of thought and strong subject matter analysis was essential. During the freshman and sophomore years of high school, we used the Institute for Excellence in Writing's (IEW) "Student Writing Intensive," "Student Writing

Intensive Continuation Course," and "Advanced Writing." Often, I would align essay topics to the current history, science, or literature selections my boys were currently studying. By writing about books they were reading, science, and/or history, their writing was a way to reinforce the learning they were engaging in otherwise.

You can't really grade reading well other than to quiz on particular facts, so having your child write and analyze a book can help convey whether your child understood what he read without focusing on nit-picky facts. Thus, grades for our English courses were based more upon clear conveyance of knowledge about what was read, proper writing techniques, and the overall excellence of the composition.

When grading papers, no matter what the subject was, I would highlight every spelling error, punctuation error, and entire sentences where the content was not clear. Yellow highlighting was used for errors, and blue highlighting was used for lack of clarity. We used a self-correction method for correcting spelling errors because self-correction is proven by research to be the most effective method for improving a child's ongoing spelling difficulties.

Within the essays, I would also make notes to let my boy know where their paper was weak and where it was strong, by saying "good attention-grabbing opening" or "your paper just ends without a good conclusion." My son's would then re-write their papers correcting errors, re-writing sections that were confusing, and they'd add in content where their papers were lacking.

Depending upon the level of quality of their first submission and second submission, I would assess the overall quality of the paper in conveying their ideas well and the number of errors that remained in their final copy. This methodology worked so well, when my younger son took English 101 and English 102 through joint enrollment with the university, he scored a 100 on every single paper he wrote. The opportunity to self-correct his own mistakes for the first two years of high school taught him how to polish up his work, and he was excellent at conveying his ideas in writing.

We "practiced" with grades during the first two years of high school. My boys then experienced third-party grading in 11th and 12th grade. Both of my boys took joint enrollment courses in core subject areas while still having the support and familiarity of homeschooling.

Both of my boys were sophomores in college simultaneously with graduating from high school, and both boys went into college with high GPA's and a solid understanding of what would be expected of them to earn good grades in college. The methods we used for grading worked excellently for my sons.

Sincerely, I believe the four years of high school are ample time for helping a child understand grading as it applies to traditional education. Thus, I don't think grades are really necessary at the elementary and middle school levels, and I personally wouldn't assign grades if it weren't required by my State Department of Education. Instead, I would recommend focusing on content mastery, particularly in the early grades.

While grading can be objective or subjective, I would recommend making the assignment of grades a learning experience. Help your child understand that grades often reflect strong study skills, attention to the details within assignment instructions, and the student's willingness to work hard to improve his performance.

It's important for you to understand grades in college will be an accurate reflection of the quality of work produced by your child, so high school grades should also be an accurate reflection too. If you give your child high grades he hasn't actually earned, you will be setting your child up for shock and disappointment when he encounters third party expectations and grading. You need to be certain your child understands the level of dedication required for making good grades in college.

Help your child understand how grading is applied; help him understand the criteria used for grading in different courses. Colleges often use grading rubrics to clearly specify the grading criteria. Teaching your child how to use a grading rubric to assess the quality of his own work can help your child make a leap in his academic performance.

Also help your child understand that demonstrating his full knowledge about the question or subject is the primary goal for most assignments and tests. If your child knows that conveying his full understanding and knowledge of a topic will help him earn higher grades, your child will be more successful if he attends college.

Does my child require an accredited high school program?

This question is covered depth in the Q&A *"What if I change my mind and homeschooling isn't working; can I put my child back into school?"* but I will add a bit more here to address the question as it relates to high school and college. Unlike elementary and middle school, if you have to enroll your child into public school during high school, his homeschool coursework is less likely to be accepted by any regionally accredited high school without rigid proof of completed coursework.

Keep in mind, placing a child into public high school mid-stream is different than applying to colleges and universities with an unaccredited high school diploma. Many colleges accept unaccredited diplomas from children who have been homeschooled, but not all do, so you need to investigate the requirements of any college your child may have in mind as a destination. Public high schools seldom accept a child's unaccredited high school coursework without testing or requiring a child to repeat coursework.

Having a regionally accredited program is not required, but I think any parent is wise to consider the long-term effects should a family tragedy happen. What if you go under a bus tomorrow? What if your spouse asks for a divorce tomorrow? What if you become gravely ill and can't handle homeschooling? Would you have to put your children into a traditional school? If not, fabulous! If you're like most of us, there may be a very real possibility your life circumstances would dictate that homeschooling was no longer feasible.

At the high school level, the long-term ramifications for using a non-accredited program have been known to cause major headaches and heartaches for a handful of homeschooling families I know. In our local school system, if a child is not being taught through an accredited program and the child is then enrolled into a public high school, the child does not automatically receive any credit for unaccredited coursework done through his homeschool program. The school system administers end-of-course tests in every subject taken, and the child must pass every exam to get credit for coursework already completed.

Simply put, if a child can't pass the corresponding course test administered by the school, the child must retake the course from the beginning through the public high school under their supervision. The possibility a child will lose all of his course credits is a real possibility. I doubt many publicly schooled kids could pass the end of the course tests three years after taking the course, but that is nevertheless the reality faced by homeschoolers.

Thus, if something happens, you can no longer homeschool, and you have no accreditation, your child might have to take tests for each completed subject (Biology, American History, Algebra, World Literature, etc.). If your child does not test well, or if it is later in high school, it could be very difficult for your child to recall content he learned in ninth or tenth grade, and the school will only grant credit for those courses in which your child can pass the exam.

We have known families where divorce, cancer, and the death of a providing father have forced the families to stop homeschooling. Except in the case where the parents had been using a fully accredited program, accredited by the same accrediting agency that accredits the public high schools, the high school students who were placed into a public school mid-stream all had to repeat some level of their coursework. For some it was just a couple of courses (for which exams were not passed), but for at least two students they had to repeat the entire ninth grade set of classes. The sad fact was that the children had to suffer double trauma by having their high school coursework tossed out the window while they were dealing with family trauma.

So, as you can probably surmise, accreditation for high school level coursework requires your serious consideration. Although regional accreditation is not required in most states, it may be advisable, particularly if there is any chance your child may need to be enrolled in a public school at any time during her high school career. While you have to give up a degree of control over your child's coursework when going through an accredited program, the oversight, reporting, and involvement of an accrediting body can ease the road of transition if changes in your schooling plans are needed in the future.

If you are going to seek an accredited program, be sure you use one accredited by one of the agencies accepted by the public school systems in your state. Most public schools readily accept accreditation from regionally accredited institutions. Those institutions include:

- Middle States Association of Colleges and Schools (MSA)
- New England Association of Schools and Colleges (NEASC)
- North Central Association of Colleges and Schools (NCA)
- Northwest Commission on Colleges and Universities (NWCCU)
- Southern Association of Colleges and Schools (SACS)
- Western Association of Schools and Colleges (WASC)

As a final note for the high school years, if your child works well independently and is passionate about learning, you may not need to concern yourself with accreditation, even if something tragic were to happen. There are several online high school programs, GED programs, and other avenues for completing high school which can be completed independently by a diligently working student. Although it can be problematic to leave a high school student to fend for herself with her studies, if your student is independent, strongly driven, and able to work hard on her own, she might be able to work independently to finish high school even if something happens to pull the primary homeschooling parent away from home.

8 BEHAVIOR MANAGEMENT AND MAINTAINING FOCUS

One of the most common challenges parents of children with disabilities face is behavior management. Whether your child has a specific learning disability, ADHD, Asperger's syndrome, autism, or any other disability, your child's neuropsychological profile is different from typical children. Thus advice commonly given by other homeschooling parents who don't have children with disabilities or by well-meaning family members often doesn't quite meet the needs of you or your child. Seeking out specialized techniques and solutions will help both you and your child cope with behavioral difficulties more easily.

Should I medicate my child to manage his ADHD?

If it helps at all, one teacher-parent said she'd medicate her child if the child were in school, but not if the child was homeschooled. ADHD can have a pervasive affect on a child's learning and ADHD affects a child all of the time. ADHD, whether it's inattentive type, active type, or combined type, can make it difficult for a child to learn any subject. Your child may be cognitively bright or even gifted, but inability to focus attention when needed may make your child seem incapable of learning.

In public school, it is difficult to control your child's environment sufficiently to enable learning, so it is often easier to make your child fit the traditional school environment by medicating. Homeschooling parents can usually modify their child's learning environment and school situation sufficiently, so the child doesn't have to be medically 'modified'.

Whether you choose medication or not is likely to be dependent upon your child's daily functioning, the impact of the ADHD on his learning, and the severity of his ADHD symptoms. As a general observation, I think fewer parents who homeschool choose to medicate, but that is because they can better control the environment, their child's diet, and the physiological needs of their child as a way of mediating the affects of ADHD on their child's learning.

While it may be difficult to think of modifying your child's attention functioning through medication, medication is sometimes the best decision for your child in the long-term. If you decide to medicate your child, find a doctor who specializes in ADHD issues. A specialist will be able to direct you in aspects of dealing with ADHD better than a general practice doctor, who may not have sufficient knowledge of the underlying problems associated with ADHD.

Benefits of medication for ADHD may include more immediate control of your child's behavior, immediate improvement in your child's ability to concentrate, and more 'availability' for learning-based tasks. The degree and immediacy of improvement will depend on the appropriateness of the selected medication and dose for your individual child. If your doctor happens to select a perfect medication and dose for your child, you are set. However, often modifications to the type of medicine or dosage are required through an adjustment and refinement phase in order to find what works best.

During the period when your doctor is trying to determine the best medication and dosage for your child, you may go through periods when your child has notable behavior changes, changes in appetite, disrupted sleep patterns, etc. Talk with your doctor about any symptoms that are of concern, particularly those having a significant impact on your child. Finding the right medication and dosage can be difficult. You may want to discuss the benefits of going through the process with your child, so he will better understand the emotions and changes he will be experiencing.

Parents who have chosen medication give mixed testimony. Some have dramatic and outstanding results. Others have a difficult road with many modifications in the child's medications with few notable improvements. Some parents mourn the loss of a 'spark' their child once had, whereas others say they noticed no personality changes in their child. Some people who initially decided against medication had poor results and realized a tremendous turn-around once they decided to medicate. Other parents give up on medication after months of trying to find a medication that works.

The specific affect of medication will be unique for your child, and the outcome cannot be accurately guessed without trying medication to see how it affects your child. I feel that some kids' brain chemistry responds well to the medications, and other kids' brains do not respond well. Thus, whether medication will work for your child is something that can only be determined through trial and error while working with a qualified doctor.

That said, if medication is causing problems for your child, perhaps medication is not the best choice. Maybe your child's ADHD symptoms aren't caused by an imbalance in brain chemistry and the medication throws your child into a state of imbalance. If that's the case, you may have better results by managing your child's ADHD symptoms through diet, sleep, exercise and other natural methods. Check out the next question and answer for more about taking a non-medicated route.

What ever your decision may be in regard to medication, you can always change your mind and your approach if you need to. In all likelihood, it will take a period of adjustment, no matter which route you choose.

How do you manage ADHD without medication?

A common concern for parents of children with ADHD is fear of the long-term affects of using medication to manage ADHD symptoms. Many parents don't want their children to be dependent upon a brain stimulant in order to maintain focus. There are alternatives for raising the level of attention-regulating chemicals in a child's brain without medication. While natural methods aren't as easy as taking a pill, if your child's symptoms are manageable through natural means, then you may find the required changes will benefit your whole family.

One way of meeting your child's need for additional brain

chemical production is through intense daily exercise. Thirty to forty-five minutes of intensive physical activity EACH day can boost the levels of endorphins which help a child focus on school work, improve memory, and help the child be less impulsive.

Exercising can vary daily, and can be accomplished through physical activities that interest your child. The activity level may be a bit much for you, but it is a sacrificial decision you'd make to cope with your child's ADHD.

As an example, your child could take karate lessons two days a week, play tennis two days per week, go for a walk at the park two days per week, and sometimes do other things like wash the cars, vacuum the whole house, etc. Although maintaining an active schedule might seem like it will empty your bank account, you can find inexpensive community-based classes or engage in activities that have no associated cost.

Being active for the sake of your child can be difficult for you if you are not a high-energy person, but you will adjust to a more active schedule over time. To read more about the use of exercise as a means of mediating ADHD symptoms, check out "ADD/ADHD Drug Free: Natural Alternatives and Practical Exercises to Help Your Child Focus" by Frank Jacobelli.

Another means of addressing ADHD without medication is through diet. There are several experts who have written books about ADHD and its correlation with artificial chemicals in our foods. Probably the most widely known expert source of ADHD-diet related information is the Feingold Association. This is a non-profit organization dedicated to helping children and adults understand and apply proven dietary techniques for better behavior, learning, and health. At the very least, eliminating "junk" food can help lessen your child's ADHD symptoms. However, eliminating junk food is seldom sufficient for eliminating ADHD behaviors altogether. MOST packaged foods contain some sort of food dye or preservative which can have negative effects on your child's body, so going toward natural eating as much as possible may bring noticeable improvement.

As a third step, establishing good sleep practices with regulated bedtime routines and bedtimes can improve ADHD symptoms. There are countless studies about sleep and the affect of poor sleep on people's ability to focus their attention. Children are no different. One of the best things about homeschooling is the ability to let your child sleep until he wakes up. This generally means your child will have a full night's sleep and will be well-rested. By establishing good sleep practices, you will be establishing a good baseline of brain functioning and brain chemistry, which should help with learning.

If you are not going to medicate your child, then making dietary, exercise, and sleep changes will be beneficial. It takes all three to set up a good foundation for your child's brain and to provide him with optimal functionality.

We managed our son's ADHD naturally through most of our homeschooling. He chose to try medication before going off to college and that choice worked well for our son. I'm thankful we were able to homeschool and avoid medication for the better part of his childhood, and I believe it was a wise choice for him to begin using medication for symptom management in college since his schedule there is more haphazard and more difficult to control by natural means.

There is a lot of neuroscience behind brain development and the treatment of ADD/ADHD through neuro-developmental programs. Programs such as Brain Gym, Balametrics, or treatments at the Dore Centers can help stimulate your child's cerebellum, thereby alleviating some ADD/ADHD symptoms. Some people report excellent results with cerebella stimulation exercise programs, but there aren't many controlled scientific studies (yet) to document the effectiveness of such programs.

Another way of learning to cope with ADHD is through ongoing family counseling. Counseling helps you deal with ADHD issues and helps your child learn more appropriate behaviors and reactions. Sometimes your child may visit with the psychologist one-on-one, sometimes the psychologist will see each person in your family one-on-one, and sometimes everyone in the family will see the psychologist together.

You can get a psychological referral from your pediatrician. Ask specifically for someone who 'specializes' in working with children who have ADHD or have learning disabilities, or a neuropsychologist.

I feel psychologists who specialize in ADHD, learning disabilities, and family counseling tend to approach ADHD management differently than typical medical doctors (who may see medication as a quick cure all). A good doctor will be willing to work with you either way you want to go. Whether you choose medication or no medication, your family will need wise advice from a qualified professional who is willing to accept your family's decisions.

Counseling for ADHD issues doesn't have to occur weekly. Counseling can take place once or twice per month, depending upon the intensity of the situation in your family. Counseling needs to be frequent enough to help deal with issues that have surfaced since the last visit, so your frequency of visitation will be dictated by the number and kinds of issues you are dealing with.

Your counselor can help you come up with ideas for helping your child understand he MUST do school work, and for helping your child stay focused. The counselor will listen to you vent when you're exasperated, which can be worth every penny to prevent you from venting at your child.

For your child, a counselor helps him reflect on appropriate or inappropriate behaviors and expectations, and helps him with ideas for dealing with frustration or tasks he's disinterested in completing. With regular counseling, your household can run smoother, and everyone will cope better. Family counseling helps everyone be a lot less frustrated, and there is less chaos.

I feel regular counseling, combined with other non-medicated solutions, makes a difference similar to what you'd see with medication, it just takes a while to get settled with good routines and practices. Medication can make an immediate difference, but it can take a few weeks up to six months or more to find 'the right' medication and dosage. Thus, going a either route isn't necessarily faster, and either route can feel slow, so seeking to do what works best for your family is the best advice I can give to you.

My child has sensory issues; how do you manage SPD?

Sensory Processing Disorder is a much bigger issue than can easily be addressed in a short answer format. There are entire books written about sensory processing disorder management. Some books I recommend are:

1. The Out-of-Sync Child: Recognizing and Coping with Sensory Processing Disorder

2. Understanding Your Child's Sensory Signals: A Practical Daily Use Handbook for Parents and Teachers

3. Raising a Sensory Smart Child: The Definitive Handbook for Helping Your Child with SensoryProcessing Issues

On the practical end of giving a short answer though, I will say that a child's sensory issues are so much easier to address and manage in a home environment than in a traditional classroom or school setting. When sensory overload and meltdowns occur, or sensory stimulation is being sought, the behaviors can be allowed to happen in your homeschool environment.

When you are homeschooling, it is feasible to manage your child's sensory issues with responsive environmental changes. Throughout the day, you can include therapies and behavior management techniques to help your child cope with his or her sensitivities. While a teacher or administrator at a school is unlikely to know what triggered your child's meltdown, you are better able to recognize patterns in your child's sensory issues and you can respond directly if you homeschool.

On a day-to-day basis, a child with sensory issues may have meltdowns at what seems like minor issues to typical people. Problems can include tags in clothing, wrinkles in socks, fabric that is too rough, wearing shoes at all, loud noises or noisy environments, foods with textures, traveling in cars where a child is strapped in a seat that is uncomfortable to him or where images move quickly and are overwhelming, including a wide variety of other possible over stimulations. You can manage these behaviors in your homeschool by trying to avoid any triggers.

It is relatively easy to avoid overly noisy environments and to make sure your child's clothing is soft knit fabric without tags, etc. You can buy your child some seamless socks, which I highly recommend if your child has an issue with socks and shoes. Because of the neurological difficulty your child may have in coping with riding in a car and with unfamiliar or noisy environments, you may choose not to do much outside of your home while your child is young. Thankfully many sensory-overloaded children begin outgrowing some of their sensory issues as they progress through the elementary years.

Some children with sensory issues seek stimulation through touching, feeling, making noises, etc. These behaviors can be difficult to manage in a typical classroom and are less of an issue when a child is homeschooled. In a traditional school, when prevented from "stimming" (as it is called), a child can build up stress within and have outbursts or meltdowns. When your child is schooled at home, you can let your child stim to some degree, and help manage the behaviors at a level that allows your child to function. You can help your child develop coping skills with less harshness in behavior management than is typically used in a traditional school environment.

I know many children with sensory issues don't outgrow their sensory issues easily, so you may need to undertake specific therapies to help your child cope. Sensory diet techniques include brushing arms or legs with a soft brush, weighted vests, and other stimulations that help a child develop the ability to cope with varied sensory inputs.

Occupational Therapists (OT) are professionals who most frequently develop treatment plans for individuals with Sensory Processing Disorder. If you suspect your child may have SPD, I would suggest having an evaluation with an OT to help both you and your child cope with this often stressful disability.

My child refuses to do his schoolwork; how do I make him do it?

You are not alone! This is a problem faced by virtually all parents at one time or another. First and foremost, remember you are the parent and it will be your job to force the child to engage in learning, whether he wants to or not. Sometimes this can be accomplished with logic and reasoning, sometimes willingness to comply can be accomplished through positive behavior reinforcements or incentives, and sometimes a parent must resort to disciplining the child.

At the heart of addressing refusal to complete schoolwork is the underlying reason why the child is refusing to do his school work. If your child is refusing to do his schoolwork, there is usually some aspect of performance or ability that is proving to be difficult for your child. If his school work is too challenging or too boring the majority of the time, your child will develop an aversion to his school assignments. If your child was previously in public school, his feelings about schoolwork could be based upon struggles he had in a traditional classroom, the difficulty of completing the work, peer influence, or any number of reasons including instruction that did not meet the child's learning needs.

If your child has always been homeschooled, I find aversions to schoolwork are usually due to curriculum and instruction that does not match a child's learning style, a failure to identify and address learning difficulties or disabilities, or a harsh, critical, perfectionist parent who seldom finds a child's work praiseworthy. In the last case of the perfectionist parent, a child often feels any effort he puts forth will be criticized anyway, so why should he bother to try very hard?

Therefore, to solve the problem if your child is refusing to complete his schoolwork, you must become an open-minded detective. You must be willing to examine all aspects of instruction that you are providing, consider your child's educational history, and pay particular attention to any struggles or traumatic experiences your child has had. Additionally, you must be willing to examine yourself for ways in which you may be robbing your child of the joy of learning or in which you may be failing to adequately meet your child's needs. These can be tough things to examine and face, but they are necessary if you want your child to willingly engage in learning.

Figuring out what needs to change to motivate your child toward a desire to learn is not easy. The detective work is difficult because of the level of unbiased introspection you must undertake in order to figure out what needs to change. I think perhaps the best way to talk about issues and problems when your child refuses to do his schoolwork is to start by giving a few examples of the issues we dealt with in our homeschooling.

In the beginning of our homeschool days, my older son sincerely believed he was incapable of completing school work. He had assimilated this belief through his five years in public school where they, in fact, told him he "couldn't" do certain assignments because he had not yet learned to read. Thus, when we began homeschooling, my poor son would refuse to even try because he believed he couldn't do the work anyway. Many times when I would ask my son to complete an assignment he would have a meltdown, and proclaim, "I CAN'T!" He didn't even want to try, which made it very difficult for me to provide him with meaningful instruction.

Admittedly, I was frustrated and at a loss as to what to do, but I also understood my son's public school background had instilled very low self-esteem and a true belief within him that he could not learn. I also knew because of his low self-esteem it was essential that I treat him with the utmost respect and understanding.

On one hand, I knew the tasks were difficult for him when we were working on reading, which was his primary area of disability, but I also knew that he was an intelligent individual who was capable of learning to read if he practiced and would at least attempt the skills. We were not at a point where I could determine whether the program I was using was an issue because we hadn't really begun using it yet. My son's refusal to complete school work was at a very fundamental level and deeply rooted in the beliefs my son had developed about himself.

In problem solving his refusal to attempt his schoolwork, I decided to take a positive behavioral intervention approach. With this approach a child is given positive feedback and incentives to do well. Our primary focus was on simply trying without the drama of a meltdown. Therefore, I developed an incentive plan called the "Blow Pop Plan." Since my primary goal was to engage my son in trying to work with me on reading skills, my only requirement was that he engage with me at the table, practice the skills I requested, and not have any angry outbursts or meltdowns. If he was compliant, he would earn a Blow-Pop at the end of our lesson.

Blow-Pops were chosen because my son loved them. We placed a nice bouquet of Blow-pops in the center of our table in a small vase, so the reminder that a Blow-Pop awaited him was always in view. I explained to my son that he didn't have to get the answers right, he just had to give his best guess to try to see how many he could get right. For each answer he got right, he earned a sticker for a small sticker chart. When the chart was full, my son received a trip to the Dollar Store with two dollars to spend, which were almost always spent on plastic snakes or lizards.

Yes, it was bribery, but I call it positive behavior reinforcement. Some people have objected to me saying, "A child sometimes has to do things he doesn't want to do because it is required, and he shouldn't be bribed."

I say there is little to no benefit in engaging in daily battles of "Please try!" and "I can't!" which is where we were stuck. We probably would have remained stuck there without a different plan to move us forward.

Our Blow-Pop and incentive chart plan was short-lived, and only lasted for about four months. At that point, my son was confident he could try anything. He even began to see that he could sometimes be successful, so bribery to put forth effort was no longer necessary. From that point forward, our reading lessons were much less of an issue.

As another example, let's look at cases where the curriculum is a bad fit. When we began to homeschool, my sons both willingly sat down to work on their math, but they found the workbook problems were confusing and the teaching component often didn't make sense to them. About six weeks into the school year my boys started expressing that they "hate math," whereas they had always loved math previously.

It was evident to me there was something wrong with the math program, not with my boys' esteem or their ability to learn math. I suspected my boys' difficulty came from the curriculum's lack of adequate visual representations of the concepts being taught and the confusing nature of the instructional portion of the program. Thus, I began looking for a math curriculum that would better meet my guys' hands-on and visual learning styles.

I researched every math curriculum I could find and chose Math-U-See, which turned out to be an excellent fit for my boys' learning styles. Once we implemented the Math-U-See program, my boys began liking math again. So, the first math program I bought was wasted money, but it was far better to change programs than to continue suffering through math lessons each day or to have my boys develop a hatred for a subject they previously enjoyed.

My last example is when my older son dreaded, hated, and was frustrated by the use of Switched on Schoolhouse (SOS) for his schoolwork. Because of his dyslexia and difficulty with spelling, his fill-in-the-blank answers were virtually always graded as incorrect by the program. Even when setting the most liberal spelling error setting within the SOS program, my son's answers were graded as wrong even when they were nearly right.

For example, when the answer was Abraham Lincoln, and my son typed in Aberham Linkon (a typical phonemic spelling for a child with dyslexia), the SOS program did not realize my son knew the correct answer. The program marked his answer as incorrect. This was very frustrating for my son and he disliked using the program immensely because of the constant negative feedback.

In this case, since the program was expensive, our problem solving involved an agreement where I would check all of his answers and override the grading, marking his answers as correct when the errors were phonemic in nature. It was a labor intensive and frustrating school year for both of us, but we continued using the program until we finished out that particular school year.

While it was frustrating, having the agreement that my son could ignore the grading until I checked his work helped. It was by no means an ideal solution. Thus, SOS turned out to be a poor fit for my older son's learning and we ceased using SOS for him in future years. My younger son, who has fairly keen spelling ability, was able to use SOS without much difficulty at all and he liked the immediate feedback in knowing whether his answer was correct or not.

It's important to remember that virtually all young children begin their school experiences eager to learn, eager to do their schoolwork, and eager to succeed. It is through early educational experiences that this eagerness to learn is often squashed. Thus, if your child is refusing to do his school work, then past school experiences, the curricula itself, and possibly the levels of the lessons are more likely at fault than the development of a sudden character flaw in your child.

Think back to when your child was three or four, and excited to learn new concepts and make new discoveries. "Look mom! Look!" your child may have exclaimed. Or perhaps he said, "Guess what?"

I think it's important to recall your child's natural desire to learn when he was young, and to seek creative solutions to your child's learning rather than blaming your child, yelling at him, or punishing him for his resistance toward learning. Using punishment or negative feedback only deepens a child's dislike for schoolwork and is likely to cause escalating defiance if the root of the problem is not fixed.

It's not an easy task to figure out why your child may be resistant to completing school work, but examining the situation with open eyes and an open mind will help you see and understand your child's emotions. Be sure to read the next question and answer to gain additional insight in how to find a viable solution for your child.

My child hates school work; what can I do?

Like the previous question, the answer to this question is often found in a child's past learning experiences, his learning style, and how well your teaching meets your child's learning needs. I almost left of this question out of the Q and A because it is so similar to the prior question, but I think hatred of schoolwork actually comes from a deeper place than simply not wanting to do it. Defeat and unwillingness to try is one thing, hatred is another. Thus, I decided to go ahead and address this question as a separate entry.

If your child hates schoolwork I think it's very important to make sure you undertake a thorough assessment of your child's learning needs. This includes using tools mentioned in the earlier Q&As about learning styles and multiple intelligences to accurately identify your child's learning style(s) and area(s) of special intelligence.

Assessing your child's learning style and specialized areas of intelligence should enable you to see if the materials and teaching style you are using are a proper or poor fit for your child. If there is a divide between your child's preferred learning style and the instruction you are providing, then the solution is relatively straightforward. You can change how instruction is provided to your child to make the teaching/learning process easier for both you and your child.

Most often, when a child hates school work, it is because he is being forced to use traditional textbooks and workbooks when he is a visual or kinesthetic/tactile learner. If your child is an active, hands-on learner—yes, he is going to dislike having to sit in a chair reading a boring textbook, followed by completing boring worksheets. It's a fact—your child will not like sitting with the books. The same thing goes for a highly visual learner who prefers to learn through audio-visuals such as documentary television, computer simulations, highly visual books, etc.

The provision of instruction using a dynamic teaching style or engaging learning activities may be more difficult for you because it may not be your preferred teaching style. However, it does make homeschooling easier if you—the teacher—adapts to meet your child's needs rather than expecting your child to adapt to a traditional teaching style or program.

Many children are not able to learn if the teaching materials are a poor fit for the child's learning style, and the child will really dislike having to work with a program that is difficult for him. Given your child has a learning disability, learning is already difficult enough, so making the instruction fit your child's preferences will enhance learning.

If you have assessed your child's learning style and areas of intelligence, and are meeting his instructional needs, then you may need to dig deeper to see if you can find what aspect of the instruction makes your child hate trying to learn. I have found that children who start off well in school, but then develop a dislike for schooling often have underlying "invisible" learning disabilities, or—as was addressed in the previous Q&A—the curricula is a bad fit for the child's needs.

Given you've ruled out a bad fit with your child's learning style and a poor choice of curricula, if your child is in third or fourth grade or above, and he's having ongoing difficulty with schoolwork, I would highly recommend taking your child to a highly qualified neuropsychologist for a comprehensive evaluation. A neuropsychologist can determine if there are any underlying learning processes that are interfering with your child's ability to complete his schoolwork.

Parents are often unable to make an accurate determination about what issues a child has with his schoolwork. Therefore it is important to consider the possibility your child has difficulty with attention, processing, comprehension, memory, or some other neurological process for learning. Any unidentified learning disability can make learning difficult or stressful for your child. You will want to refer back to the section titled, "How do I find a highly qualified evaluator?" To find someone who can properly evaluate your child for hidden disabilities.

It's important to keep in mind that "hidden" or invisible learning disabilities, such as stealth dyslexia, often mean that a child is exceptionally high functioning. Because of high intellect, a disability can remain hidden for a number of years and the child is often accused of being lazy or not trying hard enough. Invisible disabilities usually begin to surface at critical points when curriculum content makes a notable jump in required academic skill. Typically significant jumps occur in the

3rd, 6th, 9th, and 11th grades, and upon entry into college.

At the third grade level, reading transitions from one and two syllable words to more advanced wording with many multi-syllabic words. In the sixth and ninth grades curricula typically makes a notable jump in the required level of comprehension and understanding. The material is more complex, so underlying learning disabilities can hinder a child's ability to make the cognitive jump to higher level of reasoning and comprehension.

At the 11th grade and upon entry into college, understanding of concepts taught often requires advanced logic and reasoning skills, as well as advanced oral and written communication skills. If a child has difficulty with the logic and reasoning, he may easily make it through elementary and middle school by memorizing information well enough to pass tests. Sophisticated reasoning skills aren't required until a child approaches the completion of high school or college entry.

Don't let neuropsychological evaluations scare you. An evaluation can be a very insightful tool. Given your child functioned well the early grades, but then seemed to hit a wall, then your child is probably of good intelligence—average, above average, or even of superior intelligence. Often an intelligent child will develop strong compensation skills that allow him to be successful to a point. Thus, if your child was successful with schooling for several years, his learning challenges are likely to be manageable through assistive technology, and educational success is likely to be found through well-targeted instructional programs that meet your child's specific needs.

For example, a student who has stealth dyslexia may get by with poor reading skills by memorizing when a passage in a book is read aloud and/or by accurately reasoning about content based upon the pictures in a book. Stealth dyslexia can be compensated for by an intelligent child until the required reading skills reach a level of sophistication where compensatory skills no longer provide the ability to appear successful with his schoolwork.

A child who has previously done well is often blamed for being unmotivated or lazy by outsiders because they only observe the child's shift from good grades to poor grades on the outside. Observers don't see the struggle the child is suffering in his mind when he can no longer use familiar coping tricks to get by. A child with invisible learning disabilities is least likely to have his learning needs adequately met, and most likely to be treated as if he has suddenly become lazy or unmotivated.

For the sake of your child, I implore you never to take a stance of blame toward your child if your child is struggling with learning, having difficulty completing his school work, or expressing hatred toward learning. It is far more productive to take a problem-solving approach to any learning difficulties you encounter, and doing so can save the esteem of your child and your relationship with him.

Adopt a team attitude. Say to your child, "We are going to figure out why this isn't working for you and we're going to find a solution together." No matter what age your child is, discussing learning difficulties non-judgmentally, with an eye toward problem solving, identifying the root causes for struggles, and seeking solutions together can make a world of difference in preserving your child's self-worth. Not to mention, taking a problem solving approach is the only way to find learning solutions that work.

So if your child is struggling to learn, put on your detective hat and see if you can sleuth out the root causes of your child's learning problems. Try to return to the days when learning was exciting, captivating, and a joyful experience by partnering with your child as learning detectives. If you can recapture your child's early love of learning, then you will find all future schooling much easier to complete.

My child seems depressed; what can I do?

Having a depressed child is disheartening. Depression can have any number of causes, whether situational, clinical, health-based, social or otherwise. Depending upon the cause of your child's depression, you may be able to help your child develop a sunnier outlook through changes at home, but whatever you do, don't ignore depression. Ongoing depression is a cry for help and it requires compassion and loving intervention.

If a child has previously been in public or private school, it's not uncommon for the child to mourn the loss of daily contact with old friends initially. You can lessen the effects of this type of depression by planning social outings with old friends and new homeschool friends with relative frequency. In the beginning, it is helpful to schedule biweekly or monthly sleepovers with your child's closest friends from public or private school to help them stay in touch with one another. It's also beneficial to schedule weekly or biweekly outings to homeschooling activities, so your child can establish new friendships.

If your child was involved with clubs or sports at school, she may be missing those regularly scheduled activities. As soon as possible, try to identify any local homeschooling groups who may have similar or alternate activities that would be of interest to your child. If you live in a state where your child can continue to participate in the schools clubs or sports, you may want to take advantage of that opportunity. Continuing participation in school activities will make the transition into homeschooling easier from a social standpoint.

If your state does not allow homeschooled children to participate in any public school activity, then you should seek out homeschooling groups which offer similar clubs, sports, or activities. Refer to the section titled, "What about socialization and homeschooling?" for additional information about finding local groups that offer homeschool activities.

When a child is taken out of a highly social environment and is brought home to school, she is likely to need a comparable level of social interaction to the level she had outside of the traditional classroom. In other words, during class time at school, children are not socializing anyway—at least they're not supposed to be, so this is not social time a child is likely to miss. However, time spent in PE, recess, or in the cafeteria are times when a child typically has opportunities to socialize with classmates. Therefore, you may want to have planned outings to participate in a homeschool sports program, park day, or going to lunch with family or friends, which will simulate social interactions like those the child had while in traditional school.

If your child is involved in church, scouting, community sports, or any other regularly scheduled activity, keep her in those same activities to minimize the feelings of change and loss that your child may experience. The last thing your child needs to feel is alone and isolated, so it's part of your homeschooling-parent job to make sure your child has opportunities to spend time with old friends or to make new friends.

While a change in social circles can lead to depression some children, many are sorely depressed before they ever leave the public or private school. Bullying and belittling experienced by children with learning disabilities can cause significant depression. If your child is already depressed when you begin homeschooling, then providing a loving and supportive home environment can improve your child's feelings of self-worth and lessen depression over time.

Getting your child involved in an uplifting, encouraging circle of new friends can help restore his feelings of self-worth and give him hope as well. The change will not be overnight and takes a great deal of love, compassion, and understanding from all family members. In cases where a child was depressed before homeschooling even began, homeschooling in a loving environment can be a great way to help turn things around.

It took my older son about six months to come out of his deep depression, which was the result of his traditional school experience, and it took about 2 ½ more years for him to socially engage with the other homeschooled children once he figured out that they were not going to tease, bully, or belittle him. One of our greatest joys in homeschooling was discovering the level of compassion and respect which the homeschooled children provide each other. I believe the high level of civility occurs because homeschooled children are closely supervised by their parents and are disciplined when necessary.

Aside from changes in your child's daily social opportunities, low self-esteem, or other situational causes, depression can be caused by an altering of a child's brain chemistry. The changes in brain chemistry which lead to depression can be the result of a poor diet, inadequate sleep regulation, not enough physical activity, Seasonal affective disorder (SAD), or other underlying body regulation issues.

Let's consider a few possible causes of depression and possible solutions, but before we do, let me say that ***clinical depression can only be diagnosed by and treated by a licensed physician. I am not a doctor or a medical professional, so if your child is chronically depressed, please seek medical attention.*** The information I share below should be considered only for informational purposes as possible avenues to improving your child's well-being overall. Again if your child is chronically depressed, please seek help from a medical doctor. I am not a medical doctor and this is not medical advice.

That said, what follows are a few common sense recommendations which can improve a child's mental clarity and brain functioning. They are basic, health-related steps you can take to ensure your child has the best learning foundation you can provide from within your home. Health-improvement steps you can take include:

1. **Providing a well-rounded, natural diet** - Some children are sensitive to dyes and chemicals in processed foods, others are sensitive to gluten or have other food allergies which affect a child's mental clarity. By eating whole foods such as unprocessed fruits, vegetables, whole grains such as rice and oats, nuts and seeds, eggs, milk, and meats, you can eliminate artificial chemicals, preservatives, colors, and flavors from your child's diet. Some parents follow a program called the Feingold diet and find it to be an effective solution. Whether or not your child is sensitive to processed foods, eating natural whole foods is undoubtedly better for your child's health and mental clarity.

2. **Establish well regulated sleep habits** - Inadequate sleep regulation or highly variable sleep patterns can affect a child's ability to pay attention and his level of alertness throughout the day. By establishing regular bedtime routines, a set bedtime each night, and letting a child sleep until he wakes naturally in the morning, you can instill good sleep habits in your child. A sound night of sleep always helps a person to think more clearly. If your child has difficulty sleeping through the night, snores a lot, or seems pervasively tired, then you may want to ask your pediatrician about a sleep study to see if your child has any physical problems that are interfering with his sleep. Good sleep will go a long way in helping your child have a happier disposition.

3. **Exercise regularly** – A lack of physical activity can make a person feel sluggish, and research has shown time and again that increased oxygen to the brain through exercise helps with attention, focus, and learning. Programs such as Brain Gym or Balimetrics use physical activity as a means for improving learning outcomes. Vigorous exercise, over an extended period of 30 to 60 minutes, helps increase the dopamine and serotonin levels in the brain. Given that low dopamine and serotonin levels are factors in depression, engaging in vigorous exercise on a regular basis can help improve the brain chemistry to some degree, which is helpful for children who have attention deficits and/or

depression. Given that exercise is free; having a daily period of P.E. can energize your homeschool and improve the mental disposition of your child.

4. **Seasonal affective disorder (SAD)** - Some people are affected by decreased levels of sunlight or cloudy climates during the winter when the number of daylight hours is fewer. SAD is treated with light therapy. Thus if you live in an environment where your house is dark, the days are cloudy, or the days are too short, your child may show signs of depression if he is affected by SAD. If your child was previously in public or private school, then SAD may not have been evident while he was in a well lit school building for several hours every day. Therefore, if you think SAD may be an issue for your child, you can increase the light levels in your home to the equivalent of a sunny day. You will want to seek out research about the best types of lighting to use to help your child overcome SAD, but creating a bright environment is an easy step to take as a preventive measure.

5. **Omega Oils** - These healthy oils are required for the brain to function well. Healthy oils are found in nuts, olive oil, fish and other natural foods. If your child's diet does not typically include foods that contain natural omega-3 oils, then you may want to supplement with omega-3 capsules or liquid. Our favorite omega-3 supplements when our boys were younger were Nordic Naturals. These omega-3 supplements were lemon flavored and our boys highly preferred the lemon over the fishy smell and taste of typical omega-3 capsules. We have since found the "Nature Made" and "Finest" brands of omega-3 supplements, which have virtually no flavor at all when you swallow the capsules.

Taking any of the listed steps, or all of them, may help your child to some degree. If you take all of the steps together you may see a significant improvement in your child's disposition, but if you see little or no improvement I highly recommend discussing your child's depression with your pediatrician.

One other aside that I would like to cover as a factor in children who become depressed: I have seen in the past, moms who scream and yell at their children, call them belittling names, accuse their children of being lazy, worthless, and otherwise treat their children as if they hate them. The moms are frequently angry with their children. If you treat your child as if he is stupid and worthless, then he is likely feel stupid and worthless and he will be depressed. If this happens to be your case, please take it upon yourself to improve your parenting skills.

Additionally, yelling at your kids frequently can have the same lasting effects as physical abuse, so you really don't want to communicate with your child by yelling out of anger and frustration (Wang, 2013).

All children want to be loved by their parents, and part of feeling loved is to be treated with kindness, love, and compassion. If you have trouble with yelling at your children, I highly recommend the following two resources for understanding how your way of speaking to your child affects his self-esteem and depression levels. You will find both resources helpful and they will equip you with effective parenting skills.

"How to Talk So Kids Will Listen & Listen So Kids Will Talk" by Adele Faber, and

"Building Self-Esteem in Your Child: How to Give Your Child a Healthy Foundation for Life" by Dr. Susan Baile

Believe me, I know that many parents did not learn effective parenting skills when growing up, and it is difficult to overcome the inclination to parent as you were parented if you were parented by a yeller. However, if you ask yourself if you felt love and compassion when being yelled at, or if you feel love when you are yelling at your children, I know you will find your answer to be, "No love there." So, hug yourself, love yourself, work on your own self-esteem if you need to, and seek to take a more dignified path of parenting your children with respect.

You won't regret one minute spent in loving direction and discipline rather than angry outbursts. The countenance among all of your family members and the love in your home will expand if you learn from the two books above (I listened to the audiobook versions, which I think are great for hearing inflections in the "How to Talk" book). Know that you are a wise and caring parent when you take steps to lift up your child. If you're a yeller, I send a hug to you along with encouragement to find a better way to talk with your children instead of yelling at them.

Depression is a difficult subject for any parent to deal with, but there is a lot that can be done to help a child. Sometimes it's difficult to admit your child has a problem and go for help, but it is essential if you want your child to live and live without depression.

9 FAMILY MATTERS WHEN HOMESCHOOLING

What do I say to disapproving relatives or friends?

This is a tough question for any of us to answer. The family members or friends who question you about your child's education usually mean well, but sometimes their questions can be downright judgmental in nature. Truly, most people who ask questions really don't know anything about homeschooling, so it becomes our job to educate family and friends about the positives of homeschooling.

I feel the majority of people are teachable, and not too hard to appease, but some are so anti-homeschooling that it becomes problematic. It can be particularly difficult to answer people's questions if they are critical, or if they are judgmental teachers, school administrators, or strong supporters of public schooling. Most often disapproving questions center around two aspects of concern:

- The questioner's perception that your child won't be properly 'socialized' if he's not in a traditional school, and

- The questioner's perception that it takes someone who is highly qualified to teach a child who has learning disabilities.

Both of these concerns are rooted in ignorance about

homeschooling, and are based upon perceptions rather than facts and data. Anyone who has not homeschooled a child, who hasn't walked in the shoes you have with your child, or thinks they know better about what your child needs than you do, probably doesn't know the facts. Assumptions are based upon a belief that public schools always do what is best for all children, that public school personnel know what is best for your child, or a belief that the schools provide the best learning environment for every child. These beliefs are not supported by research data or school graduation rates for students who have disabilities.

Many children in public schools are not adequately taught to read, write, or do math. Children with disabilities are passed from grade-to-grade, fall further behind year after year, and many eventually drop out of school. Public schools' graduation rates are poor when you look at the data for the number of students who enter school versus the number who exit with a high school diploma. Educational outcomes are more dismal for students with learning disabilities where graduation rates lag well behind those of typical students.

Conversely, study data shows very high academic achievement levels for children who are homeschooled. If you read research data regarding homeschoolers, you will learn that homeschooled children outpace their peers academically whether the child has disabilities or not, regardless of the parents' level of education, socio-economic standing, race, religion, or any other demographic criteria. Research shows the one-on-one instruction that homeschooled children receive enables them to learn more and at a faster pace. Children who are homeschooled have a higher level of academic engagement.

For any parent who homeschools after pulling her child out of public school, I feel it's easier to give questioners and naysayers a response. Because you gave public school a try, you can say, "We tried public school and it didn't work very well for us. We are giving homeschooling a try to see if it meets our needs better." If your child failed to make academic progress, you can add commentary about how little your child's academic progress was while in school, and explain that one-on-one teaching provided through homeschooling has been proven by research to provide better academic progress.

If your child has never been in public school, but friends and family think your child should be enrolled in public school due to a newly diagnosed learning disability, then you can respond with research data. Let them know that graduation rates for students with disabilities are much lower than for typical kids, and research shows homeschooled students with learning disabilities outpace their peers in public school. Let your questioner know that one-on-one instruction provides better learning progress for children with disabilities and your child will not get that level of attention in school, so you intend to continue homeschooling in the best interest of your child.

In regard to socialization, the social environment in public school, with the level of bullying that occurs, is often psychologically harmful for children with disabilities. Kids are cruel, and they are very cruel to those with learning disabilities since the disability is not visible like being in a wheelchair. The kids call children who struggle with learning all kinds of names, and they bully socially awkward children relentlessly.

People sometimes think a child is socially awkward because of homeschooling, but that is almost never the case—the child is likely to be socially awkward in public school too, which will make the child a target of bullies. People perceive that all public school socialization is worthwhile, but you don't have to search far to discredit that notion. Often, the damage to a child's self-esteem, when he has disabilities, is significant when the child is not socially accepted in public school.

Seldom do concerned people consider the negative effects of socialization in public schools which causes a child to become depressed, to suffer from post-traumatic stress disorder, anxiety, and low self-esteem. If your child was bullied in school and suffers from low self-esteem due to the bullying, then you can easily answer concerned citizens by saying your child needs a safe and loving environment, not one where he is belittled and bullied each day.

If your child has never been in public school and people think your child needs to be in school for better socialization, you can point out to them that socialization is often negative in public school. You can further address their concerns by letting them know about activities your child is involved in and by pointing out social interactions your child has through homeschooling. You can also cite research that shows homeschooled children are socially well-adjusted. If you want to read the actual research, visit the NHERI.org website.

As we covered earlier in the socialization Q&A, children who are homeschooled are seldom bullied, and often develop the ability to interact with individuals of all ages in varied situations. Generally speaking, homeschooled children develop great social skills. You may have to be direct and tell your questioner, "Please support our decision to homeschool. Homeschooling will meet <child's> needs better (than they were met in public school)." By saying this, you can set the expectation of support from your family and friends.

If you have not had your child in public school, you are more likely to encounter relatives who judge your homeschooling and seem to think your child would not have learning disabilities or learning struggles if he was in public school. Again, this thinking is based upon ignorance, not facts. There are adequate and inadequate programs in traditional schools and just as there are adequate and inadequate educational programs among homeschoolers. However, no matter what the adequacy of an educational program is, schooling of any kind never <u>causes</u> a learning disability.

Children in public school with learning disabilities have very low graduation rates as compared to children without disabilities. Children with learning disabilities may attend public school for years, but that does not mean the children are making adequate educational progress. Learning disabilities are not caused by inadequate instruction, but a lack of educational progress is caused by failure to adequately meet a child's needs. Public schools frequently fail to provide adequate instruction and appropriate learning accommodations, so it is not overly likely that your child would receive a better education in public school.

If you are facing pressure to enroll your child in school because of a newly diagnosed learning disability, you can tell your family and friends that educational outcomes for children with learning disabilities are very poor in public school. Let them know you intend to seek and use appropriate programs now that you know your child has a learning disability, and using one-on-one instruction is best.

Most concerns about how qualified you are to teach your child are based upon a perception that teachers in public schools have special abilities and insights for teaching children with disabilities. Recent research shows that teacher preparation programs do not adequately train teachers to meet the needs of students in their classrooms. In a recent research study, the 2013 NCTQ Teacher Prep Ratings found "None of the undergrad or grad programs focused on elementary education earned a four-star rating" (Sheehy, 2013). Teachers in general education programs seldom have any meaningful depth of instruction in how to teach children with learning disabilities, so they are often at a loss when it comes to adequately teaching a child with unique learning needs.

Given the poor academic progress of many children, even if a teacher has training, she is not always adept or able to provide the best educational outcomes for every child in her care. She has a variety of students to work with and simply cannot give the one-on-one instruction some children need. When it comes to being able to work one-on-one with your child for extended periods of instruction, you—as a parent—are better equipped to meet the needs of your child. Additionally, research cited earlier in this book shows children with ADHD taught at home, one-on-one by a loving parent, make more academic progress than children being taught by in a small classroom setting by a teacher with a Master's degree.

Our personal story is clear evidence for the inability of a public school to meet the needs of a child with severe dyslexia, and I turned out to be the most qualified to reach and teach my own child. After all, my boys were in public school for five years before we began homeschooling and my older son still couldn't read. At one of our IEP meetings, one of the administrators told us our son would probably never read well and we just needed to lower our expectations. They had already lowered theirs.

We began homeschooling with the thought that our son hadn't yet learned to read, so what did we have to lose? My goal was simply to do better than the school had.

Luckily, outperforming the public school was not difficult at all. Through homeschooling, my son was reading on a 13+ grade equivalent level after our third year of homeschooling. While my son was in public school, he had teachers with Master's degrees and a lot of training, but they failed to provide adequate instruction. When we began homeschooling, I had a Bachelor's degree in computer science, and I taught my son to read without much difficulty. Our experience and research both provide evidence that homeschooling often works better than a public school placement for a child with a specific learning disability.

Other students in our same school district with similar levels of dyslexia, who went through K-12 with the school system reached the end of high school still unable to read effectively at a sixth grade level. Being in public school was probably not the best educational choice for those children, and I'm certain our outcome would have been poor if we had left my son in public school. It breaks my heart to see the educational outcomes experienced by those who left their children in the public school for the duration. It's the child who is paying the price for an ineffective education.

If you have not had your child in public school and you have relatives pushing you to put your child into school because they think the school will do a better job, go to your state Department of Education's website and find their graduation statistics for students with disabilities. Search online for the U.S. graduation rates for students with disabilities listed by state. Arm yourself with facts about the success, or lack of success, in your state when it comes to adequately educating students with learning disabilities. Since the graduation rates for students with disabilities have been notoriously low for decades, it is likely to be a long-time coming before the majority of children with disabilities graduate with full high school diplomas at high rates in every state.

Also consider the level of proficiency at which the children graduate. Many graduate with "minimal proficiency," but they do graduate. How many of the graduates from public school have a high level of academic proficiency?

Your decision about educational placement for your child may ultimately be about the level of educational achievement you expect for your child. In most cases, your child's achievement will be higher if he is homeschooled and taught through a loving, one-on-one instruction model.

Whatever you do, don't let anyone convince you that they know what is better for your child than you do. They don't. No one can possibly know your child and his needs as well as you. You are the authority on your child. You know his passions, his learning strengths, his learning weaknesses, what motivates him, what frustrates him, and you know when he is making learning progress and when he is not.

As long as you are willing to seek solutions to meet your child's specific needs, and you are willing to provide him with the educational programs he needs, then there is no doubt you are the best teacher for your child. Assure your family that you are in tune with your child's needs, you have a higher vested interest than anyone else in your child's education, and *no one* has a stronger desire to see your child succeed than you do! NO ONE.

Sometimes, it helps doubters when you simply acknowledge that schools do well with typical kids, but they don't meet the special educational needs of children with learning disabilities very well. You can point out that your child has needs you are able to meet with more speed and flexibility than is provided in the framework of the school bureaucracy. Since you don't have to convince the school to provide services you know your child needs, you can just go ahead and provide the needed instruction. There is a lot to be said for your ability to meet your child's needs in a timely manner.

Additionally, you can provide instruction and support with love, compassion, and encouragement, whereas teachers in school are often on an impersonal timetable where getting through the material is of greater priority than insuring your child masters each concept. You are insuring your child actually learns what is being taught.

If your family still badgers you about homeschooling, you may have to get blunt and tell them you've made your decision. It is final. Their interference is not helpful. Tell them not to bring homeschooling up again because it isn't open for debate and you won't discuss it with them further. If they say anything further, wave them off and don't respond. It's never pleasant if it gets to that point, but if someone can't respect your well-reasoned decision, then he needs to be told to keep his opinions to himself.

How do I handle it when my younger child is more academically advanced?

One of the best things about homeschooling is your ability to meet each child's individual needs and your ability to do whatever works for you and your children. I took on homeschooling with vastly different needs between my two boys, with my younger son being advanced in learning and my older son being well behind grade level.

In the interest of trying not to repeat myself very much, in this

Q&A I'll mention some possible teaching strategies, but most of the information that is specific to how to teach multiple children is shared in the "Homeschool Management" section, "How do I meet the needs of multiple kids?" Q&A. In this Q&A, I will primarily address behavioral issues since they are at the heart of a parent's question about having an advanced younger sibling.

Some families have issues where there is tension between siblings because of a younger child being advanced and an older child who is struggling. If you have tensions and teasing due to differences in learning abilities, I implore you to control any degrading of one child by another. You must correct any expressions one child may have of superiority over another child.

Too many times people dismiss bullying within the family as "sibling rivalry," but letting siblings harm one another mentally or physically is not healthy when one child ends up feeling like the family scapegoat. Being belittled or bullied in the family can cause a child to become depressed or suicidal, so you really need to be in control of your kids' behaviors toward one another. In a loving, supportive family, there is no excuse for letting one child be belittled by another member of the family, whether the belittling is by your spouse or a sibling. It is a parents' job to protect the mental well-being of each child.

If you don't prevent belittling, bullying types of behavior as your children grow up, you will end up with an arrogant bullying child and a victim-child with very low self-esteem. Your children deserve to be shaped into respectful, respected individuals. It may sound like a tall order, but you have the ability to teach respect and control respectfulness within your home. It isn't always easy, but it is necessary.

Let me share a bit about how we handled the issue of respectfulness when the superiority mindset began showing up in our home. Early in our homeschooling years, when my younger son was little, he didn't really understand how hurtful his words could be to his older brother. My youngest was just proud of his abilities. Sometimes my youngest would exclaim, "You can't read that? It's EASY!" He was gleeful, and not necessarily intending to put his brother down.

It was easy to tell from my older son's countenance that the gleeful, "it's easy" kinds of comments from my younger son were hurtful. In order to protect my older son's already low esteem from further erosion, we began requiring our youngest to only say something was easy for himself. He could say, "This is easy for me!" He could not compare his skills with his brother's skill level, and he must include "for me" as a qualifier to any specific statement. He could exclaim, "Reading is easy for me!"

We also began pointing out areas where our older son was exceptionally skilled, like drawing and having beautiful handwriting, and we noted to our youngest that handwriting wasn't as easy for him. This wasn't done to demean my youngest as much as it was to give him a realistic perspective that everyone has strengths and weaknesses.

We explained that some things are easy for one person, but difficult for another, and everyone has strengths and weaknesses. Our goal was to establish a mindset of mutual respect and dignity between our boys, and to establish awareness of each individual child's strengths and need for personal improvement in some areas.

As time progressed, our strategy worked fabulously and both boys began to adopt a focus on their own skills without comparison to each other. My older son's feelings of self-worth improved. Our youngest developed a healthy respect for his brother's strong abilities. Additionally, our youngest developed a realistic perspective of his exceptional abilities with a reasonable awareness that some skills were difficult for him.

The mutual admiration and respect our boys developed made our household very pleasant. As young adults, my boys value each other, respect each other, help each other, and are great friends with each other. They are upstanding young men who look for the strengths in each of their friends and people they meet.

Thus, you can establish compassion and understanding between your children. You have to be willing to correct, direct, and discipline your children whenever a mean behavior occurs. In the beginning, it is tiresome and sometimes you may feel like your children will never stop picking on each other. However, over time, applying consistent discipline and correction when mean behaviors occur will make a difference.

I think parents often forget they run the household and the level of contention and fighting among the children is controllable by the parents. If you have difficulty with discipline and controlling rivalry types of issues, I highly recommend reading "Siblings Without Rivalry," as well as other parenting books about instilling values in your children through effective discipline techniques.

From the practical side of teaching two learners at vastly different levels, you can use alternating block scheduling or teach your children together in spite of their age differences, you can use subject-based groupings or other strategies. Refer back to the "Homeschool Management" section, "How do I meet the needs of multiple kids?" Q&A for specific information about how to teach multiple children who are at different levels of academic ability.

How do I spend adequate time with my typical child?

This can be one difficult aspect of homeschooling a child with special needs along with siblings, whether the siblings are typical learners or also have special learning needs. How the matter is handled depends upon many factors such as the ages of your children, the type and extent of disability your child has, how independent each child is able to be, and whether your child can attend to assignments without constant supervision.

Each of your children will need some amount of one-on-one time for receiving instruction. However, even if your children are young, you can often engage one or most of your children in educational activities that can be completed independently. Viable independent activities include watching an educational program on TV or DVD, listening to an audiobook, making an art project, working in a workbook, playing an educational video game, or working with a computer-based learning program.

In our early homeschooling years, working one-on-one with one child was required on a daily basis. Therefore, I laid out a carefully planned, alternating time-slot schedule. I worked with one child while the other was engaged in an independent learning activity.

For example, when I was working with flashcards with one child, the other would be working on a computer-based learning program, watching an educational program, or listening to an audiobook. After I finished working with the first child one-on-one, my children would switch locations. While I worked with the second child, my first child was engaged in independent learning activities I had laid out for him.

If your children are young and need a nap, naptime is an ideal time to work with your other children. If a child doesn't nap, but could benefit from quiet time or a "free play" period, you can have him go to his room and play quietly for a period of time.

Given three children, you can have two play together, work together on a project, or have one help the other with a lesson while you work with the third child. One of the benefits of having multiple children is that the older children can help the youngest ones as they transition from one activity to another. This can enable you to spend time with one child while the others tend to their individual work and assist each other.

If you have multiple children, you will have to be creative with your scheduling and instructional grouping. You should be able to schedule a one-on-one period for each child while your other children are occupied with appropriate activities and pairings.

A few parents I know have hired a "Mother's Helper" to come in and complete school work with or to entertain some of the children while the mom works one-on-one with each child as needed. Basically, a mom hires someone to come in for 3-4 hours in the morning two or three days per week. The helper is usually a homeschooling teen who almost always appreciates earning a little bit of money.

The helper guides the children as they work on assignments given by the mom. This allows the mom to easily work one-on-one with individual children in another room. The hired teen may complete her schoolwork alongside the other children, or she may treat it as an ordinary job and not attempt any schoolwork of her own while helping out.

Generally speaking, a "Mom's Helper" is hired when all of the children are elementary age or younger, and unable to stay on task very well without an older individual around to keep them on task. Although this is not a heavily used option, I have known it to work exceptionally well. Hiring a Mom's Helper meets the goal of allowing the mom to work one-on-one with each child quite well.

One note: I've seen family relationships that were contentious and demeaning toward a child with disabilities when the siblings were jealous of mom's time. It's heartbreaking to witness and it isn't loving or right. Simply said, no child should be allowed to put another child down. Set strict guidelines for your children to treat each other respectfully. When every child feels respected and loved within his own family, he is much more likely to thrive socially and academically. It is worth every effort to maintain compassion and understanding within your home. See the previous Q&A for information regarding the need to and how to help your children have positive interactions with each other.

Managing jealousy over your time is often easier said than done, so I won't pretend there is a quick-and-easy fix for meeting the needs of each of your children equally well. You may have strong demands on your time and attention that make equitable parent-time quite difficult to create. Sometimes the best you can do is repeatedly explain special needs along with copious reassurances that you love your typical child just as much, but you feel she is more mature and able to understand that you can't be everywhere at once.

When you feel you haven't been able to spend enough time with your typical child, a parent-child date night with dinner and conversation can go a long way in helping your typical child feel valued and connected. Please consider providing this one-on-one time regularly, whether your typical child shows any signs of jealousy or not. Letting her know she is loved and appreciated is essential for your typical child's feelings of self-worth.

10 MAINTAINING YOUR PATIENCE AND SANITY

HELP! I feel so stressed out! Love Breaks

I HEAR YOU! Truly, I think every homeschooling parent has days where she feels so stressed out, frazzled, and on the edge of tears, she wonders, "WHAT was I thinking when I decided to homeschool?" When you have days like this, give yourself a break!! LITERALLY! You can't do everything for everybody every minute of every day, and your children will survive if you don't.

Some days nothing seems to be going right, and tensions start running high. On such days, it is better to pop an educational DVD in the player, tell the kids to watch it, and go have yourself a nice cup of coffee, or a soda, or go lay on the couch for a small mental break, or call a friend and vent. I was known to go to my bathroom and cry, although I really wanted to go out on my deck and scream at the top of my lungs like a Banshee woman!

Whatever you can do to give yourself some time to clear your mind and to disengage from the homeschooling stress will go a long way in helping you be more effective when you return to working with your children. Your children will appreciate the break and the adjustment in your attitude.

If you are feeling stressed because life's demands are making it impossible for you to stick to your planned teaching schedule, or you're stressed because the curriculum you chose is not working, then give yourself a few days or a week to regroup. Back-up and re-examine your program, curricula, and plans. Taking time to deal with unexpected problems can make your year proceed more smoothly and the refocus time is almost always time well spent.

You can take a break from your standard schooling by using educational games, educational DVDs, or you can send your kids on quests to find as much information as they can about a subject they are passionate about. Have your child create something—a lapbook, a diorama, a poster, etc.—to show what he or she learned independently. While your children are pursuing interests of theirs, you can take time to refocus your mind and your efforts.

One of the glorious things about homeschooling is that you are not on anyone else's schedule. You can pace your schooling, go an extra week at the end of the school year if you need to, take extra days where you need them, and make your schedule as flexible as you'd like it to be. Most of the time, when a homeschooling mom feels stressed out, it is because she is not meeting with her own expectations for what she feels should be happening in her homeschool. Generally speaking, no one is judging you or criticizing your efforts other than yourself, so it is usually up to you to give yourself a bit of leeway and not be too harsh on yourself.

Practically speaking moms ask, "How can I teach everything when I can't keep up with my planned schedule? The solution is usually found in reassessing where you may be trying to cover too much material or where you might need to manage your children's study time more effectively.

Having too much material to cover can be a result of your attempt to teach everything under the sun, it can be because your child has a slow working speed, or it might be both—over planning in relation to how fast your child can do the work. Whether your child can work faster depends upon his neurological processing speed as well as his ability to focus on his work as needed. Either way, you have to balance the amount of school work you are assigning with your child's ability to complete the work in a day's time.

Having too much school work and not enough time to complete it requires you to evaluate and see if you can find the cause of the problem. For example, one year we were having difficulty getting our work done. I realized our problems were due to over scheduling of extracurricular activities. In order to get more of our school work done, we began taking certain workbooks and reading books with us in the car. My guys would do some of their schoolwork in the car while commuting to and from activities.

When my younger son was participating in swim team, I would spend time working with my older son on his math. When my older son was kayaking, I would work with my younger son on his school work. After we completed that school year, we all agreed we needed to limit the number of activities in following years, which we did.

If life is getting in the way, such as caring for an ill relative, your family is moving, or illness is spreading through the household, then it is generally easier to declare a short suspension of your school year. The one year we had to do this, we explained to our boys that we weren't going to be doing school work for a few weeks, but "by law" we would have to make up the study days. We simply extended our school year into the summer and finished up the required number of school days then.

Suspending a school year isn't always possible, so car schooling, working wherever and whenever you can sometimes be the best way to continue with schooling. The good news is that those very stressful years seldom last too long, and the situation itself can be a learning experience for you and your children.

It's important to be kind to yourself. Get out and spend time with other adults, whether you do that through park days while your kids go play, through planned time with friends without children, date nights with your husband, or simply going for a walk. Take time to refresh your spirit and recharge your mind. Doing so will serve both you and your children well. Lift yourself up, be proud of the dedication you have to your family and your children's education, and try really hard not to judge yourself harshly.

Am I failing my Child?

I've heard many moms ask this question in a lamenting fashion. Unless the parent is engaging in gross educational neglect, I highly doubt many moms fail their children by any measure. This concern stems mostly from insecurity when comparing various homeschooling families with each other and seeing highly gifted children soar. So many parents will look at super-achievers and then question whether they are doing enough.

As a homeschooling parent, if you must measure yourself against anyone, turn your view in the other direction. Determine whether you are failing your child or not by looking at the outcomes of children similar to yours who are attending public school. Are other children like yours getting out of reading resource programs, going through high school, and graduating with college-prep diplomas? Or are the children with learning disabilities spending years in remedial classes and earning certificates of attendance rather than actual diplomas?

Surprisingly, a lot of public schools do not complete their textbooks each year. Homeschoolers usually do. Public school kids memorize to regurgitate facts for an exam and then rapidly forget those facts in order to memorize for the next test. Homeschoolers often work with the information for meaning, understanding, and conceptual knowledge that enables long-term retention even when no exam is ever given.

As long as you are working with your child, exploring and learning on a weekly basis, your child is likely to be progressing just fine educationally. If you are concerned about your child, homeschooling, or considering homeschooling, it is highly unlikely that you are going to fail your child.

The two ways I know parents "fail" their children are by being lazy in their homeschooling efforts or by ignoring a known academic problem. Those parents might be failing their children, so to speak.

Truthfully, there are only a couple of moms I've known whom I felt like were actually 'failing' their child(ren). I don't know what stymied those moms into inaction when they were fully aware their children were struggling, but the moms did nothing to help their children move past their disabilities. In those cases the moms were not action takers, nor actively involved in educating their children, but I'm suspecting you're not that kind of mom since you're reading this book.

Sincerely, if you make an ongoing effort to guide your child educationally, if you work to teach your child to read, write, and perform math calculations, your child will be well-enough educated—or at least as educated as she would have been in a special education program for 12 years. You will not have "failed" your child unless she is capable of learning, yet reaches high school graduation without the most basic of academic abilities.

Given you want your child to be employable as an adult, please take action where you know there are learning problems. Seek an evaluation of your child, seek specialized programs, help your child, and make sure he can read, write, and do math. If you insure your child has mastered those essential academic skills, you will not fail your child.

That said, most homeschoolers I know move far beyond the basic academic skills. Because home-based, one-on-one learning is usually more efficient than classroom-based learning with 20-30 kids in a class, homeschooled students typically make more than adequate educational progress. Learning is more efficient when a student can have his questions answered immediately and when he doesn't have to sit through questions and answers he does not have. When you're homeschooling, your child can move as fast as he or she is able to learn.

Even if your child has a learning disability, if instruction is provided one-on-one at home, your child is highly likely to make better progress in areas of disability than he would in a public school classroom with multiple children. The fact that homeschooled students outpace their public school peers has been documented through studies and is often seen when comparing standardized test scores. Even if your child is behind in reading due to dyslexia or behind in math due to dyscalculia, he is still likely to be ahead of his peers in public school who also have dyslexia or dyscalculia, but don't receive one-on-one teaching.

If you still question whether you are failing to meet your child's educational needs, seek out annual standardized testing. You can usually find someone in the homeschool community who can administer the Stanford Achievement Test or the Iowa Test of Basic Skills. If you have a college degree, you can administer one or the other, depending upon whether you are willing to test with other children or not. You can check with the [Bob Jones University Testing Services](http://www.bjupress.com/nav/TesterLocatorView) tester database at: http://www.bjupress.com/nav/TesterLocatorView to see if someone near you is a certified tester. By having the same achievement test each year, you can see if your child is 1) above the 50th percentile, which puts him ahead of most children, and 2) whether your child's test scores are trending upward.

Even if your child's scores fall below the 50th percentile, they may if he was in public school anyway as many children in public school have low scores. The most important indicator is whether your child is at or near grade level and advancing academically from year-to-year.

Although we weren't required to test our children every year, I tested my boys because I wanted to make sure we were moving in the right direction. I was shocked by our first year's results because they were so far ahead of my sons' previous scores from public school.

Our first-year jump in achievement has been our testimony to the value of one-on-one teaching. After all, the resource teacher my son had in public school had training and was a "highly qualified" teacher, but she made no progress while working with my son. I was not so highly qualified and my son's reading ability soared. You be the judge.

I can say with confidence that any fear you have of "failing your child" is virtually always an unfounded fear if you are actively teaching your child. You really have to withhold instruction and academic support to neglect your child's education to such a severe degree that you are "failing" him. If you are academically engaging your child, planning and providing curricula, guiding and teaching your child, and providing specialized help when needed, you are NOT failing your child.

So, keep your head up! You are NOT failing your child. Keep up the good work!

Where can I get support or connect with other moms?

Homeschooling is an increasingly popular means of educating a child and there are a couple of million homeschoolers nationwide. There are support groups in every state. You can find local groups through forum providers such as Yahoo! Groups, Google Groups, Facebook, or other social networking sites.

In most of these sites, you can search for <your state> and

"homeschool". For example, search for "Colorado homeschool" or "Michigan homeschool." Homeschoolers generally spell the word "homeschool" as a single, compound word rather than two separate words. Searching for "home school" is likely to lead to results related to a child's zoned "home" public school, which does not help you find homeschooling connections.

Look for state level websites and organizations that may have listings of all of the homeschooling groups in your area. Likewise, you can search on Facebook for local groups at the county or city level, look through various homeschooling websites for information, or request information through state homeschool organizations.

Be aware, you will find the kids and parents in most groups are often "typical." In other words, they are just like the general population in ability levels. Many of the families are not dealing with any significant learning challenge or disability, so the majority of children in the homeschooling community will be of typical academic ability, and you will have a number of academically advanced children. Thus, if you are seeking other moms who can relate to the challenges you are facing in trying to teach your child, you may find yourself feeling isolated as if no one really understands.

Also be aware that some homeschooling parents, who mean well, but who have no experience with learning disabilities in their children will advise you to wait and let your child outgrow his disabilities. However, children never outgrow true disabilities. If your child has an identified learning disability, he needs direct instruction to progress in learning. Even while making progress, a child's underlying learning disabilities will always be present.

Early intervention does not hurt a child and is more effective than waiting if a child has a learning disability. Additionally, 85% of children who struggle early on with reading will not outgrow their challenges. While 15% of children will spontaneously overcome their difficulties, chances are much higher that your child will require specialized instruction whether you begin now, next year, or five years from now. The earlier you begin specialized instruction, the more likely it is that your child will be able to make good academic progress, so don't let moms who think all kids outgrow their difficulties convince you to wait for your child to outgrow his problems.

There are not many groups in any location that specifically offer support for parents who are homeschooling children with learning challenges. That is why I created the Learning Abled Kids' support group early in our homeschooling years. I needed and wanted support from other moms who understood the challenges we were facing in our homeschool endeavors. Thus, I believe the best group for receiving support while homeschooling a child who has learning disabilities is the Learning Abled Kids' group, which can be found in Yahoo! Groups at http://groups.yahoo.com/neo/groups/LearningAbledKids/.

Learning Abled Kids also has a Facebook Fan Page where I post helpful information at https://www.facebook.com/LearningAbledKids. It is a public fan page and not a place where many people want to openly discuss their child's specific learning challenges.

I do hope you'll join us in both locations, so you will feel supported and find camaraderie with other moms who fully understand the struggles you face. We dole out hugs and support whenever needed.

How well has homeschooling worked for you?

Although our early months of homeschooling were sometimes stressful, the thought of homeschooling through high school was scary, and I wasn't always sure we were on the right path, in the end—I wouldn't have had it any other way. Out educational outcome has been phenomenal when compared to the dire predictions one administrator at our public school had made.

Both of my boys graduated from high school and completed their freshman year of college simultaneously with their high school graduations. Both boys began their on campus college careers ranked as sophomores with high GPAs. They have achievement based scholarships and are succeeding fabulously in college.

Just for comparison sake, my older son scored in the "Above Average" range in all categories on the OLSAT (Otis-Lennon School Ability Test) while he was in the third grade and in public school. The OLSAT showed my son has above average ability when it comes to his cognitive understanding.

However, my son scored at the 5th percentile on the Gray Oral Reading Test and at the 2nd percentile in spelling. In every single category of my son's 3rd grade Stanford Achievement test, my son scored in the "Low" range with the exception of Science and "Using Information," which were in the "Middle" range. In other words, his academic achievement levels in public school were WELL below his cognitive ability level. The school was unable to teach my son effectively, he was well behind his peers and behind his own ability level when we started homeschooling.

After eight years of homeschooling, my son with severe dyslexia enrolled in a Georgia University where he received an Honors Scholarship for his housing and a state funded honors scholarship that pays 100% of his tuition. On the ACT college entrance exam, my son's composite score was at the 95th percentile. He scored at the 97th percentile in math and at the 99th percentile in Science.

My older son started his freshman year with 39 credit hours earned while he was in high school, he has been on the Dean's List each semester, and was inducted into a couple of Honor's Societies at college. My son will graduate from college soon, and has been successful throughout his college career. I expect he'll be just as successful in his life and working career, and I am immensely proud of his academic finesse, fine moral character, and the loving young man he is.

Keep in mind, my older son is the child our public school said would probably never read well, they said he was not college material, and we were told we just needed to lower our expectations. Clearly, the school—the trained professionals—were wrong. Homeschooling worked fabulously for us. If you suspect your child is much more capable than your school believes he is, you should trust your intuition and homeschool your child with confidence.

Similarly our younger son, who has ADHD, took dual enrollment courses at college throughout his junior and senior years of high school, and completed all of his college coursework with A's and a couple of B's. He scored very well on his college entrance exams and is receiving scholarship funding for his tuition also.

Thankfully, our youngest wasn't in public school long enough (only three years) to be severely impacted by his experience there. Thus, he retained his self-esteem throughout his schooling. My younger son is highly capable of managing studies and has grown into a clever, quick-thinking, charming individual. I'm pretty confident my youngest will do as well with his coursework as his older brother has, so I'm one happy mom! I am tremendously proud of both of my boys.

In conclusion:
Homeschooling works.
Homeschooling works well for learning abled kids.

I think for a child who is not typical, whether gifted, twice exceptional or with learning disabilities, homeschooling can support your child's social development, self-esteem, and academic progress better than a traditional school environment. Given you are a parent who cares about her child, I think the loving support and one-on-one instruction you will provide for your child will lay a great educational foundation.

Go for it and enjoy the process!

One final note:

If you have found this book helpful and informative, on behalf of others who may be considering homeschooling a learning abled child, I would appreciate it tremendously if you could take a minute to leave a review and rate the book on Amazon.com.

Your review will help other parents of Learning Abled Kids know if this book might help them, particularly if they are at that panic point of realization that they may need to homeschool. Of course, I sincerely hope I've earned a five-star review, but most of all I hope you've gained a lot of information and insight which will help you meet the needs of your child well.

Thank you so much in advance for taking a moment to let me and other parents of learning abled kids know if you've found this book informative. If you'd like to know more about homeschooling, check out "***Overcome Your Fear of Homeschooling***," which focuses on the pros and cons for homeschooling your Learning Abled Kid. There are many hidden benefits and the one-on-one teaching is an instructionally sound way to teach your child.

If your child has dyslexia, be sure to read ***The Dyslexia Help Handbook For Parents*** for detailed information about how to help your child overcome dyslexia. Remember you can also visit http://learningabledkids.com at any time to learn about new technologies, new programs, and new ideas that may help your learning abled child.

Happy Homeschooling, and thank you so much for your time.

SANDRA K.COOK

ABOUT THE AUTHOR

Sandra K. Cook is a veteran homeschooling mom. While homeschooling, Sandra, a.k.a. Sandy, earned her Master's Degree in Instructional Design and Technology and graduated Summa Cum Laude. Sandy completed Orton-Gillingham Multisensory training (for teaching reading to children with dyslexia), Georgia Advocacy Office's Parent Leadership Support Project Advocacy training, Georgia Charter School Association's "Organization and Concept Development" Training, is a Petitioner for American Sign Language for Georgia Students, is a Lifetime Member of Phi Kappa Phi Academic Honor Society, and an educational change advocate.

Sandy provides resources, information, and support for parents homeschooling children with learning disabilities through the company she founded, Learning Abled Kids, L.L.C.. She operates an online support group hosted on the Yahoo! Groups platform, which has well over 1500 members, and provides information and resources through her website: (http://LearningAbledKids.com). She is also the author of:

- *Overcome Your Fear of Homeschooling,*
- *Reading Comprehension for Kids,*
- *The Dyslexia Help Handbook for Parents, and*
- *Cook's Prize Winning Annual Meal Planning System,*

which are all available on Amazon.com.

Recreationally, Sandy enjoys spending time with her family, photography, bowling, kayaking, writing, and walking with God.

REFERENCES

American Educator (2004). Waiting Rarely Works: "Late Boomers" Usually Just Wilt. Accessed at: http://www.aft.org/newspubs/periodicals/ae/fall2004/editorssb1.cfm

Cleary, M. E. (1945). "A Study of the Relationship Between the Intelligence Quotient and Reading Ability Before and After An Intensive Remedial Reading Program with Sixth Grade Pupils" Master's Theses. Paper 104. http://ecommons.luc.edu/luc_theses/104.

Cognifit.com (2012). The Brain Plasticity And Cognition. Accessed at: http://www.cognifit.com/brain-plasticity-and-cognition.

Delquadri, J., Duval, S., & Ward,D., (2004). A preliminary investigation of the effectiveness of homeschool instructional environments for students with attention-deficit/hyperactivity disorder. School Psychology Review, Volume 33, Number 1, 140-158. Copyright 2004 by the National Association of School Psychologists, Bethesda, MD. Reprinted with permission of the publisher. www.nasponline.org.

Ensign, J., (2000). Defying the stereotypes of special education: Home school students. Peabody Journal of Education. Volume 75, Number 1 & 2, 147-158.

Gardner, H. (1998) A Multiplicity of Intelligences. Scientific American Presents. p18-23. 6p., Database: MasterFILE Elite. Accessed at: http://ehis.ebscohost.com/eds/.

Griffiths, Mark, Ph.D., (2002) "The educational benefits of Videogames," Education and Health, Vol. 20 No.3., accessed 13 June 2013 at: http://sheu.org.uk/sites/sheu.org.uk/files/imagepicker/1/eh203mg.pdf.

Hikaru, T., et al, 2011, Effects of Training of Processing Speed on Neural Systems, The Journal of Neuroscience, 24 August 2011, 31(34): accessed 9 May 2013 at: http://www.jneurosci.org/content/31/34/12139.full.

Langsford Learning Center, The (N.D.) Teaching a Child to Read Early Intervention for Reading Difficulties. Internet Special Education Resources. Accessed at: http://www.iser.com/resources/Teaching-children-to-read.html

Martinez, M. E. (2000). Education as the cultivation of intelligence. Mahwah,
NJ: Lawrence Erlbaum Associates. Accessed at: http://books.google.com/books?id=BXnDezh6DEYC.

NAGC, (2009). Position Statement: Twice-Exceptionality. National Association for Gifted Children. Accessed at: http://www.nagc.org/index.aspx?id=5094.

Nouchi, R., et al, 6 Feb 2013, Brain Training Game Boosts Executive Functions,
Working Memory and Processing Speed in the Young Adults: A Randomized Controlled Trial, accessed 9 May 2013 at: http://www.ncbi.nlm.nih.gov/pmc/articles/PMC3566110/.

Ray, B., (2010). Academic Achievement and Demographic Traits of Homeschool Students: A Nationwide Study. Academic Leadership Journal. Volume 8, Issue 1.
http://contentcat.fhsu.edu/cdm/ref/collection/p15732coll4/id/456.

Romanowski, M. H. (2006). Revisiting the Common Myths about Homeschooling. Clearing House. Vol. 79 Issue 3, p125-129. 5p., Database: MasterFILE Elite. Accessed at:
http://ehis.ebscohost.com/eds/pdfviewer/pdfviewer?sid=665b200d-d57f-4ef8-8a5a-d7ca0cb2c127%40sessionmgr115&vid=1&hid=102.

Sheehy, K. (2013) U.S. News Releases NCTQ Teacher Prep Ratings. Accessed at:
http://www.usnews.com/education/articles/2013/06/18/us-news-releases-nctq-teacher-prep-ratings.

Slosson, S.W. (N.D.) (ALDA) Analytic Learning Disability Assessment description. Accessed at: http://www.slosson.com/onlinecatalogstore_i1002639.html?catId=51434

Wang, M.-T. and Kenny, S. (2013), Longitudinal Links Between Fathers' and Mothers' Harsh Verbal Discipline and Adolescents' Conduct Problems and Depressive Symptoms. Child Development. doi: 10.1111/cdev.12143

INDEX

A

academically advanced sibling, 261
accommodations, 177
accreditation, 229
accrediting organizations, 58
ADHD, 142, 233
ADHD, natural management, 235
assistive technology, 177
attention deficits, 142
audiobook providers, 43
audiobooks, 185
auditory learning style, 112

B

begin, where to, 123
behavior management, 233
benefits, 9

C

change your mind, 56
colleges, 229
computers, usage, 180
curriculum, 135

D

depression, 248
documentation, 213
doesn't want to, 14
dyslexia, 136

E

early intervention, 85
evaluation, 61
evaluation report, 87
evaluation, cost, 93
evaluations, 79, 84

F

failing your child, 270
family, 255
find an evaluator, 74
Foreign languages, 157
free resources, 201

G

gifted, 130
grades, 215, 223

H

hands-on learning, 114
handwriting, 148, 187
hate schoolwork, 145
hates schoolwork, 240, 245
high school, 229
household management, 209

I

insurance, 76

J

judgmental, 255

K

keyboarding, 187
kinesthetic learning style, 114

L

labeling, 67
learning styles, 101, 245
Learning Styles Inventory, 102, 121
length of school day, 207

M

Management, 193
math, 152, 155
math facts, 188
medication, 234
memory, 158
mentally impaired, 128
Mom's Helper, 265
Multiple Intelligences, 103, 118
multiple kids, 204
Multi-Sensory teaching, 106

N

neuropsychologist, 74

P

patience, 31
portfolios, 219
Power Hour, 210
public school, 18, 24
public school testing, 70

R

reading instruction, 190
References
    HSLDA, 19
regression, 210
report cards, 215, 223
reporting requirements, 213
requirements, 21
Research
    Delquadri, 46

NHERI, 257
proficiency data, 45
Resources
    Council of Parent Attorneys and Advocates, 75
    Hi-Lo publishers, 41
    IDEA, 71
    National Parent Technical Assistance Center, 75

S

Sensory Processing Disorder, 238
smart enough, 28
socialization, 34
spelling, 149
spousal objections, 44
stressed out, 267
summer break, 210
support, 199, 272

T

tactile learning style, 114
time with each child, 264
too late, 49
transcript, 215, 221

U

Unit studies, 173
Unschooling, 169

V

VAKT, 104
visual learning style, 109

W

what to teach, 39
word processors, 187
working while homeschooling, 199

Made in the USA
Monee, IL
11 July 2022